Money Isn't Everything

A book in the series Latin America in Translation /
en Traducción / em Tradução

This book was sponsored by the Consortium in Latin American and
Caribbean Studies at the University of North Carolina at Chapel Hill
and Duke University.

Money Isn't Everything

Buying and Selling Sex in
Twentieth-Century Argentina

· ·

PATRICIO SIMONETTO

Translated by SARAH BOOKER

The University of North Carolina Press Chapel Hill

*Translation of the books in the series Latin America in Translation /
en Traducción / em Tradução, a collaboration between the Consortium
in Latin American and Caribbean Studies at the University of North Carolina
at Chapel Hill and Duke University and the university presses of the University
of North Carolina and Duke, is supported by a grant from the Andrew W.
Mellon Foundation.*

*A complete list of books published in Latin America in Translation /
en Traducción / em Tradução is available at https://uncpress.org
/series/latin-america-translation.*

Set in Charis by Westchester Publishing Services
Manufactured in the United States of America

Library of Congress Cataloging-in-Publication Data
Names: Simonetto, Patricio, author. | Booker, Sarah, translator.
Title: Money isn't everything : buying and selling sex in twentieth-century
    Argentina / Patricio Simonetto ; translated by Sarah Booker.
Other titles: Dinero no es todo. English | Latin America in translation/
    en traducción/em tradução.
Description: Chapel Hill : The University of North Carolina Press, [2024] |
    Series: Latin America in translation | Includes bibliographical
    references and index.
Identifiers: LCCN 2024035425 | ISBN 9781469681221 (cloth ; alk. paper) |
    ISBN 9781469681238 (pbk. ; alk. paper) | ISBN 9781469681245 (epub) |
    ISBN 9781469681252 (pdf)
Subjects: LCSH: Prostitution—Argentina—History—20th century. |
    Prostitution—Argentina—Buenos Aires (Province)—History—
    20th century. | Prostitution—Social aspects—Argentina—History—
    20th century. | Prostitution—Government policy—Argentina—
    History—20th century. | BISAC: SOCIAL SCIENCE / Ethnic Studies /
    Caribbean & Latin American Studies | SOCIAL SCIENCE /
    Gender Studies
Classification: LCC HQ168 .S5613 2024 | DDC 306.740982/0904—
    dc23/eng/20240820
LC record available at https://lccn.loc.gov/2024035425

Cover art courtesy of the photographer, Ricardo Ceppi.

A portion of chapter 2 was previously published in a different form as
"Perón and the Female Visitors: Masculinity, Sex Consumption and
Military Opposition to the Abolition of Regulated Prostitution, Argentina,
1936–1955," in *História, Ciências, Saúde-Manguinhos* 26, no. 2
(April–June 2019): 427–43 (translated by Catherine Jagoe).

This book will be made open access within three years of publication
thanks to Path to Open, a program developed in partnership between
JSTOR, the American Council of Learned Societies (ACLS), the University
of Michigan Press, and the University of North Carolina Press to bring
about equitable access and impact for the entire scholarly community,
including authors, researchers, libraries, and university presses around
the world. Learn more at https://about.jstor.org/path-to-open/.

Contents

Illustrations

Preface for the English-Language Reader

This book is the outcome of many long years of research that carried me through the dusty libraries and archives of the Argentine jail and justice system. As with many projects, this one began with frustration. Within my first week as a PhD student in Argentina, I found that the medical records I was hoping to use to study the medicalization of sexual dissidence were no longer accessible. As an archivist would reveal, they had been destroyed some months before. It was thanks to the inexhaustible support of my supervisor, Carolina Biernat, that I persevered, jumping from one archive to another, determined to write a new research proposal that allowed me to explore Argentinean sexuality.

An unexpected but delightful encounter in the national archives sparked this project. I was reading a collection of confidential letters from Juan Domingo Perón and other generals of the army. In these letters, they claimed their rights to purchase sexual services as a method to prevent homosexuality and masturbation. These documents read like a comic sketch and quickly caught my attention. They sparked the questions: What does the politicization of male heterosexual sexuality tell me about being a man? How vital was access to the service of sex workers for these men? These documents, and the questions they inspired, constituted my first impulse to work on this project.

In the silent archival room, I read dozens of letters from soldiers who craved sex, pleading to the government to provide their sexual pleasure. This in a time when the state was abolishing regulated brothels. I had to contain my laughter as I read. There was something strange and familiar in those requests; some of their words were similar to the stories my friends in high school would tell about their experiences in brothels. As a queer young man these stories used to make me nervous and isolated, a feeling of total distance between me and those who felt the need to publicly proclaim their heterosexual sex. It was the sudden and notable resemblance between these conversations that forced me to write this project. These strange and familiar words became something I needed to unpack. They represented the erratic histories and cultural meanings of something ever-present (at least in conversations) in our lives: buying and purchasing sex. At that point, I knew that—like other scholars I deeply admire, such as Donna Guy—I had the chance to return to "prostitution" to explore the commercialization of sexuality as a terrain for the articulation of embodied experiences of social class, gender, migration, racialization, age, and sexuality.

I am very grateful for the opportunity to make this research available to a new community of readers. This book is an exploration of Argentine (hetero)sexuality, an endeavor to retell Argentina from its wet dreams, and a call to engage with sexuality as a vital component of the making of everyday life experiences. This book wouldn't be available for a new community of readers without the work and talent of Sarah Booker to carefully capture the meanings of my overly extensive and complicated sentences in Spanish and the always supportive work of Andreina Fernandez from the University of North Carolina Press. Paulo Drinot, Donna Guy, and Ernesto Semán were also behind the nomination that made it possible for this book to be part of the series of Latin America in Translation.

In academia, we usually speak about the conditions of knowledge production, sometimes as an abstract reference that rarely translates to how scholarship and knowledge in general are valued beyond the anglophone world. For many years, even after moving from a very southern country to the United Kingdom, I usually found myself a little conflicted with big terms such as the Global North and Global South, that represented distant, vague concepts that I couldn't connect with the complexities of other intellectual ecosystems and my own experience. I am not referring here to their intellectual value. I am aware that these concepts have their own traditions, and they became useful tools to unpack unequal geopolitics of intellectual production. I refer here to what they meant to me back then. Taking some distance, I wouldn't be surprised if I was just reproducing Argentinean exceptionalist narrative, our constant (failed) attempts to separate ourselves from other southern contexts. But to honor this translation, I would like to capture the backstage of the production of this research, what back then was this South for me.

I wrote my dissertation on an old desk computer with Windows XP at the National University of Quilmes, funded by a major institution of science in my home country, the National Scientific and Technical Research Council (an institution that today sadly faces underfunding and in which many scholars are currently being harassed online by far-right libertarian fanatics). Back then, due to the increasing restriction in access to anglophone literature produced by the lack of foreign currency that still affects Argentina,

I depended on alternative paths of circulation of articles and books—as many researchers in other parts of the South of the world still do. I don't want to praise this history as any type of narrative of victimhood of someone who, in fact, was and is privileged enough to have time and money to write and read, but rather to make transparent what exactly the South meant for me.

Like many other authors, I am tempted to see all the issues that I left uncovered—and the decisions that encompass them. The readers of this book will find on its pages the energy to open new research questions and jump to other exciting texts recently published, too. Since its origins, this book is a call to demoralize our understanding of the past and to open our imagination to how the experience of selling and buying sex is a well-known and present component of everyday life. I hope that readers in English will find in the fragments of the lives of these women and men—who are usually marginalized from historical narrative—an opportunity to expand their understanding beyond our morally constrained historical imagination. Luckily, far from being a lonely path, years after finishing this work, I met colleagues working in the same direction, such as Mir Yarfitz—among others. However, my focus on what I define as the "short twentieth century" and my avoidance of urban spaces usually fell short of acknowledging sex workers and pro-sex feminist organizing in urban spaces as a driving force of transformation in the last decades of the century. I invite readers interested in this final topic to read the work of authors such as Débora Daich and Mabel Belluci, who have analyzed the genealogy of pro-sex feminism in Argentina by bringing to light the figure of Ruth Mary Kelly, a pioneer in the advocacy for the rights of sex workers since the 1970s in Argentina. While this book focuses more on rural spaces, readers might also like to read other works that stress how, in postdictatorial Argentina, sex workers (at the time, terms such as "prostitutes" were much more commonly used), *travestis*, and feminist movements formed coalitions to dismantle police persecution of sexual and gender dissidence. This is something that I have recently addressed in my book *A Body of One's Own: A Trans History of Argentina*, and that coalition had a major victory in 1998 with the end of some of the police codes governing the city of Buenos Aires. I hope this book becomes a starting point for many readers to do their own exploration of the rich living literature on this topic—from scholarship to the most recent publications written by activists and unionists fighting for the rights of the sex worker community.

Patricio Simonetto

Acknowledgments

The authorship of a long-term research project, like almost any other, is a fiction. Faithful to my concern for the conditions that make human practices possible, I want to mark the debt this book owes to my colleagues, family, and loved ones.

I am indebted to colleagues who nourished me in various ways. To my mentor Carolina Bierna for her invisible labor, her friendship, and her ear. To my dissertation committee members, Dora Barrancos, Paulo Drinot, and Mario Pecheny. To renowned researchers and friends: I especially thank María Bjerg, Karina Ramacciotti, Adriana Valobra, Gabriela Cano, Patricia Vega, Rodrigo Laguarda, Inés Pérez, Ludmila Scheinkman, Sol Calandria, Débora D'Antonio, Germán Garrido, Débora Garazi, Valeria Pita, Rebekah Pite, and Nadia Ledesma Prietto. To those who from other positions gave me their opinions: Donna Guy, Ernesto Semán, Marcos Cueto, Karina Bárcenas, Pamela Fuentes, María José Correa Gómez, and María Dolores Lorenzo Ríos. To the editor Mónica Urrestarazu.

To the institutions that took me in, trained me, and financed me: Conicet, la Universidad Nacional de Quilmes and the Centro de Estudios en Historia, Cultura y Memoria, entities that would not exist without the economic support of all those absent from our classrooms. For them, my irrevocable gratitude.

To the Argentine feminists, for shaking us and fighting for lives that deserve to be lived. To my friends: Noelia, Josefina, Lucas, Eugenia, Jorge, Gerardo, Maya, Ayelén, and Thomas.

I dedicate these pages to my grandmother, my grandfather, to my *nonna* and my *nonno*, none of whom finished their primary education but two generations later have a grandson who is a doctor. To my parents, Mariel and Gabriel, their partners, Gabriela and Juan, and to my siblings Pilar, Lara, and Tomás, for supporting me. To all of them, thank you for instilling in me a human sensibility without which writing would not be possible.

Abbreviations in the Text

AGN   Archivo General de la Nación, General Archive of the Nation

CEMLA   Centro de Estudios Migratorios Latinoamericanos, Center Latin American Migrations Studies

DHJC   Departamento Histórico-Judicial del Centro de la Provincia de Buenos Aires, Historical-Judicial Department of Central Buenos Aires Province

DHJS   Departamento Histórico-Judicial del Sur de la Provincia de Buenos Aires, Historical-Judicial Department of Southern Buenos Aires Province

DIPBA   Dirección de Inteligencia de la Policía de la Provincia de Buenos Aires, Intelligence Directorate of the Police of Buenos Aires Province

FATLYF   Federación Argentina de Trabajadores de Luz y Fuerza, Argentine Federation of Energy and Power Workers

GOU   Grupo de Oficiales Unidos, United Officers' Group

HCDN   Honorable Congreso de la Nación, National Congress

SPB   Servicio Penitenciario Bonaerense, Buenos Aires Penitentiary Service

UCR   Unión Cívica Radical, Radical Civic Union

UN   United Nations

UNLP   Universidad Nacional de La Plata, La Plata National University

YPF   Yacimientos Petrolíferos Fiscales, Fiscal Oilfields

Money Isn't Everything

Introduction

For what do we know of street corners, curbstones, the
architecture of the pavement—we who have never felt heat,
filth, and the edges of stones beneath our naked soles, and have
never scrutinized the uneven placement of the paving stones
with an eye toward bedding down on them.
—Walter Benjamin, translated by Howard Eiland and
  Kevin McLaughlin, *The Arcades Project*

This book began with stories scattered across court records, news articles,
and letters hidden in archives. Hundreds of names come together in these
pages as self-contained and seemingly unique biographical sketches that
give shape to the strangeness of the ordinary.

Take Catalina, a fourteen-year-old girl who in 1948 reported her husband
for attacking her with barbed wire when she wouldn't give him her earnings from selling sex. Or Mónica, who in 1959 took care of young men to
supplement her income as a laundry woman. Or Sandra, who would go on
the road with truck drivers and in 1963 was raped in a police station by a
group of policemen. The book also includes the names of powerful people
such as Juan Domingo Perón, who as minister of war in 1944 sent a letter
to President Pedro Pablo Ramírez requesting brothels be installed in the
barracks to avoid certain "pernicious effects" among the soldiers such as
homosexuality, abstinence, and masturbation. It also includes the names of
unknown men like Carlos and Rubén, two adolescent workers who, in 1959,
met at the entrance to a ranch where they hoped to meet a girl who would
let them "come in for a bit" and "make them men."

At the crux of the book are stories meant to be kept private. The many
testimonies produced as a result of state interference or the urge to express
oneself before an audience are a reminder of the tensions inherent in the
history of sexuality(ies): that this history is made up of social experiences,
practices, and meanings that are reduced to the modern model of the individual and a historical perspective that continues to be public, complete,
and temporary. In this sense, sexuality as an object of knowledge, that which

seems to be incongruous with our flesh, is just a modern construction that was crystalized in the West in the eighteenth and nineteenth centuries (Toulalan and Fisher, 2013).

These stories about people who bought and sold sex, those who built connections around exchanging sex for money, are siloed into individual bodies—products of varying levels of sovereignty and dispossession—that are inscribed in scenes that transcend bedrooms. Through the lens of the present day, the indications of contact between one body and another become opaque. How do we as researchers make sense of those common practices that intersect our own experiences as sexual beings? Is it possible to find temporality in people's words and actions? How do we study dominant (heterosexual) experiences as legible codes from a subaltern position? These were some of the challenges I faced while considering the viability of building an understanding of the past out of bodily experiences. Is it possible to decipher historical processes from people's own narratives of their bodies? How do you resolve the tension between the intimacy of a bed (when it is used) and the discourse produced by civil servants (a privileged object for researchers)?

In this esoteric task, it is necessary to enforce distance from documents as history "requires us to join the study of the dead and of the living" (Bloch, 1954: 39). In the case of a sexual relationship, historians stand before an act impossible to observe even when studying it and are thus condemned to only know what the subjects say about it (Godelier, 2000). Though striving to overcome the borders of a disciplinary turn that prioritizes the discursive over experience (Arnold and Brady, 2011), here I address the words that came out of that which was marked as natural practices of our bodies.

The central question is, Do the sexualities of our societies have anything to tell us? I optimistically argue that sexualities do not constitute a marginal aspect of society. On the contrary, they are symptoms that articulate a set of social relations; they inform both the production of subjectivities and the ever-changing narratives in which class, gender, age, and race are embodied in moments constitutive of life.

I intend to look beyond the transfer of money for pleasure. The title *Money Isn't Everything* challenges twentieth-century discourses (and their new variables) that reduced the spheres of commercial sex to the mere expression of female economic suffering or, for the conservatives, to women's "weakness" for luxury. Looking beyond the "filthy lucre" allows for transgressing the limits of morality that dictate how money should be circulated and to reconnect these practices with the production and reproduction of the sexual locus that makes it possible. Doing so attempts to capture the possible uses of the body, the actors who recreated those uses, and their interpretations as symptoms of sex primarily imagined as heterosexual and masculine. Thus, the multifaceted subject frequently subsumed under the term "prostitution"—relationships in which someone offers an ephemeral good such as a sexual act in exchange for money or other forms of payment—is also a source for understanding the production, organization, and daily regulation of heterosexuality as a dominant social configuration (Herzog, 2011: 55).

This book has three objectives. First, it analyzes the diverse forms of selling, buying, and mediating sex in Argentina in the twentieth century with a focus on Buenos Aires Province. Second, it narrates social practices and meanings, trajectories, and social profiles of those who sold sex, bought it, and mediated it. Along these lines, it examines the interpretations and notions that the actors themselves assigned to the exchange. Finally, it explores how state interventions shifted once the system of licensed brothels was abolished.

The spatial scale of analysis connects global, national, and local perspectives. Based on the core problems addressed in the book and the corpus of documents, I examine the transatlantic circulation of prostitutes and pimps that connected Buenos Aires to Warsaw, Rio de Janeiro, Montevideo, Mendoza, and other cities; the national disputes over the definition of state oversight around the consumption of sex involving the military in Patagonia and northern Argentine provinces, Catholic activists, doctors, and union members; and the social practices and meanings of pimps, women who sold sex, and customers in Buenos Aires Province. This selection showcases the analysis of social actors generally relegated by historiography in favor of those from the metropolis (Suriano, 2009) in order to also connect their practices with the specific social, economic, and cultural dynamics that make up their multiple forms.

The project's temporal framework encompasses events. The first is the Anti-Venereal Prophylaxis Law ("Ley de Profilaxis," 12.331), which abolished regulated prostitution in Argentina in 1936. During its regulatory trajectory, the law was modified: In 1944 and 1954, its scope was limited when the installation of brothels in military barracks was allowed; in 1955, it returned to its original state; in 1947 and 1960, provisions were made that expanded the punitive capacity of the law on women who exchanged sex for money. These provisions allowed police to take more action. Also, during this final period, administrators applied this law with other regulations, such as the misdemeanor codes, that expanded police power in the country. This situation created tension with the judicial interpretations that tended to give lighter sentencing or quickly release detained women. Finally, in 1984, through a presidential decree, the law returned to its original state, restoring classic abolitionism in Argentina.

Second, the period chosen for this study shows how, despite the swings between civil and military governments from 1930 to 1984, the continuity of punitive practices associated with moral precepts that affected prostitutes (as well as gay men or the urban poor) remained a priority. In the specific case of selling sex, even though the abolitionist policies targeted pimps rather than prostitutes, the interpretations made by public officials and additional punitive regulations—such as article 202c of the penal code that sanctioned the spread of venereal disease—were valid tools used to shape legal interpretations. In that sense, the legal project of abolitionism became an instrument of state coercion that disproportionately affected women offering sexual services. Within this framework, I emphasize how the dissolution of the ties to direct mediation handled by the state (through licensed brothels) increased the conflicts that arose from judicializing the diverse relationships of paid sex.

Though the abolitionist policy was an administrative watershed, it is evident that these sexual practices persisted beyond the changes. Indeed, the policy of public officials was not new: during the first third of the century, they used unclear notions of pimping to curtail activity outside the brothels as well as watched with concern the so-called clandestine activity that frequently included self-employed women who tried—with difficulty—to gain their independence from men. That is, this is a study of continuity rather than rupture.

Only Problems to Offer

This book considers how the body acts and contextualizes how these bodily acts are interpreted. Cultural histories of sexuality first explored the categories that were created and made possible thanks to modern transformations, the emergence of the notion of individuality, and relationships of power at stake (Gallagher and Laqueur, 1987). Later studies examined erotic practices and regulatory patterns (Toulalan and Fisher, 2013). The definition that sexual practices were not separate from crystalized identities meant that definitions could be understood as a history of borders, limits of different orders, invariable but conceivable (Sedgwick, 1998).

This book underscores the continuity of mutable practices that transcended the political regimes of the "short twentieth century" in Argentina. This focus shows how these practices function, are reproduced, and change social relations over time. I test theoretical hypotheses, charging them with the conditions of temporality and space (Sewell, 2005). The search for a nonbinary perspective that provides information on the quotidian construction of heterosexuality and the patriarchy as normative narratives is a challenge.

My objectives contribute to three lines of analysis. First, I reconstruct the multiplicity of configurations for buying and selling sex to dismantle the binary conceptualization between slavery and free labor as valid categories of historical analysis. The consideration of gray areas is inspired by recent contributions to labor history that define social classes beyond the distinction between paid labor, unpaid labor, and owners of the means of production (van der Linden, 2008) as well as the reflection on productive and reproductive labor, both paid and unpaid (Federici, 2017). I agree with Mir Yarfitz on the need to move beyond a model that reduces women performing sex work to passive victims to understand instead how the hierarchies of race, sex, and class constrain the repertoire of practices and decisions (this happens with other migrants, workers, and other economic activities). As this research shows, women operated within their possible margins but engaged with the sex market at different times in their lives, not as permanent work but as an activity to survive (sometimes they dealt with male violence and others with broader degrees of independence). In turn, my approach draws two conclusions from the historiography of Brazilian slavery: it is necessary to pay attention to how goods (and the workforce) are circulated, produced, and commercialized from a position of inequality, and the categories that defined labor in the past had a positivist charge that denied the diversity of forms developed during the nineteenth century (Cooper, Holt, and Scott, 2014). This book reads the commercialization of sexual services as a porous vector in the broader universe of working-class life; it contextualizes specific points in the market and reconstructs the variable meanings with which the people involved made sense of it. Saying this is not by any means a way to avoid recognizing the rights of sex workers (quite the opposite as this book shows how state abuse has historically affected the lives of those supplying sexual services), but to offer a perspective that reads the multiple experiences of sexual commercialization in the broader context of working-class lives.

Within academia, many scholars are positioned on either side of the debate about prostitution and its legality. Radical abolitionism (Jeffreys, 2011) introduced the term sexual contract (Pateman, 2018) to argue that the state is the great pimp that guarantees the exploitation of women as it is constructed in a public space that minoritized them by associating them with the domestic. Not coincidentally, some authors making this argument have also criticized (with morality) trans communities for allegedly reproducing the structure of gender norms and stereotypes, which can be seen as part of a broader minimization of subaltern agency in redefining social norms. In turn, this approach emphasized that any attempt to find nuance within the figure of the prostitute comes across as complicit and that defining this activity as "labor" is to consider it socially necessary. This is why the focus on female agency coincided with the exaltation of the neoliberal perspective. Nevertheless, Jane Scoular (2004) warns that the radical abolitionist feminist perspective does appeal to prostitution as an ontological image from the masculine domain, and it has downplayed the conditional and situated nature of these relationships (undermining the agency of sex workers). In opposition to radical abolitionism, various studies echo the demands from sectors organizing for the recognition of sex workers, which in Argentina led to important research (Corrales and Pecheny, 2010; Daich and Varela, 2014; Morcillo, 2014; Schettini, 2016).

While attempts to avoid reducing women who sold sex to victims through restoring their capacity for agency made great contributions, some scholars pointed out that the focus on choice tends to obscure and minimize deep relationships of inequality (Widdows, 2013: 158–59). While in this text, I depart from rejecting any evaluation of people's (constrained) choice in moral terms, I establish a dialectic between the practices of historical actors considering the deep social contexts that have shaped their options. In this sense, this book engages with the challenges of historizing agency (beyond sex work) (Thomas, 2016: 324–25). The emphasis on agency as the primary goal of social history (sometimes the only thing to find in the archive) always encompasses the risk of disconnecting the active role of subjects from the broader cultural, social, and economic relationships (and the structured practices—the available repertoire of practice—that guides any potential human action) (Thomas, 2016). The excessive weight of that individual action, as it relates to this book, does not outweigh the structural relationships, such as the divide between productive and reproductive labor, which structured the relationships of buying and selling sex (Bourdieu, 2015).

We owe ourselves a reading of the past that considers the risks of projecting onto apparent "strategies" a vision of the neoliberal present that promises transparent, hypercognitive, and rational subjects. Agency should be historicized by considering the complex interdependencies and contradictions involved in people's actions; it should go beyond thinking of agency only as resistance to instead relocate this concept in an uncertain (and imbalanced) world (Thomas, 2016: 331–32). This book explores how the risk, the short-term stakes, advice, ephemeral knowledge, errors, and social verdicts play out in people's lives; this is necessary to narrate the actors who are always open to contingent ratios, motivations, and desires moved by social and individual fantasies (Scott, 2016).

Money Isn't Everything traces the available practices and social structures involved in buying or selling sex. As such, I analyze them in the terms in which they were constructed at the time. I depart from the premise that all forms of exploitation established in patriarchal and capitalist relationships are denigrating, which is why it is necessary to overcome dichotic oppositions that hinder the understanding of the mechanisms that make them possible and the ways in which these are negotiated.

I recognize that the term "prostitution" captures a universe of plural relationships, spaces, and modes of agency. It can allude to socioeconomic relations and forms of exploitation of larger or smaller scale that range from the tutelage managed by the procurers to the independent sale of sex; it can also refer to the representation of pimping—that is, to the ways in which legislative, police, journalist, medical, and legal discourses codified the sex market.

By focusing on multiplicity, this historical narrative tries to think beyond closed and static categories to encompass the pleasure, movement, and permeable movement between jobs, a source of rich information that presents scenarios that don't always fit into the debates between abolitionist moralism and proregulation. The question of how to recontextualize a contemporary category (before its own existence) provides tools for thinking about a more expansive designation of sex commercialization.

Therefore, this project attends to the individual language used to describe personal experiences and make sense of an activity and asks which words were available to avoid impositions that could overshadow personal judgments. In the sources studied here, the first question the police asked about an individual's occupation triggered a consideration of the available and chosen meanings used before the law as well as the existence of daily activities not reduced to prostitution. Defining women as servants, laundrywomen, or homemakers reveals prostitution was a supplementary way to access money, not the only way nor the one that would constitute an identity; it also reveals the social fantasies of the domestic and respected world with which individuals negotiated their identity. Nevertheless, this statement is also disrupted by the unequal condition before the state. How subjects are defined determines their relationship with the world in which they do not operate in hermetic, differentiated spheres.

One way to overcome these dichotomies resides in the growing appeal of the terms "trade" or "sexual market," which open up the analysis and include other actors such as clients, bar or motel owners, and pimps (Lamas, 2017). While this category offers an analytical direction coherent with my perspective, I understand that in twentieth-century Argentina, a stable market did not exist. Therefore, I prioritize studying the relationships and organizations involved in buying and selling sex. The loss of state tutelage that took precedence during the regulatory period from 1875 to 1936 created even greater instability and made the diversity of the process visible.

In this attempt to move historically beyond a false opposition between coercion and free labor, this book explores some of the many individuals and phenomena that mediated the commercialization of sex. From this first objective, I move to other questions: Has there always been a sex market? Is it stable? If it does exist, what are its rules? Was there an "invisible hand" in the sex market that is (or was) smaller and more rudimentary? As such, I interrogate, as I have maintained from the beginning, the potential uses of some bodies, their limits, and their experiences.

A second goal of this book is to reposition the place of sexuality in how two key problems in Argentine historiography are interpreted. As I will show in chapters 3 and 6, the apparent continuity of police agencies' interpretation of a punitive abolitionism—at odds with the decisions of the courts—was used to negotiate how spaces were used and to obtain sexual and economic privileges. This is to understand—beyond any overinterpretation—the deeper legislative objective that maintained the punishment of sex workers at the core of the existent abolitionist policies. There was a set of legal dispositions used by police forces that impacted vulnerable communities. The local impacts of updating the regulation in the practice of the police and judicial agencies forms part of a longer process of institutionalizing moral violence as a constitutive practice of state intervention in the production of sexualities. The conjunction of the professionalization of the mechanisms for territorial intervention and the approval of a set of regulations (such as the codes of local or provincial misdemeanors) intensified debates on public morality spreading throughout major cities starting in the 1930s. It created a moral metaphor in which sexuality and politics were connected to a sense of order so as to curtail specific forms of socializing, especially those associated with youth, poor urbanites, dissident sexualities, and prostitution.

Moral violence was in dialogue with other legal policies that extended throughout the twentieth century as a symptom of medium- and long-term processes (Ansaldi and Giordano, 2014). Specifically, interpretations grew out of the collapse of the liberal regime as a result of the global economic crisis that mobilized views of a nation threatened by the disintegrating effects of urban modernity and that had greater mechanisms to draw social borders and redefine its citizenship.

Finally, this book complicates the general time frames of the history of sexuality(ies) in Argentina. Dora Barrancos (2014) notes that the foundation of modern sexual subjectivities crystallized—with profound disparities between social classes and regions—during the national modernization of 1880–1930. A series of later studies reflected how these standards evolved, noting phenomena of expansion or contraction of permissible moral borders that legislated the body. While some studies found in the discourse a continuity impermeable to change (Miranda, 2011), others emphasized how the growth of modern cities created spaces of freedom in which, for example, sex between men was allowed in certain settings, a situation that would be contradicted with growing state interference following the 1930s (Ben, 2009). In turn, two historiographic interpretations present complex and contradictory processes of the transformation of modern, affective, and moral sexualities. Omar Acha (2014) found in Peronism and its challenge to certain hierarchies a process of deep transformation of sexuality, while Isabella Cosse (2010) stressed the 1960s and 1970s as a period of modifications in the loosening of heterosexual relations.

This book offers a counterpoint to these narratives, noting that women found an anchoring in the urban zones and neglected the resistance that grew in the peripheries. That is, I emphasize how certain patriarchal relations were resistant to these modifications and presented their own temporalities, dialogued with them, but also marked limits to these cycles of transformation, elaborating thus a heterogenous view of the past. The focus on these stories no longer depicts the changes of modern sexualities as indicators of the changes in the city centers, but rather as part of the diverse map of sexualities and moralities in twentieth-century Argentina. This project demonstrates how the sensibilities and sexualities of the peripheries (both social and geographic) reorient analyses of social hierarchies and their reproductions.

From the History of Prostitution to the
Buying and Selling of Sex

From its beginning, women's history has focused on life in licensed brothels in the nineteenth and twentieth centuries, and, concerned with tracing the figure of the victim, it has established the agency of prostitutes (Corbin, 1988; Rossiaud, 1976; Walkowitz, 1982). In the decades that followed, women and their spaces (generally urban) were objects of analysis conducive for examining matters of gender, class, and race that mediated modern sexualities (Drinot, 2006; Gilfoyle, 1999; Guy, 1991; Howell, 2004; Schettini, 2016). Donna Guy (1991)—along with other authors (Hershatter, 1997)—displayed a renewed perspective through the lens of cultural history and emphasized how sex in brothels allowed historians to reflect on topics such as modernization, the nation, and family. Soon local historians examined the world of pimping beyond the city of Buenos Aires, focusing on the period of regulation (Múgica, 2001).

In recent decades, studies of prostitution rapidly changed due to the recognition of sex work as a political demand and the proliferation of objects in the history of gender. While the thematic margins widened, prostitution was transformed into an object apt for reflecting on the transformations of heterosexuality and its redefinition in the construction of modern states (Drinot, 2006; Herzog, 2011). While it is impossible to present a map of this expansion in broad strokes, I can indicate new points of consensus.

First, there were global networks of social reformers and public health hygienists who, through a classist and sexist moral discourse, created narratives about the trafficking of women and intervened in public policy (García, 2012). Second, there are descriptive limits of the term "prostitute" and the connection to such practices as they relate to regional, local, and global social dynamics (Putnam, 2013). This viewpoint allowed for a focus on the act of selling sex in dialogue with the broader histories of labor; though the scale broadened, the metropolis continued to be the main point of focus (Rodríguez García, van Nederveen Meerkerk, and Heerma van Voss, 2016). Third, there was increasing importance given to other actors, such as pimps (Chaumont, Rodríguez García, and Servais, 2017; Peralta, 2015; Yarfitz, 2012) or men who traded sex for money in cities (Revenin, 2005).

In Argentina, historians have taken three approaches. First, they have studied the transnational movement of pimps and prostitutes as well as the intervention of philanthropic, medical, and civil associations in drafting policy (Guy, 2000; Mirelman, 1984; Yarfitz, 2012). Along this line, Cristiana Schettini (2014a) questioned the appeal to categories produced by cultural elites and the state to explain the migration of women and men associated with the sale of sex. Her work revolved around women's ability to move with an eye toward inserting themselves in sex markets to earn a living. This approach thus followed a historiographic tendency concerned with the difficulty of absolving the life of pimps (Chaumont, Rodríguez García, and Servais, 2017), the ambiguity of state categories to determine the movement of women (Schettini, 2014), the concern for the conditions of global sex markets (Laite, 2017), and the moralist character of the discourse and global representations of prostitution (Knepper, 2011).

Second, historians have studied prostitution as representation and regulation. The imaginaries of the world of prostitution, with special emphasis on medical ideas and connections with state intervention, were ascribed to concerns over the disciplinary modes of production of sexualities and moralities. These studies emphasized the dialogue between local and international groups in favor of the abolition of regulation (Biernat, 2013; Guy, 1991); they stressed the representations of gender deployed around the Antivenereal Prophylaxis Law in a context of transforming sexualities in Argentina (Grammático, 2002; Milanesio, 2005; Queirolo, 2014); their connection with venereal diseases to understand the step from the model of individual illness to the collective notion of public health and the appropriation of certain metaphors in the reproduction of a patriarchal interpretation of the body (Biernat, 2018; Biernat and Simonetto, 2017); and focused on the role of civil, medical, and public service organizations in building an agenda around venereal illnesses (Biernat, 2007; Miranda, 2012). The studies have focused on the regulatory capabilities of the discourses or concrete practices and have examined the possible categories to make prostitution tangible. They therefore provide tools to understand the documents that this book analyzes.

Third, researchers have produced a rich analysis of the lives of women who sold sex during the regulation period (Ben, 2014; Guy, 1991; Linares, 2016; Múgica, 2001; Schettini, 2005; Schettini, 2016). This last group, drawing on social history, constructed a detailed picture of life in brothels. Nevertheless, the studies were largely restricted to a time frame (regulation), space (urban), and actors (women). *Money Isn't Everything* proposes to open up this history in three directions to make an original contribution to the understanding of the buying and selling of sex.

First, the book presents a shift in scale in terms of space. Throughout the chapters, I first explore the transnational circulation of women and pimps and the acts of governmental institutions on a global level in the construction of "white slavery." I then move to the national modifications of regulation in response to pressure from political, social, institutional, and union groups, and then to the social practices and meanings of women and men who bought or sold sex in the southern and central peri-urban areas of Buenos Aires Province. This all to say, the use of a broad scale demonstrates the many ways that sex is exchanged for money connecting a wide range of actors regarding social, economic, and political dynamics, and global, national, and regional cultures.

Playing with scale draws on the presumption that relationships of commercial sex were built in close connection with exogenous phenomena. I demonstrate this in chapters 3 and 4 by observing how women from the interior of Buenos Aires Province moved from one city to another to sell sex to an also mobile male workforce in order to avoid conflict with local police and sometimes found temporary employment in midsize or large cities. In chapter 6, I also underscore how the circulation of a male workforce along the highways from the center and north of the province shaped a kind of sexual service specifically connected to the shift in demand. Finally, chapter 1 is also telling of the construction of transnational routes for pimps within a context of a significant intercontinental flow in the Atlantic.

Second, the time frame broadens understandings of the transformation following the abolition of regulated prostitution. I argue here that its study is relevant for understanding the changes and continuities in the redefinition of state mediations: from a direct one (tutelary through licenses and registrations) to an indirect one (marked by the intervention of various agencies such as the police and the courts, among others). For that I take as a reference the Anti-Venereal Prophylaxis Law and its respective modifications up until its stabilization in 1984.

The time frame aims to evaluate how, despite the swings between civil and military governments between 1930 and 1984, there was continuity in the punitive practices associated with institutionalized moralities that restricted how prostitutes, young people, poor urbanites, and homosexuals used public space. As I stated at the beginning of this introduction, the legal interpretation of abolitionism on the part of local police and the respective tensions with the judicial apparatus evolved due to the expansion of the legal authority of these forces. The study of the permanencies and changes of this aspect also contributes to a vast understanding of the contradictory actions of governmental power to regulate the production of sexualities.

Third, this study entails an expansion of the actors analyzed. The historic narrative proposed here reconstructs the ties between buying and selling as well as mediation in how various commercial sex relationships are set up. Thus, in chapter 1, I explore the knowledge and practices of men who lived off appropriating the money made by two or more women. In chapter 2, I study the struggles in the construction of a political representation of those who consume sex and the disputes on the part of members of the Argentine military to restore male privileges they felt were in danger due to state intervention. In chapter 5, I focus on the practices, rituals, and meanings constructed around paying for sex as a mechanism for revalidating masculinity.

Broadening the analysis introduces a process for removing morality from the historic gaze: to recount the stories while also attending to the actions of pimps and clients (among others) in order to observe how hills, streets, and thin-walled rooms provide settings in which life also played out. While I seek to deconstruct the cultural principle that justified the demand for paying for sex as a natural right of men—that is, as a social need—I also underscore its relevance in the reproduction of class and masculinity. It was also a tool to satisfy the demand for sexual pleasure that stemmed from the mandate of the male subject as well as a useful way for families to earn a living when their own material reproduction was at risk, an oft-ignored reality that allows for an expectation that individuals act in a way that we consider morally acceptable. I want to thus erect an extensive, frank historical imagination that breaks fixed, good-natured, or disturbing images of workers, judges, police, prostitutes, or pimps. I have tried not to make them out to be either angels or demons but to understand them through the traces they left behind.

On the Sources and Their Use

The abolition of regulated prostitution meant a drastic change in the sources classically studied to understand life in brothels. The records in municipal registries and notebooks from health inspections that had been previously documented by the state were instead managed by police stations, judicial offices, and jails. For this reason, the heart of this book lies in the analysis of a registry of deportation of foreigners from the Ministry of the Interior, in the records of the Historic Judicial Department of the South and Center of Buenos Aires Province, and in the files of the Buenos Aires Province Penitentiary Service, among others. Through these sources, I have reconstructed the narratives, trajectories, and profiles of 109 men and women deported for pimping, and 285 women detained in the women's prison in Olmos, in La Plata, Buenos Aires Province, as well as the testimonies of 142 women, 308 clients, and 91 witnesses contained in judicial records. All the names in this book are fictional, and some geographical information has been replaced to avoid potential identification.

This work was also supported through consultation with other documents, such as the report by Paul Kinsie, a private investigator hired by the League of Nations in 1924. The document presents a set of interviews with pimps and prostitutes from Buenos Aires, Latin America, and Europe along with the report by specialists published by the League of Nations in 1927.

Furthermore, I examined a considerable set of letters included in a secret document trumpeted in 1943 by Coronel Juan Domingo Perón that contains the military demands and their plans for installing licensed brothels with the intention of curtailing homosexuality and masturbation among conscripts. I also brought together letters from Catholic groups presented in Congress that were meant to slow the reforms driven during the Peronist government to return to the system of regulated prostitution and, to a lesser extent, letters from union leaders written to the Ministry of the Interior in which leaders filed complaints about the application of law 12.331 (the Prophylaxis Law) that affected their affiliates. Finally, to cast a wider net for records and thus reconstruct the available discourses in the period under study, I consulted many articles, books, instruction manuals, and studies produced by doctors, lawyers, judges, union leaders, and police on prostitution, as well as serials.

To conduct this research, I worked in various physical and digital archives. These included the General Archive of the Nation, the National Archive of Defense, the National Library, the Library of the City Legislature, the libraries in the schools of medicine (University of Buenos Aires), law (University of Buenos Aires), and judicial and social sciences (La Plata National University), the digital collection at the Center for Latin American Migration Studies, the records in the Chamber of Deputies of Argentina, the Polish National Library, and the Digital Periodical and Newspaper Library of Spain. I also explored the Historical Judicial Department in Central and Southern Buenos Aires Province and the files of the Buenos Aires Penitentiary Service.

The history of sexualities questions the use of documents originating from judicial, medical, or state institutions because of the idea that they restrict analysis to matters of "social control." These documents usually speak more about elite anxieties than working-class sexual practices (Ben, 2014). Here I understand that, because of the conditions under which these documents were produced, it is possible to imagine that the state and its civil servants exalted their tutelary attributes, restricting thus the styles of the practices and acts with which the actors who did not leave written records constructed sexual connections mediated by money. Because of that, I address the narratives of victims, defendants, prosecution, witnesses, and civil servants as words that would not be said were it not for the disruption of daily life, an act that forced actors to speak when they generally did not leave written records about naturalized processes (Farge, 2013). The documents were read with the precaution of balancing the actions and discourses from the subaltern sectors with those of the public agencies, knowing that these latter groups acted as mediators and tended to exaggerate their influence in social life (Putnam, 2013).

In this sense, throughout the chapters, I am attentive to the materiality of how judicial proceedings are produced—that is, to the social connections that made them possible. I understand the records not as monolithic entities but as textual spaces with various moments in which the tensions between various actors change over time, and in turn, the participating actors modify their possible locutions (Premo, 2017). I thus understand, as I will highlight in chapter 5, that the testimonies from a man about his sexual adventures with prostitutes in front of male civil servants would be more eloquent than those from the minors narrated in chapter 3, given they were subjected to vaginal touching by adults and interrogated in clinics about their private lives.

I focus on life stories, understanding that it is there that the intersections between individuals and society, institutional plots and social dynamics become palpable. The prominence of court cases in the corpus of documents should be understood within the polyphonic discourse of the court documents in which different hierarchical declarations coexist that mediate our access to information (Ginzburg, 1991). As such, the "reading against the grain" used in cultural studies is at the heart of salvaging the meanings that sellers and buyers of sex gave to their practices (Tenti, 2012).

Meanwhile, the use of judicial and legal sources had a major impact on local historiography (Caimari, 2004; Palacio, 2004; Salvatore, 2013). Here I turn to the judicial arena as a space of conflict in which not only actors with different capabilities of action and speech interact, but they also disrupt what is understood as natural order, and that forces the proliferation of meanings regarding quotidian practices rooted in the buying and selling of sex. In this sense, I understand that the court records exacerbate the conflict and present the subjects as unique authors of their reality (Palacio, 2004). As I will explain in the following chapters, my intention is to balance the agency of the actors with the conditions that made these options possible—that is, to use the information from the documents to extend our historical imagination not only about the act of buying or selling an ephemeral moment in bed but rather about everything this act can say about social relations. In sum, I use the ensemble of these stories as an entry point to the actions that interconnected in sexual acts these social narratives, that reproduced and modified them in the everyday. They also reveal the forms used to name and understand them.

· · · · · ·

This book is organized thematically into six chapters. The first chapter explores the transnational circulation of pimps and prostitutes throughout the Atlantic with a focus on the European continent as well as its installation in Argentina and its circulation to Brazil and Uruguay. The chapter also analyzes the narratives used to construct ideal images of pimps and the role pimps played in redefining the national imaginary.

The second chapter explores how soldiers, physicians, Catholics, and union members reacted to the abolition of regulated prostitution. It expounds on the strategy and proposed bills of a group of military personnel—including the young coronel Juan Domingo Perón—who felt their right to the consumption of paid sex was violated following the abolition of the system of licensed brothels. Through their speeches and practices, the chapter studies the construction of the political representation of the consumers of sex in a context of redefining masculinity in Argentina and its impact on the relaxation of law 12.331. Moreover, the text investigates the actions of Catholic activists to dismantle the framework assembled by military leadership and oppose the Peronist reform attempts that in 1954 tried to restore the regulation system.

The third chapter offers a medium duration overview of the living conditions, social profiles, meanings, and practices of the women detained for selling sex in the Olmos prison in Buenos Aires Province. It proposes a re-reading of the police punishment for the sale of sex and its tensions with the judicial proceedings as part of a controversial mechanism that established a regular path through police stations and holding cells for short periods. It analyzes these forms of control in a context of punitive moral exaltation that affected prostitutes, homosexuals, the poor, and young people.

The fourth chapter analyzes the variables in the relationship between men and women in the formulation of supply of paid sex between 1936 and 1960 in southern Buenos Aires Province, mediated by degrees of coercion and consensus. It underscores how the circulation of the workforce in response to agricultural growing seasons was connected with the movement of women to sell sex or hold temporary jobs. The chapter also recounts diverse experiences frequently reiterated in the construction of a subaltern sexual and physical experience related to class status. Finally, it describes the practices prostitutes used to resolve how their money was managed and to gain independence and affection with pimps, clients, and partners.

The fifth chapter studies rituals, notions, and acts of the consumption of paid sex in the construction of worker culture between 1936 and 1960. First, it recreates the discursive setting regarding the payment for sex as a natural outgrowth of male biology. Second, it highlights practices of paying for collective, nonsimultaneous sex, such as going with friends to brothels or flirting with girls. Finally, it analyzes the language men used to organize their experiences of paying for sex.

The final chapter presents a thematic convergence by bringing together how the three categories of actors explored in previous chapters—clients, prostitutes, police—interacted in a new temporal setting. It argues that the reforms driven in 1960 and the exaltation of public morality as an integral element of social order established a dynamic that redefined the negotiations between the police and those who sold sex. This chapter studies the three-pronged relationship in the region between 1960 and 1984 and combines how the ties between state interventions and the methods of buying and selling sex were emblematic in producing a diverse sexual market(s).

1 The *Rufianes* of Buenos Aires

Global Pimping Practices in Argentina (1924–1936)

• •

León Reiss arrived in Buenos Aires in March 1928 from Lemberg-Lwów, Poland. He told the migration authorities that he was a twenty-nine-year-old unwed carpenter (Centro de Estudios Migratorios Latinoamericanos, Center Latin American Migrations Studies [CEMLA] database). He migrated to South America along with other Jews who, due to historic persecution, bore the brunt of the war's economic consequences. Between 1880 and 1930, 100,000 Jews disembarked on the shores of Río de la Plata (Nouwen, 2013: 9). Years later, the Argentine police solicited a report from the Polish government in which it came to light that Reiss had priors for repeated larceny (Archivo General de la Nación, General Archive of the Nation [AGN], box 29, no. 143).

In 1935 he was accused of sexually exploiting his domestic partner Emma and was deported from Argentina by the Ministry of the Interior. The local bureaucracy used the term *rufianes*, or pimps, to classify immigrant procurers. Acting on the recommendation of the Committee for the Suppression of Traffic in Women and Children by the League of Nations, the Ministry of the Interior invoked the Ley de Residencia (4144) (*Boletín Mensual de la Sociedad de las Naciones*, 1 May 1927), a regulation passed in 1902 allowing all foreigners who disturbed public order to be deported without trial, especially anarchists and communists (Albornox and Galeano, 2016; Suriano, 1988). Starting in 1913, the legislature led by the Socialist member Alfredo Palacios used the law to combat the trafficking of women and children. In 1936, Reiss returned to Argentina undocumented via the Uruguayan border, a popular route for those wanting to avoid police attention (Chaumont, Rodríguez García, and Servais, 2017). He sought forgiveness from the authorities in 1937, arguing that he had "changed his profession." The ministry approved his legal reentry after he verified that he was now employed as a butcher (AGN, box 29, no. 143).

Reiss's deportation took place during a period of extensive debate in Argentina around issues of the sex trade and immigration. First, local elites had changed their attitudes toward transatlantic arrivals. For two decades there had been growing concerns around the supposed pernicious effects of immigrants, especially those from eastern Europe and the Middle East. By the 1920s, fears spread regarding the increase in social problems, the arrival of revolutionaries, and the hordes rejected by the United States following the immigration reform of 1923. In the 1930s, in addition to the decline of the liberal project, there were eugenic concerns that pushed for stricter barriers to entry for the good of the nation's human capital. As such, extensive measures were supported to refine the immigration selection process, though these were not always enforced (Bjerg, 2013; Devoto, 2001).

Second, the 1930 trial of an alleged spurious Jewish aid society called Zwi Migdal intensified nationalist fears that were then amplified in the discourse of international organizations. National civil associations, professional groups (physicians and lawyers), the press, and international organizations used "white slavery" narratives to push anti-immigration agendas. The 1875 regulation of licensed brothels, which promised to modernize and regulate prostitution, was stymied by health concerns and reports of connections to international organized crime (Biernat, 2013). Along these lines, in 1936 Parliament passed law 12.331, which abolished regulated prostitution and penalized those who managed houses of tolerance, among other measures. Beyond the regulatory impact, I argue that the imaginaries surrounding the figure of the pimp formed enclaves around which sexual notions and processes of racialization that redefined the cultural value of white masculinity for Argentina were built. It was used to valorize the criollo and elevate white, Latin, and Catholic above other identities, including Jewish and Slavic.

Reiss is representative of the social and spatial trajectories of men who scraped by taking a cut of the money women earned selling sex. These men shared a repertoire of specific practices and notions related to the selling of sexual services; they combined tasks such as taking money from two or more women, networking, and circulating knowledge on local, regional, and transnational scales. All these practices and notions were organized with reciprocal solidarity among colleagues in the construction of sex markets. As Reiss's case demonstrates, being a pimp meant moving into a nonpermanent relational category with the state, a transitory condition acquired by the sexual exploitation of a woman or an unequal arrangement with her.

The objective of this chapter is to reconstruct the practices, experiences, and meanings involved in pimping as one configuration within many possible roles involved in the sex market that connected the local and global. I examine how this unique role was constructed, imagined, and experienced as it organized the mobility of the sexual supply, the circulation of knowledge and male social capital, the networking of mediators, and the use of various degrees of coercion to take money. I also reveal how the narratives and representations of "white slavery" shaped the language of procurers as well as civil servants, politicians, and activists who promoted legislation that, they believed, would reduce its operation. This is all to emphasize how the imaginaries surrounding the figure of the rufián brought together key fears in the redefinition of national masculinity with sexuality and race.

I underscore that, while the discourse of the period tended to focus on trafficking networks as compact, homogenous criminal associations, an examination of the practices shows that the men acted in accordance with various forms of mutual reciprocity, promoted public measures, and obtained money from women in diverse networks. Thus, I also propose to study how some women, with or without previous experience selling sex, migrated by entering hierarchical networks that utilized various degrees of violence (Chaumont, Rodríguez García, and Servais, 2017).

While Zwi Migdal has been addressed by historians, this book seeks to reinstate the meanings, practices, and experiences of the pimps as actors partially marginalized in the discipline (Peralta, 2015; Múgica, 2014; Guy, 1991; Yarfitz, 2012). Far from relegating the agency of those who offered sexual services (Schettini, 2014), I am concerned with complicating the map by reinstating the role of the procurers, commission agents, and *canflineros* (pimps) in the social and cultural construction of the sex trade.

To achieve this objective, I study a considerable corpus of documents. Of primary importance is the report written by Paul Kinsie—a private investigator hired by the League of Nations in 1924 (2017)—that contains interviews with procurers and prostitutes in Latin America and Europe. As the translators emphasized, Buenos Aires's fame as one capital of "white slavery," encouraged by journalistic investigations like the popular book by Albert Londres (2007 [1927]), meant the investigator recorded a greater number of interviews by pretending to be a pimp. That is how he found his key informant, Motche Goldberg, a New Yorker who had migrated to Buenos Aires and allowed Kinsie to follow the sometimes short, sometimes long journeys of these men and women (Chaumont, Rodríguez García, and Servais, 2017). Kinsie worked under the supervision of Bascom Johnson, a member of the American Social Hygiene Association, an organization financed by the Rockefeller Foundation with explicit intentions of promoting the abolition of regulated prostitution. His reports, like those of other researchers, were used to draft the 1927 report from the League of Nations that created numerous controversies because it put a disproportionate amount of responsibility for the trafficking on Latin American and Slavic countries (Knepper, 2011). As such, it is important to be cautious when pointing out that his unpublished annotations differed from official government narratives as well as official reports published by the League of Nations between 1924 and 1927. For instance, he emphasizes that the women who were circulated by rufianes or procurers were previously involved in sex work without also diminishing the practices of pimps who positioned themselves above the women (Chaumont, Rodríguez García, and Servais, 2017).

Second, I take as reference the report published by the League of Nations in 1927 that, I understand, generated tensions among the Latino representatives (Knepper, 2011).

Third, I study the Ministry of the Interior's secret records of the deportation of 109 men and women accused of pimping between 1930 and 1936. Like other authors, I understand that these files demonstrate that the Ley de Residencia was not only enforced against leftist workers but also used to target the transnational circulation of people registered as criminals (Galeano, 2016). I use these documents with caution given that, as has been noted, they are mediated by an administrative process that reduced a multiplicity of connections to the administrative category of pimping and reveal more about police logic than that of the actors (Schettini, 2005). Nevertheless, I believe these texts elucidate certain forms of mobility and survival practices.

Finally, to a lesser extent, I include information revealed in journalistic publications, print media, international organizations' bulletins, and books and articles by physicians, civil servants, and politicians to add nuance to this analysis.

The chapter is organized in four sections. In the first, I investigate the representations of pimping and "white slavery," reconstructing the array of available discourses used to imagine pimps and their role in the first half of the twentieth century. In the second, I describe the social world of pimps. In the third, I focus on the social meanings and practices of pimping in the formation of a specific type of sexual supply. In the fourth, I study the circulation of pimps and prostitutes as an element of the profuse transatlantic mobility that marked the first half of the twentieth century.

The Imagined Procurers: Narratives of Pimping

"Paisano Díaz" was considered a canonical figure in the "world of white slaves." He was a canflinero, also called by journalists and police *canflinflero* or *panzón criollo,* an Argentine whose task it was to "introduce" women in the local brothels. The fantastic afterlives of these famous characters of the underworld survived for decades in Argentine popular culture. According to a compilation made by a *La Opinion* journalist in the 1970s, the pseudonym emphasized his local, criollo identity next to the nicknames of the rufianes or *caftens* of foreign origin. He was compared to "Tano Musolino," an Italian described as a lewd clothing lover who was generous with his allies (Urbanyi, 1976: 195–97).[1]

The press described them as men obsessed with their physical appearance, a fact that undermined their masculine image. The later compilation of journalists clips shows that media emphasized for decades that among their crowded parties there were homosexual men in attendance and that the "fags were quite visible" (Urbanyi, 1976: 80). They were represented as lascivious men who wore tailored pants, black double-breasted jackets, silk scarves, and silver cufflinks. There was a fictional aura around these figures that emphasized their perversity by resorting to simplistic aspects of melodramatic culture: they were materialist, callous, rationalist, ostentatious characters capable of forgoing a masculine libido accepted at the time as uncontrollable because of their selfish ambition for money.

Pimping as a social problem occupied a privileged place in the construction of the international agenda of the "early social question" (González Leandri, González Bernaldo de Quirós, and Suriano, 2010), as well as part of the fears of "low funding" that inspired various reformists to avoid the pernicious effects of modernity (Kalifa, 2013). In parallel, between the nineteenth and twentieth centuries, the mobility—forced or consensual—of those who participated in the selling of sex was influenced by the circulation of various global narratives with their local interpretations of the so-called white slavery (Yarfitz, 2019). The declining support for the regulation of prostitution originated from a reorganization of the heterosexual paradigm and the tutelary abandonment of a relationship considered complementary to matrimonial monogamy to instead deploy a new model that drew attention to premarital sex (Herzog, 2011).

Narratives of "white slavery" had roots around the globe. The concept of white slavery originated in the United States in the 1830s to question the low wages of white workers compared to the situation of Black slaves in the American South (Roediger, 1999). During the nineteenth century, the term was used to describe the economic and political problems experienced by citizens. At the end of the century, the circles that fought for the abolition of regulated prostitution and social reform translated the concept and added a sexual connotation. Josephine Butler, British exponent of the emerging abolitionist movement, wrote in 1870 that while racial slavery was being repealed, the tyranny over women was still permitted, a metaphor that spread rapidly among those opposed to the regulation of prostitution and the municipal licenses for brothels (Yarfitz, 2019). On the one hand, "white slavery" described the circulation of women and the forms of modern pimping that accompanied capitalist development. But on the other, it subsumed the diverse modalities of selling and buying to a singular term.

Between the nineteenth and twentieth centuries, the consolidation of national borders was key for the formation of modern states. The emphasis on international crime organizations channeled the anxieties generated among the elite about an identity they felt was disrupted (Galeano, 2016; Knepper, 2011). The notion of theft or the arrival or capture of kidnapped women sparked the spread of stories about the trafficking of deceived European women. In South American countries, these stories reflected concerns about the effects of mass immigration and helped define the relationship between citizenship and nation (Devoto, 2001; Schettini, 2014; Yarfitz, 2012). This discourse tended to define the prostitute as a sexually innocent, racially white, passive subject, which caused a moral panic that originated in multiple organizations (Doezma, 1999). As such, the historiography concluded that the campaigns against "white slavery" were also a reaction to the sexual transformations of Western culture and to globalization, which implied the "sexual access" of men from the peripheries to women from western Europe. Academics have argued that the concerns of the criollo abolitionists for Argentina's global image as a country receiving women were part of the local translation process of the moral judgments of an expanding European sexual culture (Stearns, 2017: 105).

The racial and sexual connotations of "white slavery" narratives also worked with the cultural dominance of the figures of white captives. The figure of the captive white woman has been a key cultural trope of the Argentine national imagination. One of Argentina's foundational texts, the poem "La cautiva" ("The Captive Woman" [1837]) by Esteban Echeverria narrates the saga of a white Argentine woman (symbolizing the nation) who is kidnapped by a Malón (an Indigenous group). The body of a woman becomes a metaphor for the challenges of a newly independent republic trapped by nonwhite aggressors, enemies of national modernization. The text embodied early-nineteenth-century elite anxieties about defining the limits of a nation considered empty—usually represented as an empty desert even if native communities populated it—that needed to be civilized with European descendants. In the text, the body of the white captive is always at an erotic risk of corruption by the uncontrollable and allegedly uncivilized Indigenous sexuality. Like the figure of the captive, the portrayal of white women slaves of sex trafficking reactivated the moral panic of local elites toward the unexpected effects of massive transatlantic migration. The notion of those women who were captives of the rufianes' alleged irrational, violent sexuality resurrected national anxieties about how impure sexuality could negatively affect the future of a healthy developed nation.

Here I consider "white slavery" narratives about and the role of sexuality and immigration within the complex histories of whiteness in Argentina. Alberto and Elena (2016) address the complexities of understanding the relationship between race and nationhood in a country that has historically denied its relevance. They point out that the success of Argentina's self-portrayal as an exceptional white country was based on national storytelling that erased the Black and Indigenous populations through the forced integration of these groups into the "popular world," and the elite's belief in the potential "improvement" of "lower classes" through education and discipline. While the massive European migration consolidated the conception of whiteness and Europeanness as the prioritized cultural nature of Argentina, notions of whiteness become more complicated when we examine their transformation in the first decades of the century (for example, by considering how imaginary pimping redefined the valuation of the contribution of these migrants to national development).

During the first decades of the twentieth century, the increasing influence of eugenics enhanced the idea that the "Argentine race" could be improved. The elites became obsessed with producing a homogeneous population and increased the cultural policing of the lower social world. Social reformers obsessively identified social disorders—from political affiliation to sexuality—that they believed could degenerate the nation. These concerns absorbed and atomized racial hierarchies into other languages like medicine, making racial markers even more difficult to identify and transforming whiteness into an unspoken natural reality that could be achieved through healthy reproduction, education, and social discipline. This obsession from elites and authorities for the improvement of "humankind" catalyzed concerns about racial and national belonging into languages of public health, sexuality, and social policy. In this sense, racialization was culturally organized in multiple tropes of social life such as social class, geography (the contrast between the alleged outdated provinces versus a modern European Buenos Aires), and gender (a patriarchal order in which men and women had differential roles in reproducing a society according to western European standards) (Alberto and Elena, 2016).

As we have seen, during the interwar period, the League of Nations organized the efforts of civil servants and civil organizations to prepare a global agenda to fight the trafficking of people guided by moral prescriptions of gender, race, and class (Chaumont and Wibrin, 2007; Limoncelli, 2006). Various authors noted how difficult it was for these organizations to construct categories capable of discerning the various movements of the workforce (particularly that of entertainment or domestic service) and the "trafficking of persons" (Laite, 2017; Schettini, 2014). Of utmost importance—causing pressure and tension—for these transnational networks was to write the previously mentioned 1927 report on the trafficking of persons that involved an investigation of 112 cities in twenty-eight countries and 6,500 interviews in fourteen languages. While the United States decided to withdraw from the League of Nations activities, the Rockefeller Foundation took the initiative to financially support specific commissions to influence concrete policies. As such, the investigators who started working on the report in 1924 earned wages that were supported in part by John D. Rockefeller Jr. (Chaumont, Rodríguez García, and Servais, 2017).

While it is not the subject of this book, the debates that unfolded in the League of Nations commission led to two outcomes. First, they constructed a narrative that reduced commercial sexual relations to a singular sign and established differentiated responsibilities among countries. Yarfitz (2019) shows how the research funded by the League of Nations reinforced the portrayal of the Global South as a space of sexual chaos and a dangerous space for the white women of northern countries. This usually caused Argentine and other Latin American politicians to complain about the role of the League of Nations. The emphasis on Latin American countries, especially Argentina, corresponds with a profound critique of those countries that maintained a policy of licensed brothels. As such, the debate around the abolition of brothels and regulated prostitution was spread through the League of Nations bulletins that reflected progressive adhesions to international conventions and to the deregulation of brothels. During the 1920s, sixteen nation-states dissolved their policies of regulation, reaffirming the accepted agreements. In 1936 the commission celebrated the legislative advances in Belgium, Egypt, France, and Mexico (*Boletín Mensual de la Sociedad de las Naciones*, 1936: 256). When the law was voted on in Buenos Aires, it was celebrated throughout Latin America as a triumph over a capital imagined as the center of prostitution and because it aligned with regulations in Cuba (1925), the Dominican Republic (1926), Uruguay (1927), Nicaragua (1928), and Chile (1931).

Debates about regulation and abolition brought out deep ideas about whiteness, migration, and social class. Based on my research on the *Boletín Mensual de la Sociedad de las Naciones* (the Spanish edition of the League of Nations monthly publication) and in particular on the Committee for the Suppression of Traffic in Women and Children, I agree with Mir Yarfitz (2019) that international research on white slavery also reflected the anxieties of central powers toward the postcolonial world orders, mass migration, and the consequences of interracial and cross-national relationships. The fear of white slavery articulated the broader fear of nonwhite men's access to white female sexuality, which nationalists and social reformers from the North and some in the Rio de la Plata thought would have a negative effect on their nations.

Second, the commission established its position by making policies for maternal and children's aid a central issue. In doing so, the commission symbolically took charge of the need for state intervention to restore an ontological maternal position to women that had been disrupted by the misery represented by the prostitute. That is, it intervened to construct the cultural boundary between the mother and harlot. The definition of the mother-child binary as subject of policies was expressed in the slow confluence of institutional agencies and distribution of resources that tended to represent them as subjects of a single policy, displacing human trafficking from the agenda on crime without losing the punitive pretensions toward pimping, but relocating it in a broader agenda that the League of Nations would call "social and humanitarian" questions. This shift in the makeup of the agency could be in dual records.

Argentine authorities rejected the role the commission asked them to play within the international sex market. In a letter (1927), the Argentine delegate noted that in his country the phenomenon had practically disappeared, which he attributed to the passing of law 9143, the Ley Palacios, which restricted the trafficking of women and children for sexual exploitation and that would become an international legislative model. The civil servant associated this downward trend with the fact that the war made this kind of journey more difficult. For the civil servant, the tendency to associate these practices with Argentina was part of an international campaign to damage the integrity of the country. He also claimed that the state's problems were largely caused by the moral weaknesses of the European middle class that had come to the country following the war's tolls. He refuted that the women arrived virgins; that is, they had come from Europe already "corrupted." He also said that Buenos Aires was a healthier city, both morally and physically, "than others that were older and had better regulations." Finally, he noted that they could not restrict admission into the country because men and women entered with papers, meaning state intervention would only be possible if the victim denounced her exploiters, something that rarely happened given that for the civil servant the prostitutes wanted to become independent in a clandestine system. For the Argentine representative, the state was doing as much as it could: it prohibited the entry of prostitutes and collaborated with protection groups, which in his opinion explained why the number of prostitutes was not higher than in European countries in proportion to demographic density (*Memorandum to the council on the comments submitted by the government regarding. Part II of the report of special body of experts*, 30 November 1927).

In Argentina, various actors who appealed to the ongoing discourse embraced or rejected the attempts to impose a policy regulating the selling of sex that could be adapted to broader contexts. For example, groups of physicians focused on premarital sex as a way to improve the reproduction of the "race" and populate the nation by promoting social and health policies (Biernat, 2007; Guy, 1991; Miranda, 2012). Journalists, literati, intellectuals, politicians, and police redefined white masculinity in the country by building it around the representation of the rufián. Whiteness operated as a double-sided ideology that brought together the notion of national homogeneity with the everyday construction of racial and class disparity (Aguiló, 2018). Making note of these categories is useful to understand how they prompted interpretations of morality tied to the imaginary of the nation and mediated the construction of our documentary sources. It is worth thinking, just as an example, about the tensions in the creation of census categories to measure migration and the practices of the actors to negotiate the categories (Devoto, 2001; Otero, 2006).

These narratives were saturated in language related to certain ethnic communities, such as the Jewish community, and were inscribed in the transformation of the national imagination during the 1920s and 1930s. The exhaustion of immigration as a solution for the scarcity of the Argentine population that could be used to build a modern labor force converged with tensions between a sector of the social and cultural elite's allusion to criollismo as a metaphor for the rural, agro-export country and the emergence of a *porteña* identity used to construct images of partially cosmopolitan urban layers (Adamovsky, 2012; Nouwen, 2013).

During the first two decades of the twentieth century, publications by local feminists did not morally condemn prostitutes, nor did they give much space to "white slavery" (Barrancos, 2008). It was the Swiss-Argentine physician Petrona Eyle and the Italian-Argentine pharmacist Julieta Lanteri, both pioneers of vernacular feminism, who took up the matter from two different positions. In 1924, Eyle founded the League Against White Slavery in accordance with her English peers. She joined in denouncing the sexual exploitation of women in the country and promoted children's rights and feminism. Lanteri specifically rejected regulated prostitution at the International Congress of Women that brought together socialist, freethinking, and reformist women. She demanded that the event formally reject prostitution for understanding it as an effect of the inequality between the sexes (Barrancos, 2008; Valobra, 2008).

Elite, media, and civil servant men produced narratives on the trafficking of women and images of *rufianes*. Nationalist intellectual circles disputed the racial interpretation of this concept in view of a general expression of the nation and its citizens with ethnic (white), gendered (masculine), and classist precepts. The image published in *El Gladiador* at the beginning of the century corresponds with the representations of the period (see figure 1.1). The image distilled pimping in the imaginary to a European man dominating a group of troubled women sitting on the floor. The inclusion of Black slaves and the caption critically reference "white slavery" as a problematic concept and express resentment for the displacement of a racial slavery to another, sexual one.

In his thesis "La trata de blancas" ("The White Slave Trade") (1905) presented to the School of Law of the University of Buenos Aires, the nationalist Manuel Gálvez established a stereotypical image of pimps. He defined *caftens* as ostentatious, effeminate men who looked down on women and cared about foreign issues. For the author, it was possible to see them in Buenos Aires wearing rings on their left hand and holding a cane with a gold tip in their right.

On 30 September 1930, a trial was initiated against 108 men accused of belonging to the spurious aid society Zwi Migdal. The local press made a big deal out of the information about the "shady characters" (*Crítica*, 10 September 1930). As the journalists emphasized in the various complaints presented, the Warsaw Society of Mutual Aid had been founded in 1906 and one year later was divided into the organizations Zwi Migdal, made up of

LA TRATA DE BLANCAS

LO QUE VA DE AYER A HOY

En otros tiempos las negras fueron
Las sometidas á esclavitud
Hoy á las blancas las sometieron
Pero esto á costa de su virtud.

Reid por ello, castas motosas.
Pero es que *El Tiempo*, no aparecía,
¡Oh mulatillas pundonorosas!
Cuando la trata de negrería.

FIGURE 1.1 *El Gladiador*, 1902. Digital Archive from the Iberoamerican Institute in Berlin, Germany.

Polish Jews, and Asquenasum, of Russian Jews. The newspapers described the existence of a fake Jewish synagogue with its own cemetery. A year later, the press questioned the verdict because the judge decided to release 105 detainees for lack of evidence, a judicial act executed on January 25 and signed two days later (*La Razón*, 27 January 1931). The Jewish mutual aid society caught the interest of journalists and activists and increased pressures from international organizations for the Argentine state to adopt a new policy (Yarfitz, 2019).

Argentine nationalism deemed the strength of the nation to be constructed on the heterosexual family, with full male authority and a rigid division of roles for wives and husbands, which is why the goal of marriage was the continuation of the race (McGee Deutsch, 2005). For Manuel Gálvez (1905: 15), sensuality imported from abroad was a threat to virile strength and criollo purity. Sexual energies embodied in European women in Buenos Aires brothels led to the corruption of the home, which in turn made it so that more women worked in the "sad business of prostitution." Other nationalists such as Leopoldo Lugones (1930a) blamed liberalism for problems like prostitution, abortion, and poverty. The author identified the arrival of foreigners in a context of growing urbanization as a problem caused by national decline and coincided with international stories that placed Buenos Aires at the center of prostitution and debauchery.

This worldview also appropriated an anti-Semitic story in which the participation of Jewish Poles in criminal organizations like Zwi Migdal was a reasonable explanation for pimping. In this sense, exaggerating the presence of Jews in how groups of pimps were described was used as a way to stigmatize them (Yarfitz, 2019). But the racial makeup also had political origins: for the nationalists, the perversion of Judaism and eastern European countries was tied to fables about the supposed participation of communists in crime (McGee Deutsch, 2005).

The targeting of the Jewish community was solidified into a moral panic over the pernicious effects of migration. Conservative civil servants—such as the national representative Lucas Ayarragaray (1937) from the province of Entre Ríos and a member of the National Academy of Medicine and the National Academy of History—emphasized that while this immigration harmed the ethical values of Argentina, the lecherous pretensions of the local women left them exposed to foreign corruption and argued that this must be stopped so that the country could become a patrimony of the white race.

The construction of a white Argentina functioned as a point of comparison from which the supposed developed future of the country could be held above the rest of the Southern Cone (Alberto and Elena, 2016). The spread of the "white slavery" narrative was used to dispute interpretations of the nation and, in this sense, reinforce the construction of national citizenship as a border that considered whiteness to be a passive entity suffering foreign disturbance. This was about a redefinition in the face of a white identity they considered to be at risk. As such, for the traditional ruling groups, the appeal to the criollo and rural world functioned as a reference point for affirming their legitimacy and rejecting the unsettling presence of the foreigner (Adamovsky, 2014).

Unlike the nationalists, the socialists fought to interpret the phenomenon as a social problem produced by national and foreign "capitalist poverty." Argentine reformist socialists played a central role in the legal transformations and pioneered the fight against regulated prostitution. Representatives such as Alfredo Palacios and Ángel Giménez did not hold back in their criticisms of a system they thought damaged the health of male workers because it did not limit the spread of venereal diseases (Giménez, 1930). With this point, they were in agreement on medical discourse with Catholics, conservatives, and socialists who understood health in male-centered terms. As such, they promoted methods to sanction sexual exploitation, such as the 1913 Ley Palacios, a pioneer regulation for the persecution of procurers that suggested sentences of one to two years.

The press played a central role in the national and international identification of the issue. British newspapers emphasized Buenos Aires as the capital in the trafficking of women (Knepper, 2011). Like others at the turn of the century that emphasized the problematic nature of high migration (Galeano, 2016), British abolitionists strived to contrast their legal system with the Latin one, and in this comparison, they focused on speaking against Buenos Aires, emphasizing the chaos produced by the wave of migration (Schettini, 2014).

The national press negatively presented depictions of the sexual exploiters. The reports against Zwi Migdal were meant to reveal the group's position as a powerful and limitless institution that brought together investigative journalists to carry out numerous investigations throughout the twentieth century. The 105 men accused of pimping in 1930 were marked as "ostentatious, shady characters capable of bringing down the police and justice system" (*La Razón*, 27 January 1931), and the media emphasized the ineffectiveness of the police with illustrated jokes with captions such as "Do you know why the police didn't root out the Migdal on time? Because they were suffering from *amigdalitis* (tonsilitis)." Other illustrations showed them as well-dressed men who dragged ragged women by the hair across the floor of a brothel and insisted on their foreign provenance (*Crítica*, 1 May 1930).

The appeal to the numbers was part of building representations in a unique, well-oiled machine. The *Trilogía de la trata de blancas* (Trilogy of White Slavery) by the commissioner Juan Alsogaray (1933), a police officer with a nationalist leaning, noted that the scope of the first network would be 1,000 brothels, where 30,000 women were exploited, with an average yield of 3,000 pesos a month, or 108 million a year. For the commissioner (who became an influential source for decades), the Russian-Jewish association Asquenasum produced 54 million pesos a year; thus combined with Zwi Migdal they earned 162 million pesos a year. Some newspapers with a sensationalist leaning calculated monetary figures and moreover said that 450 pimps ran 2,000 brothels (*Todo es Historia*, 1 April 1973). A portrayal that, as Yarfitz (2019) has pointed out, played a role in the stigmatization of the Jewish and eastern European communities.

In the training courses that assistant commissioner and investigator of Buenos Aires Ernesto Pareja (1937) wrote for the officers, numbers on prostitution were exacerbated and contradictory statistics were presented. Pareja drew subordinates' attention to the fact that there were 173 women registered in the licensed brothels out of 249 known by the police, which for him was proof of "clandestine prostitution." To emphasize this fact, he extolled that in 1934 there had been 24,500 misdemeanors recorded for offering sex in public. These facts speak partially to the public recognition of the phenomenon, but with more eloquence to the ways civil servants were using this data to strengthen and reproduce meaning for the interpretation of these figures.

In short, I argue that the local interpretations of "white slavery" tended to emphasize stereotypical and generic representations of a specific form of sexual supply in which the use of violence and coercion was at the forefront. The circulation of stereotypical images of procurers influenced the interpretations and production of public documents. The cultural production of pimps' imaginaries showcases the interrelationship between sexuality and race, catalyzed by the broader notion of public morality, which played a key role in the definition of hierarchies of national belonging and whiteness. At the same time, this construction is an indispensable element to rearm the discursive logic that governed the production of documentary sources from which it is possible to investigate the itineraries, practices, and profiles of the men and women involved in networks of sexual exploitation.

More Than Friends: The Social World of Pimps

Under the fantasies awakened amid a national imagination that responded to global trends—the urban dynamic and anxieties of Argentina's elite— groups of men experienced a specific form of selling sex that entailed the circulation of persons, money, and knowledge on local, regional, or transnational scales, tactics for the appropriation of money in the context of a regulated system of prostitution, and networks of horizontal reciprocity of ethnic socialization.

There are many challenges to tracing those who were at the margins of the law and were objects of (historical) exorbitant fantasies that had some grounding. The documents are scarce and limited: records of the deportation of foreigners offer some information about who were marked as procurers. That is how I gathered information on the 109 rufianes or canflineros and seventy-four women considered to be exploited that I compared to the migrant entry and egress data from CEMLA. I also compared this data with CEMLA's immigrant records of entry and egress as well as the anecdotes collected by the researcher Paul Kinsie in Buenos Aires.

The data is unclear, given the civil servants put the information together under the influence of moral precepts with which they reduced a multiplicity of activities to a single sign (Piscitelli and Lowenkron, 2015). The data also tells more about police rationale than the "networks of procurers" as complex relationships of cohabitation or movement were frequently reduced to criminal figures (Schettini, 2005). Bureaucratic language was infused with available discourse and pressured to present what the international organizations considered to be an effective solution, but once the available fantasies are isolated, it is possible to identify patterns that distinguish the fantastical narratives from reality. Thus, the stories presented in the Kinsie report—guided by his own intentions—also help present the voices of men who were in situations similar to those who were deported. Here I do not observe them with the scrutiny of the state, but as men who shared the characteristics already described to be able to think beyond the macro understanding of small individual hierarchies, daily activities, languages, and support that mediated the life and future of the pimp. Yarfitz (2019: 34–35) also critically analyzed how the studies conducted by private investigators such as Kinsie portrayed themselves as heroic male characters uncorrupted by the vice of pimps and prostitution. Even if the studies didn't describe the women as passive victims, Kinsie usually reproduced the moral condemnation against their way of life and usually mediated their voice in the documents.

The deported men recorded as procurers were older than twenty-nine, born between the last decade of the nineteenth century and the first of the twentieth. Forty-six percent were between twenty-nine and thirty-eight years old, 39 percent were between thirty-nine and forty-eight, 14 percent were between forty-nine and fifty-eight, and the rest were between sixty and eighty. In their statements before the migration authorities and the brief descriptions written by the Ministry of the Interior, they stated they came from poor working-class families whose inadequate living conditions were exacerbated by the world wars. They confirmed they had jobs such as carpenters, blacksmiths, butchers, farmers, day laborers, and factory workers. Like other immigrants, they filed the appropriate information with their respective governments to move to Argentina. In Poland, the state promoted immigration as a way to overcome poverty and the economic crisis; immigrants could consult manuals that explained the legislation and gave advice on how to act in the offices and which jobs were needed (Archi-wum Urzad Wojewodzki Katowice, Fondo 9358, "Wiadomesci dla emi-grantow," 1930–38). Some procurers Kinsie interviewed in Krakow stated that it was fairly easy to pay off the government officials or Polish police to acquire the passport and necessary visas more easily (Chaumont, Rodríguez García, and Servais, 2017: 42).

The deported men likely had little room to negotiate with the Argentine police. During the first decades of the twentieth century, the police force received little training and low salaries and was unable to respond to ur-ban social demands even though it did acquire better technologies like ra-dios and cars (Caimari, 2012). In the 1930s new technologies such as photography, and the transnational circulation of manuals and the identi-fication documents of wanted criminals converged and were added to the growing police networks in the region. Their mission was to fight "interna-tional crime" (Galeano, 2016).

The deportees were registered on state lists of procurers. In 1924, the pre-viously mentioned Motche Goldberg, key informant for Kinsie, who pre-tended to be a pimp to infiltrate their groups, recommended that Kinsie take care that the police did not put him on their list of pimps, which included photographs and made freedom of movement outside the country difficult (Chaumont, Rodríguez García, and Servais, 2017: 36). That same year, the head of identification for customs complained about the absence of adequate legislation to pursue rufianes and explained that the police used raids to persuade them to leave the country or change their professions. At the same time, he referenced a handbook of those suspected of pimping that included 500 accused men (Chaumont, Rodríguez García, and Servais, 2017: 48).

The written evidence of priors reported by the countries of origin sug-gests that the accused committed minor theft and illegal gambling from a young age. These practices would continue in Argentina and would grow to include minor injuries from fistfights with other men in bars after getting drunk or with the clients of prostitutes who refused to pay. The pimps spent a lot of their days in bars, brothels, or apartments where they collected money from the women they exploited. In the case of the group infiltrated by Kinsie, the men gathered at Havra bar and in a social club where they exchanged information and made transactions (Chaumont, Rodríguez García, and Servais, 2017: 33). Socializing in jail and on the street would put the men in contact with others at the margin of the law with whom they would share practices of reciprocity and mobility to take the money made from selling sex.

The documents express relationships based on age and social position. Based on the number of women or brothels pimps managed, it is clear they were procurers of low standing or midrank, though this could change throughout their lives by abandoning their work or growing their wealth, partnering with more men, having more women, and finding more locations. Due to their way of life, their earnings were also higher than average for workers.

The Reiss case is representative of the type of person recorded as a pimp both because of his deportation and because of the pardon the state granted him in 1937. As we have seen, being a rufián implied entering a relational and circumstantial category with the state; that is, it referred to a transitory quality acquired by a situation (the appropriation of money from a prostitute). While those at the time referred to the criminal organizations as solid and well-oiled, a deeper look at the documents shows them as complex centers of social relationships that promoted installing procurers with relative autonomy but also fostered interdependence based on ethnic origin and favors. Social relationships created by a common language and trust meant that groups tended to form around national identities. These groups were also composed through a circuit of spatial and social mobility in which hierarchies were established and knowledge was shared. Pimps established these links based on a common ethnic foundation, though once they arrived in the country, these borders became flexible and were cemented by interfamilial relationships with similar (brothers, cousins, or friends) or dissimilar partners (sisters or wives who sold sex).

Motche Goldberg understood that his circle of procurers was part of "his people" (Chaumont, Rodríguez García, and Servais, 2017: 36). It was not an organized, concentric network that the money flowed to, but a diaspora that provided resources to its members, a group of bonds in which knowledge was spread—for example, how to make a place for yourself in the Buenos Aires sex market—and that provided economic support to the recently arrived.

Goldberg bought houses that he divided into apartments and rented out to women to sell sex. According to the regulations from Buenos Aires, there could only be one prostitute per room (Schettini, 2016), which is why Goldberg gave his women a certificate of administration for the room as tenants and a certificate of good health in exchange for a blank promissory note with which he ensured he could kick them out. He advised Kinsie (Chaumont, Rodríguez García, and Servais, 2017: 36–40) that the girls be forced to give up their rooms every six months to avoid problems with girls who wanted to be independent and would refuse to pay rent.

The relationship between Goldberg and other procurers was social (an ethnic bond) and economic (credit). He would lend the recently arrived enough money for a house and charge them 10 percent of their earnings as payment for the credit. He also paid salaries to those most in need so that they would go to the houses he managed to collect fees from the women who offered their services to clients there or the madams (Chaumont, Rodríguez García, and Servais, 2017: 37). Similarly, Yarfitz (2019: 80) pointed out that the Varsovia Society (Zwi Migdal) circulated loans to develop properties to be used as brothels, much like activities developed by other immigrant groups that shows cooperation between different groups, not just pimps. At the same time, he orchestrated a system of mutual trust with which he guaranteed access to these resources. Through Goldberg's recommendation, Kinsie was able to access procurers in Paris, Florence, Rio de Janeiro, Montevideo, Warsaw, and Krakow. Therefore, their world also restricted the circulation of trusted credentials that were used to regulate exchanges and protect the group from potential intruders.

Access to property was key for the activity. The rapid expansion of Buenos Aires from the nineteenth century on made it so that access to a living space was a problem and led to the overcrowding of workers and high rent until the arrival of Peronism (Ballent, 2005), which is why workers invested a large portion of their earnings in paying for a place to live (Escudero, 1939a). There was an inherent inequality in the setup of how sex was sold where the regulation requiring a home be managed by a woman and the access some pimps had to property worked together so that they could take a portion of those women's money. Furthermore, Goldberg pointed out that the women who sold sex on the street were looking for the opportunity to move into a home to avoid police sanctions (Chaumont, Rodríguez García, and Servais, 2017: 44), which coincided with the high number of women detained for scandal recorded in city police manuals (Pareja, 1937).

In contrast with the representations of the period, the report's interviews reveal that most of the women involved with procurers sold sex before arriving in Buenos Aires. As pimps offered advice to Kinsie, they emphasized that he shouldn't look for just any old woman. They called inexperienced girls "greenies," recommended setting agreements with the women because the use of violence was considered risky, and suggested strategies to convince women they needed a "man" (Chaumont, Rodríguez García, and Servais, 2017: 36–45).

While the press exalted the Slavic and Jewish character of the pimps, the records of deported foreigners present a diversity of collaborative relationships mediated by interfamilial and interethnic connections. In addition to the accused Jews, there were also Germans, Algerians, Czechoslovakians, Spaniards, French, Dutch, British, Italians, Poles, Romanians, Russians, Uruguayans, and Swiss.

The French were part of the network called Los Marselleses, which involved men from the Provence-Côte d'Azur region. The police manuals described supposed recruitment agencies in rural zones of Paris, Marseille, and Bordeaux (Pareja, 1937: 124). Classic books, like the one written by the journalist Albert Londres, analyzed Jewish procurers protected in a chauvinist reading of the circulation of prostitutes within the context of mass migration (Guy, 2000). The men in this association who were deported from the country appropriated the money from women of peripheral nationalities. The files contain information on six prostitutes from Algeria, a French colony until 1962, and Egypt, an English colony until 1936. Between the wars, the Mediterranean was a place of mobility: women from the Middle East and North Africa were part of a massive flux in the workforce, sailors, travelers, and migrants, though generally it was read by the state as mere trafficking of women (Kozma, 2016).

The First World War accelerated the transformation of European sexualities: it heralded prolific mobility that generated anxieties among the elite regarding an apparent stability between the sexes. Couples were separated for a long time and women occupied male roles in the workforce. The war allowed new sexual experiences that surpassed class, age, gender, and racial borders, though it also involved traumatic experiences such as gang rapes. In this context, during the first postwar period, the fear of venereal diseases as a catalyst of national anxieties was accompanied by the interrelations between European women and men and inhabitants of the colonies who seemed to threaten the political and social order of supranational domination (Herzog, 2008). While the women of the colonies entered these groupings to sell sex and move to the south of the American continent, men became procurers to transform their own status. Thus, for example, Luis "Lulú" Migliario, a single thirty-three-year-old man documented as a pimp from Los Marselleses in 1932, was registered as a French criminal, even though when he entered through the Buenos Aires port in 1930 he declared he was an Algerian trader.

The ethnic basis for social relations among peers also played out in the intergroup competencies. Goldberg told Kinsie that the altercations with the police started due to fistfights and some murders between French and Polish pimps. Ethnic identity was the primary criterion used to define these groups, and this was made explicit in his testimonies. Goldberg noted that the French were "white slavers" who abused their women and tended to be spies; that's why he recommended Kinsie not mix with them (Chaumont, Rodríguez García, and Servais, 2017: 43). This description aligned with how the French procurers made out the Jews (Londres, 2007 [1927]). There are possibly two levels to the use of these terms to differentiate one group from another. First, he considered his own activity to be legitimate, appropriate, and within the framework of a mutual favor toward the women from whom he collected his fees. Second, he expressed a certain degree of adhesion to the use of the term "white slavery" as a negative label to catalog certain activities within the selling and buying of sex.

In this section I described the heart of common social relationships that sustained the meanings and practices that made up the social world of pimps. That is why I point out how the horizontal ethnic or economic connections were organized with unequal relationships (with the women) to create nodes of the incipient sex markets in Buenos Aires. In this sense, I underscore that the pimp condition was relational and changing in order to put forth a perspective that transcends these categories.

The Social Meanings and Practices of Pimps

Horizontal and vertical hierarchies shaped reciprocity between procurers. Overlapping spaces and business connections established the division of labor between rufianes, canflineros, and commission agents. The proliferation of writings on "white slavery" contributed to the existence of multiple meanings; police and procurers converged and diverged in what they called this activity. Manuals, the press, and stories used words such as canflinero, *caftan, cafishio, chulo, souteneur, maquereau, hewreman,* and *ricotaro,* among others (Barrés, 1934).

A police manual defined the rufián as a dealer in charge of selling women and the canflinero as an Argentine exploiter whose primary task was to exert physical control over women (Pareja, 1937). Other police publications identified the rufianes as those who would contact brothel owners and could exploit two or three women whereas the canflinero exploited only one domestic partner (Pinazo, 1918).

The canflineros or *canflinfleros* were notorious for implementing the so-called breaking-in—that is, using violence to minimize resistance from women who refused to sell sex under the conditions provided by the procurers. A journalist uncovered an Italian woman's report that described this modus operandi as a *clamangiamento* that involved being moved from one brothel to another and gang bangs (Jozami, 1930). Like the journalists, the communist teacher Angélica Mendoza, arrested in 1930 for her political activities in the Asilo del Buen Pastor, stated that these canflineros negotiated with the police for the release of detained women (Mendoza, 1933; Urbanyi, 1976).

In Kinsie's presence, the procurers displayed the methods they used to organize their practices. They defined their connections with the women as commercial relationships in which they had the unilateral right to a portion of the money earned by the women for selling sex, a privilege they could "sell" or "trade." They did not understand "selling a woman" as exchanging property but rather as two equals trading the right to the money and the possibility of moving her from one house to another (Chaumont, Rodríguez García, and Servais, 2017; 30–31). To sell, as Goldberg explained, referred to men trading girls with whom they could not "come to an agreement" (46). The procurers thus deviated from the journalistic narrative: for them, their relationship with the women was not one of ownership, but rather it was a contractual way for men to assert the monopoly they had on representation by managing residences. Madame Rue (a fantasy name that stressed being a woman of the street), a Polish woman who arrived at the age of sixteen in Buenos Aires accompanied by her husband, told Kinsie that the husband had tried to "sell her," and so she convinced him to go to Brazil where they would manage a brothel together (86).

For Goldberg, the "breaking-in" was not a violent act. He thought the use of physical force was ineffective and created problems with the police, which is why he advised "his boys" that it was best to show the woman there would be no other way to make a living, especially if she wanted to send money to her parents in her home country (Chaumont, Rodríguez García, and Servais, 2017: 36). One girl Kinsie interviewed in a brothel told him that she had "never practiced prostitution before" but that in Buenos Aires "everything is very dear (high-priced) here; besides, they pay very small wages," which is why she thought it was best to sell sex to earn a living (29), an account consistent with the low wages for female workers (Queirolo, 2018).

The police and procurers singled out the commission agent as the person in charge of managing the contacts that connected procurers with women interested in moving to the Southern Cone. Their roles varied: they could charge a woman for finding her a brothel where she could set up in Argentina or, vice versa, find a girl for a local procurer who could pay for her travel expenses to come to the country. For a man, getting in touch with them was complicated and required the referral of another procurer higher up (Chaumont, Rodríguez García, and Servais, 2017). Women with prior experience in prostitution went through commission agents to migrate as the authorities had restricted the entrance of single women (Chaumont, Rodríguez García, and Servais, 2017). None of this means women did not enter hierarchical, violent relationships in which they lost part of their earnings when they had to pay for male management. The commission agents also functioned as points of contact when there was interest in brothels in the country's interior. Deportation records include characters such as Pedro and Alejandro, French and Italian, respectively, who had "deep knowledge of pimping in the interior of the country" (AGN, box 29, no. 143).

Goldberg told Kinsie that commission agents charged 200 pesos to establish contacts (Chaumont, Rodríguez García, and Servais, 2017: 34). The procurer demanded those agents find women who conformed to certain criteria based on ethnicity, age, and previous sexual experience. The women entered a house for which they had to sign a blank check worth 1,000 pesos. When they left, the paper that acted as a security deposit was ripped up. For example, if the girl did not want to leave, if there was a dispute, or the mandatory medical examination diagnosed some illness, Goldberg would kick her out. According to the procurer's story, the Argentine regulation system was a "business: You see, that is why a girl must have a man. The girls have no money, and it takes her man to arrange things and pay the money" (39).

The pimps represented themselves in order to negotiate their standing among peers; creating a "reputation" was a double-edged sword allowing them to earn the respect of their peers but also potentially drawing the attention of state officials. Nicknames protected their individual identity in the eyes of the state and were also how other procurers identified them. The monikers exalted nationality or physical peculiarities; for example, "el Tano" gained recognition in Rosario along with an unpleasantly virile description that contrasted by men nicknamed "Lulú," which emphasized a more feminine attitude (AGN, box 29, no. 143).

The police used the concept of "amorality" when naming both homosexuals and procurers. It implied the supposed disruption of an ontological moral condition of the male: heterosexuality and a chivalrous attitude toward women. Media narratives that persisted throughout the century often depicted gay men as innkeepers, pimps, friends of prostitutes, or sexual servers of clients (Urbanyi, 1976). Prominent in interviews collected by forensic doctors is a young *travesti* employed as a housekeeper who went to the brothel to visit female friends and gained access to opportunities for courtship (Belvey, 1939).

The development of the Buenos Aires metropolis was a magnet for those seeking independence far from their families to engage in dissident sexual practices (Ben, 2009; Simonetto, 2017). Buenos Aires brothels were spaces for heterosexual reification but also social spaces for desire between men. There gay men could organize festive gatherings as with "la Renée," a Spanish woman who had a house on the 200 block of Avenida Corrientes that was raided by the police numerous times (Urbanyi, 1976: 80). Journalists and travelers wrote about retirees participating in the selling of sex; they were called *cocotos*. A Spanish forensic doctor described "La Teresita," who was "deported from Buenos Aires, Chile, Bolivia, and other American countries, landed in A Coruña in March 1911." La Teresita was thirty years old, the child of a former merchant, and was described as an "effeminate, not bad looking" person who "dressed as a woman and, wearing the most elegant outfits, had a knack for conquering more than a few Americans and received many gifts. La Teresita thus managed to raise some capital and settle into a truly luxurious life. At night La Teresita worked the streets in a carriage, accompanied by the most attentive suitors," which is how La Teresita "came to be part of a sodomitic scandal that is famous for causing a crisis in the Chilean government as various high ranking political figures had relations with the young man." In Buenos Aires, La Teresita "settled into a magnificent house on a Belgrano Street and threw huge parties and soirees where La Teresita turned up wearing scandalously extravagant dresses" (Bembo, 1912).

Material coercion governed the hierarchies between procurers and prostitutes. Goldberg emphasized that the women who walked the streets were exposed to abusive police control (Chaumont, Rodríguez García, and

Servais, 2017: 34). The city police reported that between 1928 and 1934 they detained 24,651 women for offering sex in public and for scandal (Pareja, 1937: 224), which is why the system of rooms managed by people like Goldberg and loans were useful for the continuation of pimping practices.

Pimps selected women based on ethnic criteria, willingness to provide oral, anal, and vaginal sex, and the ability to adapt to conditions. Goldberg stressed that Kinsie should avoid "greenies," first, because immigration law imposed administrative obstacles on the circulation of women under twenty-one. Second, these girls demanded a lot of "investment" given they didn't always "adjust" to the requirements of the clients, which is why he recommended Kinsie only look for them when engaging in a romantic relationship that would allow him to convince a woman of the benefits of selling sex (Chaumont, Rodríguez García, and Servais, 2017: 46). As Yarfitz (2019) points out, this contrasted with the images crafted by social reformers who—usually guided by the victimization of women—assumed the value of virginal women. As shown in Kinsie's study, pimps usually recommended avoiding this relationship and looking for women with previous experience in brothels.

Perhaps this is why deportation records show that hierarchical familial or marriage relationships were often in place between these men and their "girls" (AGN, box 29, no. 143). The slow access to civil rights for women (1968) strengthened male action; at the same time, state policies that confirmed the notion of women's biological inferiority and their need for protection were reflected in women's loss of power over their goods, individual liberty, and the free use of their bodies (Barrancos, 2006; Giordano, 2012).

On 25 May 1930, the Rosario newspaper *Reflejos* announced that Sabina Heit, twenty-two years old, reported her husband Isidoro Goldestein, thirty-six, as a "member of Zwi Migdal." Sabina did not speak Spanish and was assisted by a Polish laborer. She testified that she got married in Poland and that, upon their arrival in Rosario, her husband forced her to earn money by selling sex under "threat of death," which is why she was locked in a café for fourteen days. It is possible that in their reports, this pair emphasized the pressure the pimp had placed on her to create a new emotional connection, but beyond these conjectures, the frequency of these stories expresses the interpretations and experiences produced around the violent hierarchies that governed the selling of sex. For example, Santiago Petijón, nicknamed "Henry Le Doigt Coupé" (the cut finger), was the husband of Victoria Jaudalat, who worked in a brothel located on Calle Tucumán in Buenos Aires. The Russian Elías Tarnosky took his wife Rossa Lapioker Weis's money, just like the Pole Nysel Neiman, who exploited his wife, Cecilia Gelblum; the Italian José Apuzzo did the same to his wife Milena Olite as did the French Juan Pittarino to his spouse Alce Gothier (AGN, box 29, no. 143).

However, the majority of women selling sex under male surveillance in Buenos Aires were not doing so because their husbands tricked them, but because the state institution reinforced patriarchal relationships that legitimated the appropriation of money. Once married, some women transition from a social circle governed by the father to one managed by their partner. At the same time, migration entailed a breakdown of the social fabric and would sometimes place women in new linguistic territory.

The migratory reform of 1923 attempted to control the "quality" of those who arrived at Argentine ports as a response to the United States' quota policy and the increase in migrants along the southern Atlantic coasts. Within this framework, though the checkpoints were flexible, minors and women were paid special attention when traveling alone, and their entrance was restricted due to the belief that they were involved in prostitution networks (Devoto, 2001). The Committee for the Suppression of the Traffic in Women and Children recommended that women only be accepted if they were married (*Boletín Mensual de la Sociedad de las Naciones*, 1 May 1927). Paradoxically, these restrictions also made it so that women from less-favored areas needed to find a spouse if they wanted to move in search of a new life.

Other hierarchical familial relationships used these men to govern the use of a woman's body. Thus, Szmelko Markus, a twenty-five-year-old Pole, took the earnings of his sister Pesa and his wife Sarah, who cycled through three brothels. The Uruguayan Ramón Rama brought a young woman into the country making use of a fake ID obtained in Montevideo using his deceased sister's records (AGN, box 29, no. 143). That is, he appealed to familial connections to establish power relations based on gender inequality, much like situations that could be seen at the heart of other families.

The xenophobic and antisemitic discourse that surrounded the Zwi Migdal reports did not only affect pimps. The discursive power determined the amount European prostitutes could earn, given the condition of prostitutes and foreign women operated like a combination of isomorphisms of status and class that influenced their social position and economic situation both by being restricted from engaging in other work and in terms of their lives outside the brothels.

Differing status came into play for pricing the consumption of sexual services. The so-called Polish prostitution was a way of identifying a cheaper system for the clients than the French women. This was due to how long it took for Polish brothels to get set up compared with the French, which forced the former to set lower prices so they could be competitive (Urbanyi, 1976). Thus, it is possible to imagine that the proliferation of this narrative served to lower the costs for consumers of sexual services.

The procurers also adhered to dominant notions of sexual qualities for certain ethnicities. Goldberg recommended Kinzie prioritize relations with French women over Jewish Poles as the former had greater liberties and prerogatives around their sexuality and were open to fellatio and anal sex. He also emphasized that when the women were on their period, the French only lost a day while the Jews took off four (Chaumont, Rodríguez García, and Servais, 2017: 44). It is possible to also imagine that the references to women as the bounty of male property functioned as part of the symbolic rivalries between procurers and different ethnic communities.

The journalistic stories also noted that the properties associated with female morality affected the prices of services. It was believed that virgins earned more (Jozami, 1930), as an expression of male fantasies that related the lack of sexual experience with purity and greater pleasure, and as a moral condition, a healthy, never tarnished body. Furthermore, with access to a virgin, men were guaranteed aseptic sex without the possibility of contracting venereal diseases. This contrasts with the stories of procurers who recommended that Kinsie look for experienced girls to avoid conflicts with local authorities.

Other journalists emphasized how city zones and their neighborhoods established different prices. In Rosario, they noted that while in the neighborhood Pichincha prices were around two to five pesos, as you got farther away, the prices dropped to fifty cents, as they were considered railroad neighborhoods and the women, therefore, were for "worker" consumption (Jozami, 1930; Pareja, 1937; Múgica, 2014).

Some women managed to climb the ladder. Zwi Migdal allowed women and family members to participate in the organization (Yarfitz, 2019). It is possible that, as some of them aged and therefore lost their "value," they had the chance to participate as investors or managers of the places where sex was sold. This is the case of the deported sisters Hana and Blanca, of Polish origin. Fifty and forty-five years old respectively, over time they worked as madams and commission agents (AGN, box 29, no. 143). Goldberg noted that some women were mediators between procurers and other women who used the houses to meet customers. This situation avoided problems with the law, given the regulatory system required a woman to manage the brothel.

In sum, in this section I analyzed the social meanings and practices of the pimp's universe. To do so, I described a combination of common resources that defined the borders (sometimes permeable) and their social rules.

Global Circulation as a Spatial Practice

The priors reported to the Ministry of the Interior in the deportation files give clues about the movement of procurers and prostitutes (AGN, box 29, no. 143). The geographic itineraries reveal fine lines of movement that are not "routes" but interconnections between global and local scales, juxtaposed circuits that speak as much to the practices of reciprocal association between pimps as to the massive flows of migration across the Atlantic.

In Europe, movement was transnational and regional: as much from rural zones to cities as from central countries to the peripheries (South America) or centers (United States), movements in line with the high level of mobility of poor workers who moved in search of employment. This context that spurred millions of migrants to move to the Southern Cone also encouraged some women who sold sex to seek out procurers and commissioners in order to make the move. Working-class European women had already experienced a similar process between the end of the eighteenth and middle of the nineteenth centuries: female migration from agricultural work to a labor market that did not offer opportunities to all, and the low female salaries compared to the male workforce generated a mass of women prepared to sell sex (Stearns, 2017: 86–87).

A network of ephemeral contacts, the circulation of knowledge, the certification of trust, and monetary loans eased transnational movement for the sale of sex. As I explain, there were many forms of contact between procurers and women with previous experience in a brothel. The local police claimed there were job placement offices that offered women positions as dressmakers, dancers, singers, teachers, servants, or models (Pareja, 1937). The League of Nations suggested measures to control the circulation of women with an inclination for artistic activities (*Boletín Mensual de la Sociedad de las Naciones*, 1 August 1927) (Chaumont, Rodríguez García, and Servais, 2017: 34–46).

Some women who sold sex in European brothels looked for commission agents to contact Latin American brothels (Chaumont, Rodríguez García, and Servais, 2017: 34). It is difficult to know how the commission agents operated in cases of women who did not have previous experience selling sex and who migrated with the hope of obtaining one of the promised jobs. There were numerous mechanisms with which to adjust the expectations of these women to the way of life of the procurers. Kinsie received many warnings about bringing "greenies" but also suggestions for convincing them that they would earn more money to send to their families than with domestic service. On the other hand, the procurers established a strong hierarchy tied to the access to property to get some of the money, and though they denied it, it is likely they resorted to coercion to guarantee the connection (Chaumont, Rodríguez García, and Servais, 2017: 34–46).

Cross-referencing the data on the national origin of the pimps and prostitutes illustrates some of the inequities in the circulation. Though Goldberg recommended Kinsie look only for French women, the procurers did not only bring over women of their own nationality. French, English, Spanish, and Italian men could make contact with Polish, Slovenian, Russian, or Romanian women. The circulation of women and men was also an expression of the asymmetries resulting from unequal effects of the Great War on the old continent (Urbanyi, 1976).

Following the xenophobic and antisemitic narratives, Warsaw was considered the center of operations associated with Zwi Migdal. Fears around the trafficking of people were concentrated in Poland. As discussed, the term *"polaca"* seeped into the popular slang for decades among pimps to define a "cheaper" way of selling; it became synonymous with prostitute (Urbanyi, 1976). Buenos Aires was singled out as the other link in the chain. The city gained this reputation through the emphasis given by international organizations. The *Boletín del Patronato Real para la Represión de la Trata de Blancas* (1914: 66) from Spain indicates that in the Argentine capital "men have too much money in vice and there is no public opinion on morality."

Though the representations imagined the city as the center of the global sexual map (Schettinni, 2014), the movement of procurers and prostitutes was not one-directional. Records of deportations present a changing landscape that involves the ability to permeate and bend state restrictions and demonstrates how magnetic poles were moved by regional economic flows.

Attempts to deport procurers were not always effective. The Reiss case I took as a point of departure coincides with many of the impressions highlighted by Kinsie's informants and the later 1927 League of Nations report.

Goldberg indicated to Kinsie that it was possible to negotiate deportation as they had a contact in the police office that informed them when things were about to get more difficult so they could travel to Montevideo for a while (Chaumont, Rodríguez García, and Servais, 2017: 43). The important thing was to not get documented in the photographic records of pimps; avoiding that guaranteed travel without major inconveniences. He also recommended Kinsie travel in first class to avoid a search by the migration authorities.

Meanwhile, Argentine state officials, like others indicated in the report, were susceptible to illicit payments. In the Buenos Aires Health Department, you could obtain a certificate for 100 pesos (Chaumont, Rodríguez García, and Servais, 2017: 39). Procurers from cities like Warsaw, Poland, and Florence, Italy, celebrated that in exchange for a little money they could get passports and visas (as other immigrants in general) (42). It is possible that these statements were part of an exaltation of their abilities in the presence of a new arrival to whom they wanted to appear as skilled criminals. This should also be included within the general tactics migrants used to get papers in the so-called immigration business (Devoto, 2001).

What appears to be a failure of state agencies is the confirmation that for these offices being a pimp was dependent on context and was constantly in flux. The apparent "failures" also underscored the possibilities to circumvent borders, as Reiss did through Montevideo. The weakness of the state is made clear by the fact that he himself reported his country of residence during his application for entry. In his visit to South America, El Mayor Wegner, president of the German League Against White Slavery, emphasized that some pimps flocked to Montevideo to avoid checkpoints when they entered Argentina (*Boletín del Patronato Real para le Represión de la Trata de Blancas*, 1907–12: 13). Thus, the most economically successful pimps possibly were those capable of moving women to other cities or ports. The police detailed the circulation of some of them to Brazilian cities like Río de Janeiro or São Paulo as well as to Montevideo. The Uruguayan magazine *La Pluma* (1 July 1930) reproduced the notion of Poland and France in Europe and Buenos Aires and Montevideo in South America as the hubs of this practice.

Kinsie depended on Goldberg's approval to travel, which suggests that these connections operated with mechanisms that brought together social capital and credentials, like the letters of recommendation they gave him. It is thus arguable that the unified nature of these networks did not stem from a hermetic center that organized the group of operations, but that points of connection were fostered between different groups that fostered the installation and development of procurers.

The specialist report from the United Nations (UN) (*Report of the Special Body of Experts on Traffic in Women and Children*, 1927) emphasized the routes of interconnection between the countries of the region. It points out the intersection between border cities Salto and Concordio as a preferred passage for *caftens*. It reported that in the passage from Brazil to Argentina people could get documents with false identities that they bought from the police in the capital. Though the authorities denied both reports in a letter to the commission of specialists, the information remained. Israel Laperie, a forty-year-old Russian man, entered in 1924 from Brazil, where he had been deported for engaging in illicit activities. In 1936, he was thrown out of Argentina for sexually exploiting Magdalena Torres, a thirty-one-year-old Spanish woman, and for the crime of corruption and various damages (AGN, box 29, no. 143).

Kinsie's interviews with procurers and prostitutes in Montevideo reveal a lot about their connections with Buenos Aires. In Salto, a boat could carry them across at night, avoiding migration checkpoints; those with Argentine documents could elude any kind of check by migration officials. One woman told Kinsie (Chaumont, Rodríguez García, and Servais, 2017: 63) that "to come here from Buenos Aires is easy . . . the girls take the train from this city to Salto, and then across Uruguay River to Concordia, and then you are in Argentina and can go where you want." In the case of Rio de Janeiro, the woman told him they had to pay bribes to the migration officials on the trains and explained that "the way in here from Rio is over the old American-built railroad. You cross the border at Rivera. All you have to do is cross the street. The line runs through the main street. The officers sometimes hold you up, but a few pesos to an officer who only gets about 60 pesos a month is a lot of money" (Chaumont, Rodríguez García, and Servais, 2017: 64). The movement to Montevideo was also associated with the rule that in Argentina there could only be one woman per location, which is why many of them moved to the eastern city or to towns in the interior where it was possibly cheaper to share rent (Chaumont, Rodríguez García, and Servais, 2017: 73), a description that Albert Londres also gives (2007 [1927]).

The routes also show the movement between Argentina and Chile. The Spanish newspaper *El Extranjero* (10 March 1933) documented the arrest of eight men who were identified as members of Zwi Migdal (a term that seems to have been used indiscriminately by journalists after the trial) who were trying to cross into Argentina with forty women between the ages of fourteen and forty whom they had promised jobs in Buenos Aires theaters. Nevertheless, the turmoil of journalistic narratives could also channel nationalist fears about the border permeability, which makes it difficult to differentiate the reliable information that only marks crosswalks and addresses.

Finally, there was also movement toward the interior of the national territory. The deportation records detail that some of the canflineros traveled to cities like Mendoza, Rosario, Córdoba, and San Luis, four important urban centers with potential customers. Rosario ended up being a paradigmatic site; it was the country's second-largest port city and housed, in the Pichincha neighborhood, a high number of well-known brothels (Múgica, 2014). Some journalists also pointed out that the procurers moved from Buenos Aires to Tucumán, San Juan, and Bahía Blanca (Urbanyi, 1976). Because the regulation system was governed at the municipal level, many women moved to cities where, for example, they were allowed to live with multiple women and where the state and press did not apply as much pressure on the sale of sex.

In this section I analyzed the movement of actors related to the sale of sex as part of the many transatlantic, continental, and national influxes of the first half of the twentieth century. I also highlighted some of the possible migration routes as multidirectional paths, which shows the global circulation of procurers as a viable option for some migrants.

· · · · · ·

In this chapter I analyzed the discourses, practices, and meanings of procurers, prostitutes, police, civil servants, and journalists related to pimping. To do so, I investigated an extensive corpus of documents to study a specific configuration of selling sex marked by the mobility of the sexual supply, the circulation of knowledge, male social capital, mediator networks, and the use of different degrees of coercion to appropriate the money earned.

First, I examined the general outline of the local formation of "white slavery" as an argumentative thread to univocally analyze the buying and selling of sex. I considered the growing public concern in the 1930s around the trial of Zwi Migdal members as the pivotal moment that catalyzed anxieties provoked by the end of the Argentine liberal project, the waning use of immigration as a path for development, and the tensions in the restructuring of the national identity and whiteness between the Buenos Aires cosmopolitanism and criollo traditionalism.

Second, I analyzed the practices that structured this specific form of selling sex and its relationship with the system of regulated prostitution. To do so, I studied the many social meanings and practices procurers used to participate in the sex market and described a diverse set of social meanings and practices they used to create and understand their role in the buying and selling of sexual services. Among them I emphasized the reciprocity between peers founded on ethnically defined social groups, the description of relationships with women as rental markets, the techniques of suppression and appropriation of money earned by two or more women selling sex, the investment in residences as an assurance for making connections, the intergenerational relationships marked by loans and advice for the continuation of procurement as a practice, the tactics to undermine the authorities, and transnational circulation.

2 The Client Rebellion

A War for the Right to Pay for Sex (1936–1965)

· ·

In 1943, Colonel Juan Domingo Perón, interim minister of war for the de facto president Pedro Pablo Ramírez, along with Edelmiro Farrell, led a group of soldiers who since 1937 had been questioning the abolition of regulated prostitution and were demanding the installation of "houses of tolerance," or licensed brothels, for the army. The colonel was hoping this would help the soldiers resolve "issues of sexual abstinence" (Perón, 23 June 1943).[1] In *Captain Pantoja and the Special Service* (translated by Gregory Kolovakos and Ronald Christ), Mario Vargas Llosa recounts the difficulties General Pantoja faces as he installs a brothel in the Iquitos barracks to avoid an increase in the number of rapes perpetrated by the soldiers in the jungle. The novel's fictional documents resemble the reports and plans presented by the Argentine soldiers to the Ministry of the Interior and alert us to a widespread imaginary of paid sex.

The passing of the 1936 Prophylaxis Law triggered an intense epistolary exchange between government officials and high-ranking military officers. The dissolution of the regulatory system that was in place for sixty-one years had a disruptive impact beyond the legal conditions and set in motion an intense symbolic shift in dominant masculine norms: the state ceased to directly manage the purchase of sexual services. In response to this change, high-ranking military officials positioned themselves as representatives of those who paid for sex and questioned a regulation that, they believed, violated the male right to intercourse with women. Colonels and generals from Patagonia, San Luis, and Corrientes argued that the legislation left soldiers vulnerable to sexually transmitted diseases, "homosexuality," masturbation, onanism, and abstinence.

In 1944, Edelmiro Farrell, de facto president, allowed the installation of "houses of tolerance" close to barracks through executive order 10.638, which, under Perón, became law 12.912 in 1947. This situation sparked resentment in the multiclass government coalition, and some unionists questioned the regulation. In 1954, when the conflict between the Catholic Church and government broke out, Perón again attempted to regulate brothels through executive order 22.532, sparking fervent opposition from Catholic activists, but in 1955 the initiative came to a halt following the coup d'état. In 1965, Parliament formally closed the brothels near regiments in line with the United Nations convention (law 16.666). Several months later, however, some representatives reported that the military brothels were still open in certain parts of the country (Luis Merrero, Comisión de Asistencia Social y Salud Pública, file 410/65).

The objective of this chapter is to reconstruct the social meanings and practices used by soldiers, unionists, physicians, Peronists, and Catholic organizations in response to the abolition of regulated prostitution and subsequent reforms between 1936 and 1965. I present the many voices speaking to the political representation of sexual consumption in order to analyze the convergent and divergent tensions in the definition of masculinity and male sexuality as central to the Argentine national ideology.

Historians have underscored the construction of public and private agendas regarding venereal diseases (Biernat, 2013; Biernat and Simonetto, 2017; Guy, 1991; Miranda, 2012; Múgica, 2014), marked the representations of gender deployed around the law, noted how attention shifted from female to male sexuality, and emphasized the reproductive character of the male body and his responsibility to keep his family and the nation healthy (Grammático, 2002; Milanesio, 2005; Queirolo, 2014). Analyzing this new body aligns with the historical trend that focused on how patients behaved and how physicians understood their experience of illness (Biernat, 2018). It also acknowledges the tensions between the idea that masculine sexuality was presumed to be central to the national imaginary and the defense of an institutionalized double standard that, historians believed, should guarantee men have access to sex for recreational purposes.

This chapter also contributes to studies of Peronism. The epistolary exchange was crucial to understanding the active place of workers in the Peronist cultural construction (Acha, 2007; Guy, 2017). The relevance of eroticism and sexuality in the transformation of Peronist political ties gave way to important conflicts that explain the role of divorce, sexuality, gender, and filiation in the tension with the Catholic Church that marked Perón's downfall (Acha, 2014). The letters from generals and Catholic women shed light on how the Peronist movement channeled the sexual demands of its allies in the organization of networks of political loyalty.

Finally, this chapter illuminates the tensions between the transformative dynamics of Peronist policies and their limitations in dismantling structures rooted in sexual moralities (Cosse, 2006). The Peronist drive to loosen restrictions on the installation of "houses of tolerance" was based on caring for men's reproductive health, and it adopted the military's premise that paid sex needed to be managed to enhance men's performance.

The chapter shifts the focus from the positions taken by dominant doctors in the field to examine how soldiers, unionists, Peronists, Catholic organizations, and physicians appropriated or rejected these medical notions through metaphors of the body, masculinity, and nation. I also observe the dynamic following the passage of the law to study how the local tensions around the reach and limitations of the abolitionist policies in Argentina responded to international pressures from organizations like the League of Nations. I thus analyze both the cycle of how abolitionism was relaxed and the resistance to this trend on the part of unionists and Catholic groups.

To do so, I studied how members of the military tied to the United Officers' Group (GOU), a nationalist-leaning circle that played an important role in the military coup of 1943 and the subsequent rise of Peronism (Potash, 1969), lobbied against the abolition of regulated prostitution. In their letters, colonels and generals interpreted "being a man" as the natural consumer of paid sex, as a person endowed with a boundless sexual appetite. They used medical concepts to attribute meaning to the experience of consuming sex and to define male identity. This language linked the letter writers with medicine as a source of authority and with Catholicism as a moral guide.

High-ranking officers represented themselves as spokesmen for the consumption of paid sex by appealing to two lines of reasoning: the consensus that male sexuality was uncontrollable and male reproductive and sexual health were crucial to the strategic development of the nation and the defense of the prerogatives of the periphery in response to a law the letter writers thought came from the center. That is, they espoused an androcentric concept of male health as responsible for producing and reproducing proletarians, soldiers, and consumers, thereby stimulating the nation's development. Furthermore, I see the officers' letter-writing as a practice that distilled a collective articulating a specific male identity that was resentful of state intervention.

My corpus includes letters between regiments in Patagonia, Corrientes, and San Luis, the Ministry of the Interior, the Ministry of War, and the National Department of Hygiene; reports from the National Archive of Defense, union-run courses, and specialized medical journals; and files presented by Catholic organizations to Congress. I interpret the exchange of letters, reports, and secret notes between the health authorities, Ministries of War and the Interior, and the barracks as spaces of male socialization that fostered declarations, requests, and demands that would be less likely to emerge in other contexts. With the insistence with which the high-ranking officers wrote their demands, they participated in a performative ritual of their masculine identity and defined borders of belonging. Therefore, privileged documental access helps us understand the gendered structures of the state.

This chapter is organized into four sections. The first deals with the circuits for the letter-writing campaign, the participants, the background to the dialogue, and the way it was constructed as a space for male socialization. The second explores the officers' fears as driving forces and nuclei of meaning that organized their construction as political representatives for sexual customers. The third section examines the bills the officers proposed and the practices of consuming sex among the conscripts. The final section analyzes the tension between the efforts of unionist, medical, and Catholic interventions in defense of the Prophylaxis Law, in a context of internal conflicts of Peronism around this issue and the crystallization of the abolitionist policy.

Writing to Defend Virility

Military access to prostitution was a topic of global debate. In 1864 the British government passed the Contagious Diseases Acts to protect servicemen. It mandated compulsory medical examinations of prostitutes near barracks, a measure the abolitionists fought against. The French and British armies installed brothels to limit the transmission of diseases on the premise that sexual activity would enhance soldiers' performance (Herzog, 2008). In the twentieth century, Japan sought to provide women to the army to guarantee soldiers' loyalty to the state (Tanaka, 2003).

In 1937 Argentine military surgeon Guillermo Ruzo wrote a letter warning that it would be impossible "to prohibit the oldest profession in the world" and that the new law would drive up "prostitution and pimping." The doctor understood that the goal of the legislation was to ban the purchase and sale of sex and was upset by national intervention in what he felt were matters of the army. He demanded that "houses of tolerance" be set up to meet "men's physiological needs," a "mechanism for sexual relief" that would keep their bodies virile and healthy, "physically and psychologically tuned" (Ruzo, 4 July 1937).

The physician's letter encouraged colonels and generals in the south of Argentina dealing with what they considered to be the disastrous effects of the abolitionist law. They were members of organizations such as the Patagonia Association, a group of regiments stationed in Neuquén, Trelew, Río Negro, Santa Cruz, and Tierra del Fuego charged with guarding the resources of the Fiscal Oilfields (YPF). Their purpose was to strengthen the army's presence and influence in the region in order to protect national security and defend strategic natural resources (Memorias Agrupación Patagonia, Archivo de la Defensa National, 1948).

These missives were inserted into a political and institutional framework that facilitated their circulation and influence. Besides Juan Domingo Perón, the authors included Colonel Ángel Solari, the founder and commander of the Patagonia Association and first military governor of the military zone of Comodoro Rivadavia; Luis César Perlinger, minister of the interior in 1943; and Colonel Luis Alberto Gilbert, minister of the interior and foreign relations under the de facto presidency of General Pedro Pablo Ramírez (1943–44), as well as other members of the GOU.

Eugenio Galli, a government health care official, acted as a nexus between the army and physicians who agreed that abolitionism needed to be loosened. He had worked in the armed forces so was actively involved in the resistance. In 1925, he was made head of the surgery division at the Central Military Hospital, and in 1939 he became the army's director general for health. Then he began working for the state as director general for hygiene in Buenos Aires Province (1941) and became president of the National Department of Hygiene in 1943.

The secret letters, files, and notes written by members of the military, physicians, and civil servants represent a space for male socialization that enabled statements, requests, and demands that would have been difficult to make in another context. The clandestine production of these documents allowed the circulation of shared assumptions that the male body has uncontrollable sexual urges. The writers developed two topics on their agenda: a strategic concern about population quality and quantity as a national issue and strategies for solidarity among peers.

Along with other members of the military, physicians and low-ranking civil servants established a male dialogue and inserted it in political and institutional systems that considered male sexuality a matter of the state. Nevertheless, when the Peronist minister of health Ramón Carrillo tried to bring back the regulatory system, Catholic women's organizations demanded that the Senate delay the revision of the law "until women could vote on it" (Congreso de la Nación, Particulares, no. 131/49).

During the postwar period, the military grew increasingly concerned about national security weaknesses stemming from the prioritization of agriculture and the uneven distribution of the population in the territory. As a result, the state became deeply involved in local politics (Berrotarán, 2008). From the 1930s on, the military developed a perception of itself as an independent institution that broadened its margin for intervention in the life of the nation. The widespread presence of the military and its blend of Catholic culture enabled the armed forces to define themselves as an independent subgroup within the nation, with the authority to intervene to "reorganize" the fatherland (Soprano, 2016). This context influenced what the colonels wrote: they were members of a professional body who believed that although their duties were expanding, the prerogatives to which they were naturally entitled were being cut back.

Their letters were generated in the Patagonia political microclimate. The officers laid out a hypothetical conflict with Chile, the presence of strategic petroleum reserves, and low population density to articulate a southern populationist ideology driven by local nationalist movements in the interwar period (Bohoslavsky, 2007). Patagonia was the metaphor for the empty country, the idealized image of a foundational period for the Argentine army, an eternal desert that renewed the pact for state domination of a land cleansed of its early inhabitants. Life in Patagonia was entwined with the barracks. From the 1930s on, colonels and generals occupied military governorship positions, blocking Patagonian citizens' access to their political rights. The development of social policies and infrastructure broadened military control and influence on a population that was disqualified from electing their local authorities. This situation made possible the military's perception that it was crucial to the reproduction of the nation and its values in the southern region (Navarro Floria and Nuñez, 2012).

The letter writing also developed within institutional traditions and the fear of a national masculinity perceived as under threat. Obligatory military service, voting rights, and education contributed to the construction of Argentine identity in the restructuring of the mass migration of local citizens. Argentine conscription encouraged loyalty to the nation among the working-class men by using a rhetoric of hegemonic masculinity that promised they would be positioned above women (Ablard, 2017).

The 1930s also created a divide in the interpretation of social and sexual order associated with that national identity that was perceived to be threatened by profuse material transformations that modernized Buenos Aires (Barrancos, 2006). Elites responded to this apprehension with a battery of interventional policies regarding public and social space—like the misdemeanor codes—to strengthen a social order they thought was fading. This was a moment of transition in the national representation of virile identity. While virility was presented as potent, new products and policies emerged that promised to protect male sexuality as an indispensable quality for the reproduction of the nation. Law 12.331 addressed men's health care to the detriment of the mandatory sanitary protection that the state had exercised in licensed brothels (Biernat and Simonetto, 2017). In the 1940s, President Perón as a symbol as well as his public performance channeled that social angst: he presented himself as an enthusiastic, attractive, family-oriented, funny young man, an ideal of the modern man who broke the tradition of men lacking power and built part of his legitimacy on a new erotic magnetism for the public, both men and women (Milanesio, 2014). Transforming the request from the military into a policy was part of a process of reimagining the male pact between the state and the soldiers, and it was part of an ambivalent process between the traditional and disruptive nature of the Argentine model of masculinity.

In sum, these demands circulated in a space of state-sponsored masculine socialization in which members of the military articulated notions of what they saw as legitimate masculinity in their texts. The requested transformational measures were supported by important political figures and the state interpreting the context as transitional.

Male Fears: A War against "Sexual Deviation"

Colonel Perlinger criticized a law he believed could not satisfy "men's bestial needs with talks and videos on sex education" (Perlinger, 4 May 1941). Military officials saw the legal situation as a threat to the primary issue: the virility of a healthy body as the active center of the nation. Writing as representatives of their peers meant mobilizing associations in which the fatherland depended on men's reproductive health, the satisfaction of their pleasures, and the care of their bodies. It was the corollary to the proliferation of discourses that began in the late nineteenth century that ranked sexual practices in order to define the parameters of what was permissible (Ramacciotti and Valobra, 2008; Salessi, 2000).

At the same time, the supposed active nature of men's sexual desire was understood as a symptom of fragility as it was vulnerable to external threats.

Law 12.331 was interpreted as constraining men's natural right to access sexual services. Constant references to the "oldest profession in the world" suggested the innate, immutable nature of men's access to paid intercourse, which is what made the military officials see the regulations as a danger for the moral discipline and virility of the soldiers.

In the military discourse, illegitimate sexuality was not the product of the subject's individual imprudence but of a lack of state intervention to control it. The resistance to the law constituted a "crisis of masculinity," a mechanism of virile regulation of the body that assumes the masculine is vigorous but fragile, always threatened and at risk, which is why it should be exalted to protect against its enemies (Allen, 2002). These fears elicited resentment in the face of social and cultural transformations that were threatening the conditions that upheld their identity. Thus, the appeal to a past: that of a healthy and virile body that the officers thought was disappearing and that they reaffirmed in a cyclical process. The writing thus expressed a ritual of revitalization and internalization of a specific interpretation of the universal ideal of "being a man."

The concern with producing a healthy, disciplined body to occupy the territory demanded that members of the military translate concepts from the medical field to define their own identities and reclaim what they considered to be their sexual rights. Venereal diseases, onanism, masturbation, and homosexuality were listed as threats to servicemen eager for sex with no guaranteed access to brothels.

The primary risk to military leaders was venereal disease. The officers saw non-state-regulated prostitution as the cause of a supposed rise in the number of cases. Therefore, if the public's goal was to protect men's health, the changes in regulations should not delay attention to needs that were considered biologically necessary such as intercourse but should guarantee the sanitary conditions to make it possible. The agenda for venereal disease in Argentina appealed to eugenics and populationism in that it focused on reproducing workers and consumers for desirable development in modern states. Venereal diseases, as in the rest of the world, were described as causing miscarriages and nervous and circulatory conditions that weakened the working class. As such, these diseases channeled meanings used to redefine social borders (Biernat and Simonetto, 2017).

References in the letters to cases of genital damage due to syphilis and gonorrhea contrasted with the statistics of the army's own Internal Health Board, which stressed that the number of cases was going down. From 1935 to 1940, the percentage of enlisted men with sexually transmitted conditions fell from 32.54 percent to 9.27 percent of the total number of patients. The military's statistical records showed that venereal complaints were gradually losing ground to other infectious diseases such as measles (Memorias del Ministerio de Guerra, 1940). This drop can be explained by the application of prophylactic measures such as distributing medications and creating a standard treatment that was applied more efficiently in the military than in civil society (Biernat, 2007).

Far from being a false narrative, the military perceptions responded to the construction of an effective fiction based on an identity that they felt was being threatened by the state. The androcentric notion of health—that is, the understanding of the public as responsible for the health of the male body—transcended the institutional margins of the military. The records of the Buenos Aires Penitentiary Service (SPB) and judicial departments contain complaints lodged by men regarding violations of article 202(c) of the penal code, which penalized the transmission of venereal disease. In these legal proceedings, the men demanded that the women who infected them with syphilis, chancroid, or gonorrhea be penalized, with the belief that women were passive objects, vessels for disease, and responsible for managing them (Biernat, 2018).

The text of law 12.331 was the subject of interpretation by state organizations (judicial and police agencies), physicians and jurists (in favor or against), and social sectors (negotiating ways to buy and sell sex). An early group of critics organized themselves around prohibitionism, understood at the time as a system that barred the sale of sex (Biernat, 2013; Múgica, 2014). While the law did not prohibit the sale of sex but rather the licensed brothel, many critics understood it as prohibitionist. Colonel Ángel Solari defined it as "the law that bans prostitution, a law which, rather than being beneficial, has aggravated and created new problems" (Solari, 3 May 1942). Ernesto Pareja (1940), deputy commissioner for the city of Buenos Aires, claimed that the law served the interests of an idealist, ineffective cultural elite who knew little about the people's needs. According to Pareja, it put low-income youths at risk since they were "moved by organic sexual instinct" but short of money to start a family and had no "official" sources of sexual relief.

Solari also believed the law tampered with the "sexual needs of grown servicemen," a problem aggravated by the "vertical growth of the male population" (Solari, 3 May 1942). For military leaders, the demographic imbalance between men and women in the territory meant that brothels should be open. Many laborers migrated to the region for work: the census data show that Comodoro Rivadavia had 25,651 inhabitants, 15,328 males and 10,323 females; Río Gallegos had 5,880 inhabitants, 3,400 males and 2,480 females; and Esquel had 5,484 inhabitants, 3,035 males and 2,449 females. In cities like Neuquén, in which there were only thirty more men than women out of a total of 7,498 inhabitants, military advocates stressed that prostitution services were required because of the small population that made it difficult for people to find partners (Censo Nacional de Población, 1947).

In addition to sexually transmitted disease, the military pointed to onanism and masturbation as consequences of sexual abstinence. Law 12.331 was described by officials as "one that restricts the sexual needs of grown servicemen and the civilian population, which can lead to unfortunate excesses" (Solari, 3 May 1942). In 1943, colonel Juan Domingo Perón attached a report by the surgeon Ruzo to "speed up resolution of an urgent problem" (Perón, 22 June 1942). The surgeon described how sexual abstinence could interfere with the brain function regulating sexual desire in men, seriously compromising the body. "The rupture of the nervous balance of those who do not ejaculate during intercourse with the opposite sex" could lead to permanent damage to the volitional system, "permanently destroying sexual desire." It therefore led to serious damage, according to this physician, who saw servicemen deprived of any sexual contact (Ruzo, 23 April 1942). Perón described this situation as the "disorders and harm caused by the law" (Perón, 3 March 1944).

Dr. Ruzo was dismayed by what he saw as the potential loss of desire and reproductive capacity among enlisted men caused by stifling the biological impulse that defined "being a man." For Ruzo, abstinence led soldiers to engage in masturbation. Sexology manuals described masturbation as the origin of perverse forms of deviation such as "self-gratifying autoeroticism" and "onanism" (Pellegrini, 1950). These categories referred to the patient disconnecting from the world and replacing it with sexual fantasies, which generated extreme narcissism, the greatest risk of which was homosexuality, seen as an inversion that removed the subject from the masculine world (Opizzo, 1963).

Colonel Alberto Gilbert worried about the "harmful influence on the performance of military activities" that went hand in hand with sexual abstinence. He requested houses of tolerance be installed in response to the fact that "military personnel are in a critical situation given that it is materially impossible to satisfy their sexual needs," which contributed to "loosening of moral principles, loss of vigor, and lack of control over the spread of venereal diseases" (Gilbert, 28 August 1942).

According to Colonel Solari, the obstacles to having sex with women seriously affected the units' performance, weakening men's bodies and distracting them from a soldier's task (Solari, 11 May 1942). He understood that the legislation was idealist and impractical, having been designed in the federal capital in complete ignorance of the interior of Argentina. The colonel reiterated the criticisms of physicians from the country's interior who called for more resources and distribution of effective medications for treating venereal diseases (Biernat, 2007).

Homosexuality also evoked fear. The "imperious need for ejaculation through penetration" carried the risk that there might be "functional substitutions for the physiological sex act among the conscripts" (Gilbert, 3 August 1943). Homosexuality was a condition that fractured the state of virility considered necessary for combat, a sexual inversion that implied being unmanly. In this sense, the letters appealed to binary metaphors of femininity and masculinity to catalog passive bodies (weak, homosexual, penetrated) as opposed to active bodies (penetrators, strong, agile).

The definition of homosexuality as a negative otherness had major repercussions in 1944 when photographs emerged of cadets in suggestive poses at gatherings in the National Military College (Bazán, 2006). The spread of this panic was the expression of a subjective barrier seen as threatened by the consolidation of modern homosexual identity in urban metropolitan areas. The gradual gathering of dissimilar sexual practices was perceived as a threat to masculinity (Simonetto, 2017).

There was not complete agreement that "sexual perversions" were a direct result of the lack of prostitutes. For example, Eugenio Galli believed there were no reliable statistics for measuring said perversions. On the contrary, the "unleashing of sexual instincts" was due to a "growing sexual freedom" that was "splitting our society" (Gall, 20 March 1944). In sum, the appropriation of pathological medical discourse acted as a mechanism for defining borders when faced with visible otherness. The homosexual was described as a passive partner who was penetrated by a male, a situation in which the male body was inverted and entered the female universe (Salessi, 2000).

In an effort to focus their fears on the central state, the colonels exalted violent actions. Colonel Pablo Dávila elevated a report that explained a gang rape of two underage girls by conscripts that was a direct result of not having access to licensed brothels. He underplayed the incident as a collective social responsibility excused by the uncontrollable libido of the soldiers, stating that "despite the efforts devoted to investigating this matter, the perpetrators were not found." He threatened that people should listen to him if they wished "to defend towns, families, and homes" (Dávila, 23 June 1942).

Colonel Rafael Lascalea drew attention to the risks to "homes and civilian families" in Río Gallegos given men's inability to "satisfy their desire for carnal access to the female body." The provision of married housing for officers and non-commissioned officers and their families would encourage infidelity and attempts at carnal access with women in service. The military letter writers presented themselves as representatives of working-class families and noted the risks of the spread of venereal diseases and homosexuality among isolated communities of laborers such as those working for YPF (Lascalea, 9 February 1944).

The officers' attempts to broaden their representation to workers coincided with debates within the labor union movement. In 1949, José Quevedo, president of the Argentine Federation of Light and Power Workers, gave a lecture on union debates about prostitution and antivenereal policies. It was published in 1952 as a popular pamphlet, priced one peso, by the Unionist Club's Argentine Social Laboratory and bearing a Peronist slogan, "Buenos Aires, city of justicialism" and the title *Unionism and the Problem of Prostitution*. The union leader's goal was to argue with "certain worker organizations" who were claiming in a newsletter that the unions needed to advocate for opening licensed brothels (Quevedo, 1951).

In sum, faced with the first attempts to enact abolitionist policy by the Argentine state, the military combined various notions to attack those policies. Thus, they used the threats of homosexuality, venereal diseases, and masturbation as valid arguments for reform.

Purchasing Sex in the Barracks

Matías, a worker from Buenos Aires, began his compulsory military service in 1968 in Neuquén. After three months, he received his first paycheck, and he and his peers went to a shed where a group of women sold sex to soldiers. Since they were part of a mountain division, they were not always served promptly; the women wasted a lot of time waiting for men to take off their equipment and delayed servicing other soldiers (Matías, interview, 5 December 2016). Even though two decades had passed since the military's resistance to the closure of the licensed brothels, the consumption of paid sex persisted among servicemen and was encouraged by their superiors.

Matías's story provides a glimpse into the meanings and practices deployed by the army once it obtained authorization to install brothels, and it expands on the descriptions in the letters. The moralizing messages about sexuality and its practices did not always converge. Even though homosexuality was a threat the letter writers claimed could be overcome by purchasing prostitution, Matías gleefully recalls that a young man from Rosario had sex with various officers who, protected by the "isolation of the garrison," were the penetrators. They may have recorded this participation as a manifestation of their overwhelming sexuality, thinking that as penetrators, they were not damaging their heterosexual virility (interview, 5 December 2016). It is possible that Matías emphatically and ironically recalled this situation as a symbolic act of revenge for the suffering the soldiers endured and that would cause a broad antimilitary stance among workers (Ablard, 2017).

The Patagonian military's vision for brothels was based on the premise that prostitution was a necessary "evil." Understood as eternal and timeless, the only hope was to put in place measures to manage the practice. Perlinger wrote that a prostitute was "medically suspicious" and requested appropriate treatment to guarantee "risk-free" consumption (Perlinger, 27 March 1944).

From the beginning of the letter-writing campaign, colonels and generals thought of brothels as the perfect response to their "bestial needs." They imagined architectural designs to satisfy their desire for recreation under rules for medical monitoring and health maintenance. Through their project they looked for women who had possibly already served them. In 1940, General Horacio Crespo submitted a plan to the Ministry of the Interior to "cater to men's needs" between the cities of Neuquén and Bahía Blanca. He brought in two women and proposed that they manage the brothels. The women signed with a thumbprint a letter certifying they had discreet rooms, bathrooms, and a private space for medical visits. The establishments were located far from the urbanized area so as not to "disturb nor promote immorality in civilian society." They also promised not to sell alcohol or encourage dancing, which were believed to foster loss of sexual control in young men. Perhaps for these women the army was offering a way to recoup the business they had lost when the legislation changed.

As in Vargas Llosa's novel, in 1942 Colonel Ángel Solari presented a plan to install houses of tolerance in the garrisons, explicitly referencing the

French and American army policies in the First and Second World Wars (Roberts, 2010). The colonel believed the state should increase the presence of prostitutes in areas with low population density or an imbalance between the sexes. The women brought in should be strictly monitored to limit their presence in urban areas to preserve "moral order" (Solari, 11 May 1942).

Solari designed his ideal brothels to be roomy enough to house multiple women. They were to have heating, be hygienic, and possess the health care resources needed for prophylaxis: a room for medical examinations and first aid supplies for urgent venereal problems (Solari, 11 May 1942). The emphasis on the sanitary nature of the buildings reinforced the idea that women were solely responsible for transmission. Among the resources he required was that blood tests could be shipped by air to Buenos Aires.

The housing designs had separate spaces for sexual recreation for military officials, professional soldiers, and conscripts to avoid direct contact between the sexual bodies of enlisted men and officers. There were also different fixed rates for each group: three pesos for officers, two and a half for noncommissioned officers, and two for enlisted men (Solari, 11 May 1942). The differentiation in the consumption of sex was intended to establish status and allowed those of higher rank to maintain privacy from their subordinates. Secrets about their sexuality circulated in those spaces for meeting women, ensuring the officers' position of dominance and the respect they were owed by male subalterns. Even though Matías—our interviewee—and the other conscripts were stationed in a town that had a brothel with two prostitutes, subalterns were forbidden to visit them. They had to wait for the weekend to be driven in army trucks to Cipoletti, Neuquén, where they were serviced in a brothel along with all the other conscripts from the garrisons. Despite this, Matías met "Lulú" while having lunch at a local bar. She was one of the two women who serviced a colonel who enjoyed "being beaten." Perhaps magnified in his memory in defiance of the man who made him spend long hours in the cold, Matías recalled that fact as a humiliating detail about his superior.

Solari advised installing another brothel for civilians. He said it was needed to prevent young workers from crossing the Chilean border and bringing back venereal diseases to disrupt the family order. This fear echoed nationalist discourses from the 1930s on, which were involved in constructing a Patagonian identity in opposition to that of neighboring Chile (Boholavsky, 2006).

In 1944, Colonel Perlinger proposed a bill that, in dialogue with Eugenio Galli, showed a certain respect for the Prophylaxis Law. Unlike his colleagues, he saw the effects of law 12.331 as positive and described "prohibitionist interpretations" of it as biased. He suggested creating temporary brothels that could be dissolved, having women stay in individual homes where they could provide "sexual services" themselves, ruling out any intervention by third parties. These houses should be discreet and not advertised among civilians (Perlinger, 28 March 1944). His bill included a system for identifying the women, providing medical supplies, creating a blood test, and establishing a health record. This proposal had been made since 1937 by some physicians, and it was starting to replace the old identification of regulated sex work (Baliña, 1937; Russo, 1937). For this record-keeping system to work, Galli and Perlinger recommended that the Ministry of the Interior create a team of medical specialists who would examine both women and consumers three times a week and isolate women when they became ill (Perlinger, 28 March 1944).

The National Board for Health and Social Welfare created a commission of specialists to analyze the military authorities' bills. They called in leading figures in the area: Pedro Baliña, chair of the clinical department of Dermatology and Venereal Diseases in the Faculty of Medical Sciences at the University of Buenos Aires; Alberto Zwank, director of the Argentine Social Museum, who had been involved in creating the degree program for mobile doctors; Enrique Castaño, director of the Argentine Urology Society; and Pedro Scolari of the Argentine Dermatology Association (Galli, 20 March 1944). This group of specialists stressed the support for law 12.331 among the medical community, such as the Argentine Medical Association, the Argentine Medical Society, and the National Conference on Venereal Diseases. In their mission statement, they reaffirmed their opposition to regulationist policies, which they saw as deficient, and denounced prohibitionist interpretations of the law by the police and judicial agencies. The commission pointed out the advantages of the military bill and invited the state to build emergency brothels until there were women selling sex independently in the area. They also suggested creating hotels that would rent out rooms where couples could give free rein to their sexuality in more comfort; however, they thought these should be located far from urban centers (Galli, 20 March 1944).

As I have shown, the dynamics of how things changed in the law and the proposals to create loopholes in abolitionism attenuated international organizations' sphere of influence on this topic. Eugenio Galli reported his concern about the situation to Lewis Hackett, a US public health official sent by the Rockefeller Foundation to evaluate the state of hygiene policies in

Latin America. Taking a critical view of the Argentine government, Hackett wrote, "They are worried about the problem of prostitution in Argentina and are thinking of changing the law which now makes it illegal. This is a good example of how relatively ignorant men with full authority decide after brief consultation how to handle problems of the greatest complexity" (Hackett, 1944).

To some extent, these changes flouted international policy abolishing prostitution, which was generally accepted from the 1930s, even though Argentina was not the only country to undergo these processes full of contradictions. The complaints of the Rockefeller Foundation officials were also a sign of the processes of struggle that add dimension on various levels to the local and international conflicts that involved and defined political dynamics.

Once the change was decreed in 1944, the government requested a report from rear admiral Enrique García, military comptroller for Tucumán, on where to locate the houses of tolerance to "satisfy the needs" of the soldiers (Aranda, 11 November 1944). The provincial authorities created a commission to make this decision composed of the director general for health, the director of the social prophylaxis section, the army physician, and the commander in chief of the provincial police (Doll, 19 June 1944). The commission drew up a short report on the barracks but did not go on to explain how it would carry out this measure. The local government in San Luis went ahead with the process. The provincial director for health recommended setting up houses of tolerance in that province, in Mercedes, Justo Daract, and Concarán, where regiments were stationed (Carranza, 18 November 1944).

Due to the confidential nature of these documents, it is difficult to assess the extent to which these proposals were carried out. In 1955, the military dictatorship reversed course with a Peronist attempt to return to the regulationist system, but it kept the loopholes in decree 10.638/44, which remained in force until 1965, when it was abrogated by full application of the international treaties of the UN. In San Luis, the provincial representative Luis Marrero complained that the military brothels were still running even though the neoregulationist decree had been revoked (Merrero, 25 August 1965).

Despite the regulations promulgated by this legislation, as Matías's memories emphasize, the practices of consuming sex persisted among soldiers. It is also possible that these requests were carried out since the secret nature of the documents gave regiments prerogatives and autonomy to do so once they were authorized.

The Abolitionist Resistance(s)

The Peronist institutionalization of the military demand through law 12.912 put prostitution back on the public agenda and triggered the resistance of a group of actors. Between 1948 and 1955, the government initiated a debate about relaxing abolition that would culminate in the failed attempt to return to regulationist policies in 1954. The president planted a new challenge in the relationship between the state and the army that made it difficult to distinguish among the military, civil, and political. The debate involved unions, civil servants, doctors, and Catholics, sectors that were all part of a Peronist social, political, and cultural alliance.

In 1949, the government initiated an offensive and sent a first draft to Parliament with the backing of the president and the health minister Ramón Carrillo. The bill attempted to make inroads on the autonomy granted by the previous regulations to those who sold sex without a mediator or working location, by demanding that prostitutes get tested as well as proposed optional testing for clients. As such, it broadened the penalization of pimping that increased throughout the twentieth century and was used by the police to extend their legal authority throughout the country.

For the president, the bill would have to adapt the "legal regulation of the problems to the current reality for the repression of pimping." Carrillo then defined the Peronist policy as "regulationist by necessity, abolitionist by morality" (Carrillo, 1948). Humberto Messina, deputy of the Peronist Party for the Federal Capital, presented four bills between 1946 and 1951 that increased the punitive capacities of the state to force those with venereal diseases to get treatment and requested greater authorization from public agencies to install houses of tolerance beyond those requested by the military (Messina, 1946, file no. 1582, National Congress [HCDN]; Messina, 1949, file no. 38, HCDN; Messina, 1950, file no. 9, HCDN; Messina, 1951, file no. 313, HCDN). Messina wrote in a draft bill that with abolitionism "this evil [prostitution] far from decreasing, increased." And he argued that to "foster the control of prostitution" they should only leave "houses of tolerance managed by the state, which would allow the country to put a stop to evils that destabilize society." It was necessary, then, "to educate the people about venereal diseases and how they are retribution for committed sin" (Messina, 1951, file no. 313, HCDN).

The debate also extended to the union members. As previously explained, in 1949 José Quevedo, president of the Argentine Federation of

Energy and Power Workers (FATLYF), a labor union that emerged in 1943 as a product of industrial modernization and that supported Perón's candidacy, spoke at a conference about the union discussions around prostitution and antivenereal policies. His talk was later published in a cheap pamphlet. The union leader's objective was to talk with "certain worker organizations" that stated in a notice that the union members should fight for the opening of houses of tolerance. It was not new: during the first half of the twentieth century, union newspapers demanded members dedicate more time to the organization and less to brothels (Scheinkman, 2017).

In defense of law 12.331, Quevedo placed the debate within the argument of "Peronism and its values." He thus considered abolitionism a task of the "justicialism" that was part of the "social justice" agenda. The union inclusion of prostitution as a "worker's" problem is also associated with a tradition framed in the socialist discourse that argued that low wages and poor living conditions forced women to sell sex to survive (Giménez, 1919). This was part of the broader social reformist discourse that fought for policies that would address the evils generated by "poverty" (Armus, 2007).

Though in his discourse Quevedo promised to defend men and women, he spoke only to an audience of adult men as consumers of sex. His speech was meant to defend the "health of the [male] workers" and the morality of women. It implied a rejection of prostitution in and of itself, which is why "the woman who submits herself for money" was just as immoral "as the man who pays her." He proposed to defend working families by adhering to the ideal that their task was to populate the fatherland with a workforce.

Far from rejecting the military officials' premises, he also defended the search for a policy that would consider the demands of the youth and their "sexual relief." For Quevedo, prostitution was a multifaceted problem based on the economic inequities that restricted the sexualities of young men. Regarding this conclusion, he believed the union's position had to be two-pronged. On the one hand, it had to be educational: The unions would have to provide the tools so that their members would not contract infectious diseases that would threaten their descendants; he thus cited Pedro Baliña's work in which he argued for sexual education that without becoming pornography would do away with the "false morality" that hides the body's pleasures from the youth (Quevedo, 1951). On the other hand, there was an economic aspect: from his perspective, low wages kept young men from getting married, which is where they should be having their sexual initiation for the good of their "moral and physical health and that of their descendants." In much the same way, some physicians who looked positively upon the work the secretariat of labor and social welfare had been doing since 1944 believed that a broadening of social policies should have as its only objective the increase in the marriage rate with the "primordial goal" of populating the nation (Russo, 1944a).

As such, by signaling there was an economic barrier for the development of an uncontainable masculine sexuality, Quevedo argued that the issue of housing was central given it supported the nuclear family in which men could develop their healthy sexual life. For him, the "4 × 4" homes for workers led to the overcrowding that promoted "promiscuity," and he stated that in 1937, 80 percent of working families in the capital only had one room, a concern also shared by civil servants and police (Pareja, 1937).

The first two Peronist mandates accelerated a quick transformation of worker territory that involved implementing a housing plan, a cultural pattern that reaffirmed the central value of the family and made possible new social uses of the urban space (Ballent, 2005). At the same time, the family focus also introduced an excessive concern for preserving—with a certain accusatory tone—the health of the working woman who, by assuming a new role in the working world, was believed to be capable of putting the family institution at risk (Queirolo, 2018).

But beyond the "weaknesses" he found among his members, Quevedo focused on the "responsibilities of the prostitutes." In his eyes, the low wages for women did not explain their "moral degeneracy." If the consumption of sex was a natural quality of the untamable male libido that should be restrained, the supply of sexual services could only be stopped when women "have a superior morality and greater respect for their own responsibility" (Quevedo, 1951: 11). For Quevedo, accepting the regulation of brothels meant tolerating the degradation of the female status, which went against the "time of social justice" given that a woman with a criminal record could never "socially redeem herself." He thus introduced the slogan "better death than the police record."

Quevedo also questioned those who attempted to "unionize" prostitution. This approach seems anachronistic in debates taking place under Perón. At a global scale, the organizations that proposed a recognition of sex work emerged during the 1970s and '80s; perhaps the only exception to this periodization emerged in postrevolutionary Mexico when in the 1940s a union for prostitutes was created (Peralta, 2015).

Finally, Quevedo noted that any form of institutionalizing prostitution had to be resisted so as not to benefit the trafficking of persons for sexual exploitation. The argument, with which "some unions" agreed, was a request against the foreign demand for "rufianes and pimps who want to regain control of the Argentine market." At the same time, it was alarming that the "immigration wave" could not be conceived of as a "moral emergency," which metaphorically echoed, ironically, the anti-Peronist idea of a "zoological wave." Within this framework, how were these arguments connected with the exaltation of an idea of Argentineness, which associated problems with phenomena exogenous to the national territory?

The union debate was informed by broader experiences in which the unions had to intervene in the face of abolitionism. The unions in urban areas intervened in specific situations to "defend their members" through secret complaints to the Ministry of the Interior to define the boundaries between pimping and sexual consumption.

In 1953, the federal police organized a raid in the San Martín railroad facilities to learn whether "the workers were violating the decree that prohibited the sexual exploitation of women." They detained nine workers aged nineteen to thirty-five who were purchasing sexual services from three women who visited them at night in the abandoned train cars and accused them of pimping. The rail union had to intervene before the Ministry of the Interior to "clarify" the situation and seek the freedom of its members (AGN, box 120, no. 504, 1945).

Workers did not only participate as consumers. Some of them, like the taxi drivers, were in direct contact with the women who sold sex. In 1952, the taxi driver union raised a complaint to the Ministry of the Interior to protest about the "arbitrariness with which the police enforce law 12.331." The union responded to the complaint lodged by Carlos, a twenty-eight-year-old taxi driver. The police accused him of participating as a third party who made money off prostitutes in the area. The driver transported the women from one dance club to another in what was commonly called the "circuit," or making the rounds in search of clients. Because of this accusation, the man was detained for eighteen days in Devoto, causing him to lose several days of work. That jail also held detained gay men sentenced for breaking the city's misdemeanor codes. The driver filed this grievance not only for a loss of an economic good (multiple days of work and a fine for the lack of a back license plate) but also because in that act they had stripped him of "honorability," of his home he shared with his wife and three children (AGN, box 119, no. 135, 1953).

Like Quevedo, the taxi union framed their complaint within Peronist values. They noted that "the justicialism of Perón and the worker's martyr

Eva Perón" invited a "happiness that should always operate within a framework of a strict morality without facilitating debauchery." The presidential couple was the ideal heterosexual family who protected the workers and poor like their own children (symbolically). It was no coincidence that the appeal to Evita as a mother or prostitute separated her devotees from her enemies and organized the Peronism/anti-Peronism antimony. Her body as a material and symbolic trophy became a battlefield in the twentieth century (Acha, 2014; Milanesio, 2014).

Evita was evoked as a protective mother, channeling the ideal of social ascent, a champion for the popular sectors. Each group that supported Peronism created a specific representation of their Evita. Mariana Soriano de Rocha, president of the women's center María Eva Duarte de Perón and member of the Catholic Action Group in the province of Corrientes, handwrote a letter that was added to the hundreds of missives, telegrams, and communications sent by Catholic activist groups. In it, she asked the president of the Chamber of Deputies that in the name of the "loyalty to our honorable President and our Headwoman," who worked hard to "lift the lower classes" and possessed the "strongest morality of our country," to avoid reforming the law and put an end to the "brothels that in broad daylight disrupt morality in front of boys and girls." In it she affirmed, "Sir, I am not involved in politics" and reiterated that she was making the demand in the name of the "loyalty to my Leader and our Headwoman, the only ones I serve, I am at their service" (HCDN, Particulares, 1949, no. 190).

The organization's reference to Evita's full, married name defined a relationship of fidelity to the representation of Eva as mother of the unprotected and devoted wife to her husband. It also placed Evita in a parental position with the Virgin Mary, as a spiritual guide of Catholicism. María Soriano de Rocha wrote, like hundreds of others faithful to the Catholic Church, to Argentina's Chamber of Deputies to question the attempts to regulate the brothels. She connected it to broader debates such as those around the divorce law, which got heated due to the then porous borders between social, cultural, and political belonging to Peronism and Catholicism (Caimari, 1995). These tensions did not deny the pull between coexisting affective-political connections that marked the fidelity to the church and the presidential couple.

In an attempt to reconcile fidelity to both identities, María affirmed her loyalty to the leaders of Peronism, whom she identified as moral guides. Thus, the trust that permeated her writing as a Catholic and Peronist woman led her to accept in part the consensus around the necessity of buying sex as a complement to masculine sexuality. She had to negotiate with the two discourses that were slowly revealing themselves to be divergent; as such, she asked Perón to not allow the "brothels to open during the day" (HCDN, Particulares, no. 190, 1949).

Medical groups focusing on eugenics used the resurgence of this topic as an opportunity to spread their ideas. The Argentine Eugenic Society, founded in 1912 by Víctor Delfino and subsidized by the state since 1947, proposed four bills to reform law 12.331. In them they proposed subdividing the policies included in the regulation to address the treatment of diseases, sexual education, punishment for spreading disease, and state policy toward prostitution. The bills aimed to broaden the influence of their principles in the form of sexual education and strengthen the punishments for those recovering patients who spread venereal diseases. At the same time, they proposed more rigorously classifying the recognition of pimping and included among the potential victims "prostitutes or homosexuals." Additionally, they protected the attempts to create loopholes in abolitionism suggesting that the state allow women to sell sex independently or administer brothels without any punishment (HCDN, Partículares, no. 111, 1949). These bills did not catch on, perhaps because this medical tendency had already lost its hegemonic position within the professional field.

Organized Catholicism presented a resistance to the attempts at new regulations. The Committee for the Defense of the Woman's Dignity, a feminine branch of the Legion of Decency, whose objective was to "build awareness among women labor leaders, mothers, and women educators," responded to the official proposal by sending letters to the officials. These critiques can be read in a more extensive process associated with the renovation of the Catholic world, the extension of their cultural power, and the renewal of their activism, under the guise of critiquing the government's authoritarianism and resuming tasks neglected by the state, such as official censorship of shows considered immoral and the demand for family-oriented policies.

Catholic activism worked with renewed energy and invited its followers to write to the Congress of the Nation to avoid the reform of the Prophylaxis Law. The movement produced missives, sent telegrams, and gathered citizen signatures. Some parishes took the initiative to send their own letters signed by the women gathered there.

They organized meetings and public campaigns, promoted sending letters to Congress, and gathered 120 pages with thousands of signatures from across the nation (HCDN, Partículares, no. 374, 1949). Letter writing with collective signatures produced by Catholic circles was a way of uniting a common identity in response to the government initiative. In the letters, they used the abolitionist nature of the Prophylaxis Law and defined it as a "saintly, moral, divine law that makes it so that the brothels never come back." They referred to women as mothers, wives, and daughters, defined themselves as "Argentines, women, and Christians," and, borrowing some elements from the social Peronist discourse, called on the president to desist "in favor of social justice" and in "defense of the dignity and health of working-class women" (HCDN, Particulares, no. 374, 1949). In this sense, the Federation of Mercy Alumni Centers and the Association of Argentine Mothers sent a letter to national legislators, read on the floor, that expressed an "absolute repudiation and clear opposition to this reopening and its desire that this law not be addressed as long as Argentine women do not have the right to vote and cannot be heard on this floor" (HCDN, Particulares, no. 131, 1949).

With this kind of statement, Catholicism renewed the place of women in its movement as part of a transformation that shifted the role of women in public and democratic life. Women's rights appeared on the Catholic agenda in the 1930s out of a fear that women would be attracted by "dangerous ideologies" and would thus temper some of their positions and attempt to contribute to an agenda that would fight for the recognition of them as citizens from a conservative perspective. Thus, in the 1943 coup, women who identified as antifascist, communist, Jewish, and Catholic formed the Juntas de la Victoria that fought for suffrage in defense of democracy by making maternal appeals. For example, the Peronist push for the right to vote was well received by the Argentine Association for Women's Suffrage, which had a Catholic leaning (Valobra, 2008).

The network of Catholic organizations made advances in demands for expanding women's rights generally associated with the feminist and Peronist agendas. As such, Catholicism brought together a group of organizations such as the Association of Argentine Mothers, the Federation of Mercy Alumni Centers, the Catholic Action Youth, the Catholic Action, the Association of Women Catholics, the Board of Catholic Action, the Circle of Housewives, the Federation of Argentine Marian Congregations, the Committee in Defense of Women's Dignity (Rosario, Santa Fe), the Ateneo Universitario (Santa Fe), the National Professional School (Posadas, Misiones), the Catholic Women (Córdoba), the Salteña Catholic Action (Salta), the Circle of Catholic Women (Bahía Blanca), the Rivadavia Nuns (Comodoro Rivadavia), the Ministry of Our Lady of Lourdes, and the Society of Women Protecting

Orphans (Rosario, Santa Fe), among other school groups, private individuals, alumna of confessional schools, and mothers' groups (HCDN, Partícula-res, no. 276, 1949).

The criticism from the Catholic women echoed the opposition letters and telegrams from numerous women's organizations. They opposed a first ambiguous bill that did not make clear whether the installation of houses of tolerance was prohibited, though they did not reject that they be built close to military installations. Because of this, they accused false intentions behind the "dismantling of pimping." Under the premise that the state should "take care of the health of the race," they called on Carrillo to maintain the clear abolitionist nature of the regulation (HCDN, Partículares, no. 276, 1949).

Catholic circles also proposed that sexual education be understood as a disciplinary measure—that is, that men and women be given moral education to assume their roles. They rejected any kind of health intervention in the medical examinations of women, which they considered an obscene invasion of their bodies. They also demanded that the state assume moral policies to tackle "human trafficking" (HCDN, Partículares, no. 276, 1949).

The Rosario Democratic Social Action Group, the political branch of Catholicism in the city, also interceded with the "imperative of complying with their civic duty" against a reform that constituted an "offense to women, their honor, and their rights." Like Quevedo, they invited legislators to act against those who "profit and make money off white slavery." At the same time, he denounced as false the arguments that regulationism would be "beneficial for the physiological development of men." The objective of the democratic-Christian entities was thus to avoid the outrage over "social morality" that would mean for the state "an embarrassing situation upon receiving income in exchange for making a shameful business official" (HCDN, Partículares, no. 687, 1949).

In 1949 the organized Catholic Church managed to delay the first attempt at reform led by Ramón Carrillo. Finally, faced with the failure of the first draft bills and with the Catholic institution's clear position, in December 1954 the national government supported decree 22.532. Its secret nature demonstrates the government's need to present itself as cautious before the Catholic opposition that, when the regulation was approved, catalyzed a large part of the anti-Peronist discourse. In 1955, the coup put an end to the Peronist attempts at regulation.

In the 1960s, the gradual expansion and classification of the misdemeanor codes, as well as the adhesions to international conventions, transformed how the abolitionist doctrine was applied in Argentina. Institutional violence was constant and would change how it was implemented. The expansions and limitations, the consolidation of the abolitionist approach, and the creation of loopholes were ambiguous. Thus, for example, until 1965 there continued to be formal echoes requesting brothels previously won over by the military. These requests functioned as a substrate of a deeper masculine culture that considered the consumption of sex a natural prerogative of masculine sexuality.

· · · · · ·

From the practices and notions studied in this chapter, I identify some conclusions. First, I analyzed the circulation of missives that constituted a space of male socialization among civil servants and the military. In the context of redefining masculinity in Argentina, the military officials presented a successful resistance by articulating a male-centered notion of health and sexuality that defended the prerogatives of the consumption of sex as a guarantee of protection in the face of potential disturbances to virility, such as homosexuality, onanism, and abstinence. The construction of an organizing fiction of their experience of paying permeated receptive administrations that took the initiative to install brothels in military barracks. As such, military officers drafted bills in which they defined their own representations of paid sex with gendered and classist criteria. These concerns overall articulated a nationalist imaginary that made the work and reproductive capacities of men the symbolic center of national development. As such, far from being a marginal question, the concern for the recreational and reproductive qualities of sexuality occupied a central place in the edification of the considered strategic tasks in response to a disrupted world in the second half of the twentieth century.

Second, the institutionalization of loopholes to abolition and attempts to return to the regulation of brothels pushed by Peronism invited the participation of unionists, doctors, and Catholic movements in the support and dissent of the reforms. Like the military officers, union members for or against reform took as primary arguments the need to guarantee the health and sexuality of the man as the center of the debate. On the other hand, a renewed Catholic movement led by women presented a diverse group of actions and positions to resist the measures.

Both the letters from military officials reticent to a regulation they felt limited their right to access paid sex and those from the Catholic activists in defense of the same regulation express different sides of a public culture in which sexuality progressively gained ground. Their language and topics became not only stages upon which to resolve how sex was bought and sold, but also tools for the more extensive debates around defining the experience and understanding of heterosexuality in Argentina.

3 The Streets and Jail Cells

State Sexual Moralism and the Lives behind Bars (1936–1984)

....

In 1940, Josefa (thirty-two years old) was detained in Tandil for selling sex along with Elena (thirty-seven), Carolina (twenty-five), Sandra (twenty-seven), and Ernestina (twenty-two). They were transferred 336 kilometers to the Olmos women's prison (no. 8). This was not their first time; their prior records indicate they had been detained in police stations twice before. Josefa was Spanish, 1.57 meters tall, Caucasian, blond, thin lips, and round features. Elena was Argentine, 1.55 meters tall, Caucasian, brunette, thick lips, round features. Carolina was Argentine, 1.62 meters tall, Caucasian, brunette, broad thighs. Sandra was Argentine, 1.42 meters tall, dark skinned (*morena*), dark hair, thick lips. Ernestina was Argentine, 1.67 meters tall, blond, and Caucasian (SPB, file 659, 1940). Written using Lombrosian and Eugenic language, their files describe more about the measurements of their bodies than their experience with such a long journey just to spend the night in a jail cell. It was a familiar experience among those who sold sex, as the SPB files show.

The objective of this chapter is, first, to analyze the enforcement of the 1936 Prophylaxis Law that abolished regulated prostitution first instituted in 1875 by prohibiting properties where "prostitution [was] practiced." The law also fined, imprisoned, or, in the case of foreigners, potentially deported those who "support[ed], administer[ed], or manage[d]" prostitution. Though the law did not penalize the individual sale of sex, I study how state agents interpreted it as a punitive tool against prostitutes by combining it with routine practices and other laws, such as the provincial misdemeanor codes.

Second, the chapter analyzes the social meanings and practices of the women who sold sex and were imprisoned between 1936 and 1984 in Buenos Aires Province. I focus on practices (such as traveling to sell sex) and how women understood their work. By taking this approach, we can look beyond court documentation to understand how the actors replicated, reinvented, and navigated their diverse relationships based on trading sex for money.

Third, the chapter describes a broad and far-reaching sample of cases that along with other documentation outlines the social and cultural characteristics of the women who sold sex in Buenos Aires Province. I outline patterns in their lives to show larger social processes: experiences with the state (such as with educational and judicial institutions or institutes for minors), experiences with male procurers and other mediators (doctors, aid societies, intrafamilial arrangements), family unions and separations, and illness.

I argue that the police emphasized the punitive character of the law with the aim of recovering or negotiating lost jurisdiction around licensed brothels. That is, there was a shift of direct authority with which police previously regulated women to indirect negotiations, as shown by the increase in the number of judicial trials and imprisonments. This was at odds with judicial officials who tended to absolve the accused, which suggests that women who sold sex negotiated their activities and also suggests longer trends that restricted their ability to act.

It is clear that the new approach to the law and its influence on the practices of police and judicial officials are part of a longer process of institutionalizing moral violence as a practice constitutive of state intervention in sexualities. The combination of the professionalization of procedures for territorial intervention and the passage of a set of rules (such as the local and provincial misdemeanor codes)—which intensified the debates around public morality that had been spreading like wildfire in the urban centers since the 1930s—relied on a notion of morality in which sexuality and policy provided a sense of order. The convergence of written processes functioned to ban some forms of sexual-affective socialization because they were considered divergent from the national "being" (Cowan, 2016; Simonetto, 2016). These forms of violence were in dialogue with hostility enacted through social, political, and cultural arrangements, processes of medium- and long-term duration that were displayed in interventions symptomatic of a state locus as a response to social dynamics that were marked as having deviated from any kind of order (Ansaldi and Giordano, 2014).

At the same time, I argue that the multiplicity of practices and meanings leveraged by state officials and female prisoners—constantly changing and unstable—allows us to reconsider the categories for sociohistorical analysis. These categories reveal the everyday negotiations of how people usually understood sexual commerce and moved beyond binaries, allowing us to access a fragmented cultural map of a diverse sexual economy. These terms might also be signs of different moralities that mediated people's experiences of sexual commerce (or at least what they thought was convenient to articulate under police pressure).

With this goal, I assembled a primary database with records from the Olmos women's and minors' prison of the SPB. I selected 279 files of women processed under law 12.331, articles 202c and 126 of the penal code, detained between 1937 and 1968. I also consider 327 simple records of entrance and exit between 1937 and 1971 for the same crimes. As secondary information, I include the information of 143 other women processed for the same crimes held at the Historical-Judicial Department of Central Buenos Aires Province (DHJC) and of the South (DHJS).

The judicial records and prison files present an image suspended in time of the lives of these women who were forced by the state to articulate matters they considered natural (Farge, 2013). These were routine documents dictated by the moral repertories with which officials of the prison, the justice system, or the police attempted to classify and organize prisoners. These are polyphonic texts that prioritized the voice of the civil servants and police officers; thus, I consider every instance of the document where the women responded to the police, judicial civil servants, and nuns to build counterpoints. Despite their opacity, I believe these documents offer useful information about the life paths and profiles of the detained women, such as age at detention, time spent in welfare institutions, priors, charge, final result of the trial, number of children, disease, nationality of father and mother, place of birth, place of arrest, home address, stated profession, time of detention, level of education, and year of detention. I use this information to construct a counter record that considers the conditions under which women made statements to capture how social meaning and practices intersected with the experience of prison (Tenti, 2012).

The chapter is organized in four sections. First, I study the relationship between the normative trajectory and the punitive application of the law to understand the process of legal interpretation of abolitionism as a policy of public intervention in the sex market. Second, I analyze the prostitutes' daily experiences of arrest and how they struggled with different types of historical agency. Third, I observe the negotiation of identity between the women tried for selling sex and the state to understand how women gave meaning to those experiences and how they presented the experiences to public institutions. Finally, I describe the living conditions of the women who sold sex, with a focus on how the intersection among relationships of gender, class, and age informed a subaltern social and sexual experience.

Constructing "Abolitionism":
Legal Pathways and Punitive Practices

The Prophylaxis Law proposed a range of measures that included sexual education, distribution of medication, forced treatment of venereal diseases, and abolition of regulated prostitution. Articles 15 and 17 prohibited the establishment of houses or properties where "prostitution is practiced or encouraged" and sentenced those who "support, administer, or manage houses of tolerance with a fine of one thousand Argentine pesos." Between 1936 and 1984, law 12.331 underwent numerous modifications. Various government authorities—the legislative, executive, and judicial branches— disputed the scope of and restrictions on the abolition of regulated prostitution. Additionally, the police were the ones primarily interpreting the law and acting, thus establishing the actual uses of the law to reinforce their own power. Though in 1984 the law returned to its original state and the transition to democracy caused greater disputes, it continued to be a product of wide-ranging interpretations on the part of government and judicial agencies. In postdictatorial times, the police continued the violent persecution of sex workers (Daich and Sirimarco, 2015).

Police intervention was influenced by three ideal models: regulationism, abolitionism, and prohibitionism. The manual written by the police in Buenos Aires described them as such: Regulationism assumed state control of brothels through a license and medical review; prohibitionism aimed to punish any kind of prostitution; and abolitionism attempted to respect the individual liberties of women and penalize their exploitation. In any case, the same author published in that and other articles that the abolitionist laws aimed to "prohibit" prostitution by making the punitive scope of the system established by the Prophylaxis Law ambiguous (Pareja, 1937).

The punitive interpretation of abolitionism came into force during the police's territorial control in which they negotiated between government and police agencies, sellers, and intermediators (if there were any). The successive reforms enacted by civil and military governments—whether eliminating regulations or keeping them—constructed a framework with overlapping regulations that permeated a doctrine that encouraged state action through police routines.

The transitions and mixtures between regulation and its abolition were impacted by the reorganization of heterosexual masculinity—that is, both the renegotiation of access to sexual services and rising tensions between a liberal state and one that intervenes. Though regulation as a legal phenomenon assumed state action in defining the contract for selling and buying sex, abolition established a new set of issues for state agencies as they were expected to expand and have a greater reach in society through increasing intervention due to the power granted by the liberalization of regulation. Abolitionism allowed police to renew their power, intensifying the methods with which they enforced the Ley Palacios that starting in 1913 penalized sex trafficking of women and allowed them to take advantage of unregistered prostitutes (Múgica, 2014).

The police's role in defining sexual and classist (as well as potentially racist uses through the punishment of those who deviated from supposed western European moral standards) uses of the nation's territory brought together a wide range of regulations and practices that united multiple subjects. The political, economic, and cultural elite perceived an apparent disintegration of the nation's material conditions of national identity and attributed that decline to modern, urban transformations, specifically the exponential growth of cities, the mobility of the population, and the detection of new sexual and emotional configurations seen as threatening (homosexuality). In the 1930s, this perception meant that the elite promoted controlling the national space in a way that broadened their political power and impacted the youth, homosexuals, poor, and prostitutes who gathered in public spaces (Simonetto, 2016). The interpretation of law 12.331 dialogued with these other measures in that it allowed the police a tenuous use of regulations to negotiate their position within the territory in relation to the buying and selling of sexual services.

The majority of women who sold sex and spent time in the Olmos prison (75.6 percent) were accused of the crime of prostitution under the law 12.331, though the crime also converged with other regulations such as article 202c of the penal code (9.3 percent) and article 18 of law 12.331 (3.9 percent), which condemned spreading venereal diseases, and article 126, which punished the facilitation of prostitution (0.7 percent), corruption (9.3 percent), or homicide (0.7 percent).

As previously explained, between 1937 and 1955, abolitionist policies were relaxed, but then between 1955 and 1984, the repressive capacity of the policies was strengthened. In 1944 the installation of houses of tolerance in military barracks was permitted (executive order 10.638), and though Catholic activists opposed it, in 1954 Perón regulated prostitution through decree 22.532. Those reforms were then repealed between 1955 and 1965 (decree 4863/55, law 16.666/65). Law 12.331 converged with growing police power that came from new misdemeanor codes passed in the provinces that, among other measures, in 1950 effectively allowed superintendents in Buenos Aires—as well as in other provinces—to apply judgments, moving arrests from prisons to police stations (decree 850/50, provincial decree/law 8031/55).

The changes analyzed here are inseparable from the institutional transformations that expanded or shrunk provincial police scope and action. During the Perón period, the police force became centralized and militarized, a process that sought to limit the connections between the police and local powers. Meanwhile, beginning in 1955, most agencies were "de-peronized" through the ousting of many agents, reforming the police educational model, and gradually increasing power to locally intervene through new police edicts (Barreneche, 2009).

Regarding penal matters, there was a tendency to utilize different judicial tools for madams, pimps, and prostitutes. The 1917 and 1921 bills punished those who made a profit off facilitating a minor's consent as well as promoting or facilitating corruption or prostitution of adult women. The reforms of the penal code sharpened the tools for differentiating madams, pimps, and prostitutes. Rodolfo Moreno's 1906 penal code bill (1917: 25) penalized the promotion or facilitation of prostitution and required that the perpetrator have used fraud, violence, threat, abuse of authority, or coercion to try him under articles 129 and 131. The formulation of this crime was maintained in the 1917 bill and in the 1921 code, which punished those who made a profit or who satisfied their own desires by promoting the prostitution or corruption of minors, without distinguishing sex, even if they managed to get consent.

The 1937 bill, presented by Jorge Eduardo Coll and Eusebio Gómez, penalized those who promoted or facilitated the prostitution of a minor (article 125 bis) and facilitated sexual relations with a third party (article 170). When the woman was not a minor, the consent of whoever was her husband or led a marital life with the "victim" was required (article 172). The 1941 bill punished those who promoted prostitution or the corruption of a minor or a person who was sick or of psychological deficiency. For those who were not minors, there was punishment if there was the use of trickery, force, or intimidation, and it was considered aggravating if the accused were a husband, lover, brother, or teacher.

In 1951, the penal code separated the crimes of corruption and facilitation of prostitution. The 1953 bill included in article 202, under the chapter "Crimes against sexual freedom and good customs," the promotion or facilitation of persons of either promiscuous sex or habitual sex trafficking,

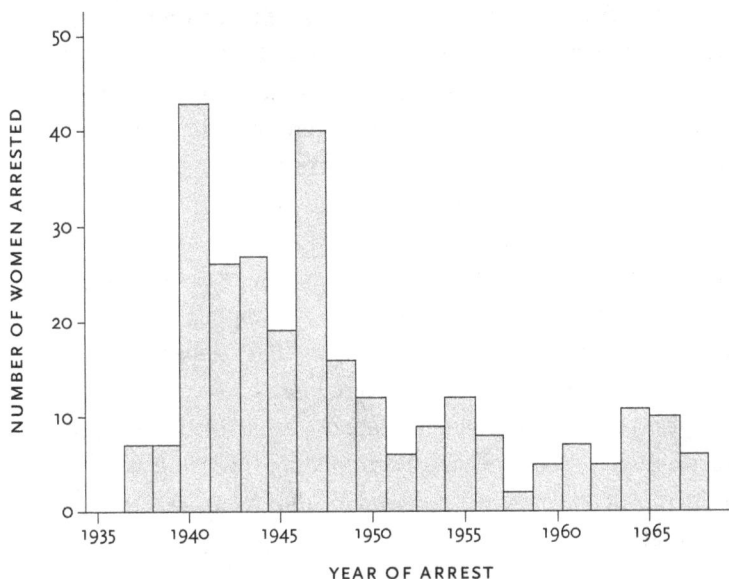

GRAPH 3.1 Arrests for the violation of law 12.331 in unit no. 8 (1936–71).

which required that cases brought by adults involve a situation in which resistance is impossible (article 202, inc. 2) or that trickery, violence, or intimidation had been used. In 1960, the government addressed the figure of the pimp with article 126, which restricted those who promoted or facilitated the prostitution of a person without differentiating for sex or age. In the cases of minors, this became an aggravating circumstance. The de facto government's 1976 law 21.338 substantially maintained the 1921 code as it addressed the promotion and facilitation of corruption and prostitution. The government added article 127 bis, which punished pimping, and 127, which penalized the trafficking of persons—women and minors—for prostitution. It was in 1984 when law 23.077 repealed the previous modifications, returned to the 1921 code, and reestablished article 17 of law 12.331 (De Luca and Lancman, 2010).

Graph 3.1 shows that the rationale for arrest varied over time. Thus, the question of whether abolition became a punitive tool should be answered by observing the changing rhythms of an ambiguous dynamic. Imprisonment at the women's prison was associated with minor crimes, such as larceny. The female prison population was low but grew throughout the twentieth century. According to the 1929 prison census, women made up 2.24 percent of prisoners on the national level (O'Connor, 1931). Prostitutes were quickly released and had the option to pay a fine or wait a few days until their case was dismissed. Sixty-four percent of the women detained for selling sex spent less than a week in prison, a situation that varied when law enforcement piled on other crimes such as theft, spreading venereal disease, corruption, or homicide. It is likely the arrest, which meant they accumulated a record, depended on how they negotiated with the police and if the officers benefited financially or sexually.

In my study of the archives of the Dolores and Mercedes prisons, I did not find records of men detained for the crime of pimping. The results of trials initiated in the courts of the central and southern departments show that men were rarely taken to prison and were more likely to be fined.

This could also be due to a previous state dynamic. In the 1929 prison census there is only one record of a man detained for the crime of pimping, or "white slavery," out of a prison population of 2,861 men (O'Connor, 1931). This suggests that the androcentric interpretation of the law tended to penalize prostitutes, especially those who did their work in groups.

As the subsequent chapters emphasize, women negotiated with local police and were subjected to requests for money or sex with the staff to avoid a charge. Some of them reported officers, though this never went far. At the same time, the police's attempts to make use of legal tools had its limitations, as 74.9 percent of the detained women were dismissed or pardoned after a short period of time. The convicts also frequently enjoyed significant reductions to their punishment. I argue that punitive abolitionism made sense in an institutional system that reinforced relationships of local power and built synergy between the institutional and social regulations founded in precepts of gender and class that confirmed police power.

The high rates of arrest between 1937 and 1955 are explained by regulatory changes. As soon as law 12.331 was in place, it is possible that the dismantling of the regulatory system was relevant to police routines because of the increase in "free prostitutes." At the same time, some courts legitimized the coercion by creating precedence, which sparked a debate around the interpretation of the regulation that divided those who thought that selling sex was proof of pimping and those who were opposed. While the courts of Rosario (9 March 1939), Bahía Blanca (31 March 1939), and Buenos Aires (1938 and 1939) revoked the sentences of tried women, the criminal and correctional court of appeals in Buenos Aires decided in 1940 that "the simple exercise of prostitution by a woman, individually and independently, in an establishment, constituted an infraction" (Jiménez de Asúa, 1953: 739–40).

In 1946 the transformation into law of the military decree that allowed houses of tolerance was accompanied by an antivenereal policy that defined all prostitutes as "foci of contagion" and established the forced submission to medical controls (Anónimo, 1946: 47).

The consensus among specialists and civil servants of classifying prostitution as a focus of contagion made these women more susceptible to wide forms of institutionalization. While article 202c of the penal code was connected with article 18 of the Prophylaxis Law, the same law that abolished regulated prostitution unleashed another slew of measures, such as the mandatory treatment of the sick while contagious (article 7); the forced hospitalization for every infectious individual who, all persuasive measures exhausted, did not regularly submit to treatment and for those whose outpatient treatment could be a danger to society (article 9); and doctors' condemnation of the focus of contagion (article 10) (*Anales de la Legislación Argentina*, 1953: 706–7).

The health inspectors' manuals show the ambiguity of these regulations. For the judicial institutions it was difficult to determine the level of knowledge on the part of the sick people about their disease and its contagious nature to define whether the tried person was willful or culpable. At the same time, officials were encouraged not to confuse the abolitionist and prohibitionist system, even though this directive highlighted the growing propagation of "bureaucratic corruption" and the abuses that were assumed by the diverging precedents that had permeated the policy thus far. As such, the manuals indicated the benefits of the loopholes created in 1944 (Domínguez, 1947: 165, 170).

Paradoxically, the decrease in those sent to prison in the 1950s is related to the increase in police power. In 1956 Argentina joined the 1949 UN treaty to suppress the trafficking of persons (executive order 14.442; decree 11.925/57). This was interpreted as an increase in the capacities of police intervention. In 1960 the UN treaty was legalized and used to punish anyone who had a place to carry out these activities or facilitate them. In 1965 decree 10.368, which established houses of tolerance in barracks, was repealed and the fine was increased from 1,000 to 100,000 pesos (law 16.666).

These reforms were inserted into the growing appeal to public morality, the rise in police edicts, and the increase of raids as a mechanism for territorial control. The police initiated a new punitive influence that impacted groups that were becoming more visible, such as youth, homosexuals, and poor urbanites. Provincial codes meant that oversight of detained women was shifted from prisons to police stations. In 1950, the chief of police was given the status of judge in absence, which allowed him to accuse and apply the provincial codes (decree 873/50), and in 1956 the first misdemeanors code was passed (provincial law 5571).

The morality institutionalized in the codes constituted a record in which state agents pictured themselves as bearers of virtues that were no longer present in civil society and that appealed to the fantasy of a past in which a disrupted order existed that could only be recovered with their constant intervention. Public morality as a matter of social interpretation was connected to precepts with a long tradition in the legal system. While the patriarchal system based on family had been in a slow decline since the end of the nineteenth century, the legal frameworks attempted to establish rules to reinforce it. As such, the laws were permeated by a dual concept of morality that protected freedoms of the male body over the restriction of female power (Giordano, 2012).

The women involved in the various forms of selling sex had diverse experiences with the law over the course of their lives: 57.3 percent had at least one prior when they were detained. The contingency between age and priors presents an accumulative scene in which a woman could have between one and seven arrests recorded in the penitentiary system, though this was likely only a small portion of the many informal negotiations with the police that did not end up recorded in a government file. Moreover, when detained in local police stations, many women usually provided fictional names to avoid creating their own record.

The 1955 misdemeanors codes included the category "public decency," which allowed for the arrest of any person who disturbed the aesthetic order with their appearance. With the 1936 Prophylaxis Law, pimps were fined 200 to 2,000 pesos. Beginning in 1966, the codes punished homosexuality by associating gay men with prostitutes to persecute the public activity of a group that socialized in the streets, bathrooms, and theaters due to restrictions in their private spaces. Police agents were thus permitted to take action against gay men in private places under the notion of scandal. The codes also defined those who "in their daily life dress and present themselves as the opposite sex" as "exploitation of public credulity" and classified it as a symptom of the gradual emergence of practices and identities tied to *travestismo*. In 1973 the codes added a prohibitionist perspective by criminalizing those who practiced prostitution and assigning it an indecorous characteristic with fines of 50 to 150 pesos and thirty days in prison.

Why were homosexuality and prostitution combined when it came to punitive action? These practices were associated with the feminine world in

which both prostitution and homosexuality would represent depository beings who were "penetrated" by the uncontrollable masculine libido. As I
recounted in chapter 2, the debate between regulationists and abolitionists
extended from the 1930s through the '50s. The 1936 Prophylaxis Law
emerged at the heart of these disputes. Protecting the double standard of
sexual morality, the health fear that focused on prostitutes as propagators
of venereal diseases pushed the abolitionist doctors to demand that women
maintain a health record (Biernat, 2013). Recall the famous episode of the
National Military College cadets who were discovered in public gatherings
photographing one another naked and in suggestive positions. This provoked "moral panic" that incentivized the modification of law 12.331 in the
aspects concerning prostitution (Bazán, 2006: 276).

That is, unlike the 1980s, the mark of individual loss of moral status tied
to illness was associated with prostitution and not homosexuality. At the
same time, homosexuality was represented as an example of the loss of masculine morality that could be recovered with the consumption of women as
prostitutes. Perhaps understanding this nexus can illuminate how a semantic code was later moved and inverted from one sign to another, from the
venereal focus of the brothel to homosexuality.

This array of regulations shows how the apparent decrease in sanctions
cannot be explained as a change in how they were applied. As we will see
in the last chapter, just as I compared in the DHJC, the new legal documents
started with approvals of the misdemeanor codes in the police station, relegating the place of the prison to jail cells in police stations.

In sum, the general reading of this framework suggests two arguments.
First, the processes of creating loopholes in the abolitionist regulations and
the prerogatives of regional neoregulationism were accompanied by repressive peaks in which state pressures to recover control over prostitution
were strengthened. At the same time, the apparent gradual decrease in detentions marked a transformation in the structuring of a punitive interpretation of abolitionism that was condensed in drills done piecemeal, such
as raids.

The Streets and Jail Cells: Experiencing Prison

The Olmos women's prison was run by the Order of the Good Shepherd
(1935–71), just like the entire women's penitentiary system between 1890
and 1970 in Latin America. In Olmos, the religious order ran juvenile detention starting in 1904, took over the women's prison in 1913, and in 1935

started operating in a building with three floors donated by the provincial government. The nuns' objective was to feminize the inmates based on the premise that crime went against their condition (D'Antonio, 2016). A decade later, Peronism strengthened this idea with policies of "social reintegration" through jobs associated with gender roles (Caimari, 2004).

Adult prisoners entered an establishment that in addition to cells had workshops where they would be educated in domestic chores (Rey, 2009). Prison and the application of the punishment of modern society were transformed by Peronism, which picked up some of these practices and, in the case of the women, proposed their reintegration in society associated with domestic labor (Caimiari, 2004). Women constituted a smaller percentage of the total number of detained persons accounted for by the national and provincial penitentiary system (Guy, 1991).

As I argued above, women who sold sex were locked up for short periods multiple times. My database indicates that 65 percent spent less than a week, 14 percent between one week and one month, 3 percent from one to two months, 2 percent from two to three months, 8 percent from three months to one year, 2 percent from one to two years, 1 percent from two to three years, 1.5 percent from three to nine years, 1 percent for nine to eighteen years, and 1 percent for more than eighteen years. Detained arbitrarily by police and freed by judges, women who sold sex received short sentences (one week), medium sentences when they were accused of spreading venereal diseases (from two weeks to two years), and long sentences when they committed crimes like homicide (from nine to eighteen years).

The women were detained in the following counties and cities: 25 de Mayo, 4 de Junio (now Lanús), 9 de Julio, Almirante Brown, Alsina, Avellaneda, Balcarce, Banfield, Bella Vista, Berazategui, Berisso, Boulogne, Campana, Cañuelas, Capital Federal (Buenos Aires), Caseros, Chascomús, Chivilcoy, Ciudadela, Coronel Suárez, Dolores, Don Torcuato, Ensenada, Esteban Echeverría, Fiorito, Florencio Varela, Florida, General Alvear, General Paz, General Sarmiento, Haedo, Hurlingham, La Plata, La Matanza, Lanús, Lomas de Zamora, Madariaga, Mar del Plata, Mercedes, Monte Chingolo, Moreno, Morón, Navarro, Necochea, Olavarría, Olivos, Punta Lara, Quilmes, Ramos Mejía, Roque Pérez, Sáenz Peña, Saladillo, San Fernando, San Isidro, San Martín, San Miguel, San Nicolás, Tandil, Tapalqué, Temperley, Tigre, Tres Arroyos, Tres de Febrero, Vicente López, Villa Ballester, Villa Diamante, Villa Lynch, Villa Madero, Villa Maza, and Zárate.

Though the women came from every zone in Buenos Aires, the arrests in Buenos Aires, La Plata, Tandil, San Isidro, and La Matanza took precedence. The transfer from the interior of the province to Olmos up-rooted the women, cutting off their ability to service clients, and was a punishment in and of itself. For example, 11.1 percent of the prisoners were detained in Tandil, which required a displacement of 334 kilometers for a detainment that lasted less than a week. Possibly, though the police officers knew the case they opened would not have major consequences, the routine constituted a complex mechanism of punishment and a threat to the future with which they consolidated their territorial power.

The information in the records coincides with the impressions collected by the communist teacher Angélica Mendoza, detained in 1933 in the Buenos Aires women's prison. She described the prisoners as daughters of working-class families who from a young age were responsible for domestic labor. Among the beggars and thieves, Mendoza (1933: 6–28) was especially interested in the prostitutes, whom (potentially guided by the paternalism and moralism of communists) she defined as "bourgeoisie in their thinking but lumpenproletariat in their social position" and recognized among them "an emotional solidarity." She emphasized that the prostitutes quickly entered and left the prison due to the payment of fines that was in effect during the regulation period.

By living together in prison, women could exchange experiences and refine expertise in their connection to the state. The "natural aura" that Mendoza described was defined by the segregation among the prisoners, a feeling that caused her as much attraction as pity. She observed that the construction of a precarious solidarity among the women was associated with the hierarchization that separated them from the other prisoners, even though, possibly, the romantic vision of the communist teacher hid the conflicts among them, erased by the empathy that arose from prison punishment. In her notes, Mendoza (1933: 29) describes forms of differentiation: the workers detained for theft did not want to be confused with the "whores," a statement with which the rest of the prisoners possibly inaugurated a performance that recovered feminine honor as the heart of their identity. They used this to navigate the stigma socially associated with being imprisoned.

In the jail cells, women talked about clients, how to dress to get their attention, daily hardships or joys, or tricks for negotiating with the police, and they exchanged prophylactic knowledge like the use of condoms or forms of douching they thought could prevent infection. These interactions created networks that allowed the women to spread across the province in search of consumers as well as find some owner in a bar who would rent them a room where they could receive clients when they did not do it in their own home with the consent of their partners. It is possible that the jail cells were spaces for distributing the scarce social capital of the underworlds with which these women articulated forms of survival as well as a set of knowledge that the intergenerational contact of the occasional prisoners transformed into a set of unofficial resources for their work.

Mendoza's description of knowledge sharing provides insight into the prostitute's active nature—that is, the knowledge involved in selling sex. There were "trades" with a set of rules that implicitly defined them and were confirmed by the participants. The link between the use of the body in the sale of sexual services required the knowledge of certain information associated with the performance of servicing clients: how to sell, dress, negotiate with the police, find locations, or charge for services. As such, these precarious networks also served as opportunities for some of this knowledge to circulate.

Forty-six percent of the detained women stated they had children, though possibly only a minority had to bring them along. Until 1962, when the Peronist regulations of 1950 that required the establishment of a different ward for prisoners with children were standardized, women could keep children under two years old with them (regulation 1373 from 1962). The demographics interpreted the presence of extramarital children as a sign of premarital sexual practices; in this sense, the data indicated that the presence of children outside of marriage constituted a long-term Argentine trend reaching an average of 27.8 percent in 1950. It was not until the 1980s that this process was divided by classes, differentiating between an average of 29 percent among unskilled laborers and between 7 and 11 percent among the middle class, likely due to broader access to affordable birth control methods (Torrado, 2003).

Peronism restructured institutional logic and emphasized that work could reintegrate the prisoners into society using binary gender models: men were trained for manufacturing labor and women for domestic work (Caimari, 2004). This situation allowed new opportunities for negotiating detention conditions. Work and education were used to measure the progress of the detained women, which allowed some women to save money to buy items such as shoes or help their families. The prisoners' change in status inspired by Peronism modified this experience as it allowed for new meanings and a wider array of available actions. This new ideology that saw prisoners as the subject of a humanitarian contract that aimed to reintegrate women in the social order functioned as a framework in which prisoners inscribed and organized their practices.

Eva was seventeen years old when she was detained by police and accused of murder in the city of San Miguel, Buenos Aires Province. Her parents were working-class, and she had four siblings. She stated that she left home at the age of fifteen and sold sex in various bars in the areas surrounding Buenos Aires. While working the bars, she met a group of thieves who regularly paid for her services. They proposed she participate in minor robberies to increase her earnings. With two of them, in a planned robbery, the guys killed a couple when they broke into their home. Though the thieves fled, Eva was abandoned to her fate and sentenced to the maximum penalty for the double homicide. Though she spent a year in juvenile detention, which in Olmos was located in a separate building, she spent many years of her life behind bars (SPB, card 37.251, 1953).

In prison Eva looked for various ways to offset the monotony of the prison regime. Using knowledge gained from agents inside—other prisoners or nuns—or outside—public defenders—she made use of institutional mechanisms to influence her standing. Her circulation through four prison establishments—Dolores, Bahía Blanca, San Nicolás, and Olmos—increased both her access to specific information and her alienation from other prisoners. Thus, supported by information she had obtained, Eva wielded three forms of agency: epistolary writing, connecting social policies, and disobedience to the prison order, which elicited reprimands.

Letter writing was a mechanism for prisoners to preserve emotional ties with family members, friends, and partners as well as make public requests. To do so, it was necessary to be literate, which was the case for 82.1 percent of the sample. Those who did not learn to read or write during their time in prison could get help from a nun or peer, which transformed the space of intimate writing into a public forum mediated by community bonds (Breckenridge, 2000). The recognition of the inability to write was used in the trials to throw out the first statements made to the police when women were not given the assistance of someone who could read or write. During her stay in Olmos, Eva sent and received letters from many people. Her exit records indicate that she wrote to her father, mother, siblings, two cousins who were prisoners in San Nicolás, her sister-in-law, and her lawyer. The writing allowed her to receive visits on Sundays. Other prisoners were visited by their partners, given the Peronist reform allowed married persons to have "hygienic visits" to maintain their sexual relations.

Just as Eva maintained affective and emotional ties with her peers, she used writing to make requests of public servants. In 1953 she wrote a letter to the governor of Buenos Aires Province Carlos Aloé—a member of the military and a politician who was very popular among the working class because of his humble origins and his role in the creation of the Eva Perón Foundation—to ask that they transfer her to the Buenos Aires prison. The letterhead displays the legend "Long live Perón and his immortal Evita." The justicialist narrative is inscribed in the polyphony deployed in the letter writing that the government solicited in support of the Segundo Plan Quinquenal (Elena, 2005; Guy, 2017).

It is not possible to say whether Eva wrote her letter motivated by her empathy for the Peronist political project, but she did think it was pertinent to permeate the discourse of her request with the values of the justicialist narrative: the condemnation of inequality and the request for "social justice." In the letter she sent to Governor Aloé, she told him she was the victim of a group of thieves who committed the murder and accused her. At the same time, she was emphatic in pointing out the state action as malicious: she emphasized that the events of the crime were not reconstructed, that her status as a minor was not respected, and that she was subjected to police violence. She argued that in the jail cells of the San Miguel police station she was humiliated: "They had the right to do whatever they wanted with me." As such, she begged the governor that as reparation he give the order for her to be transferred to the Buenos Aires prison so she could be close to her parents, who were getting old, given her younger brother would begin obligatory military service, leaving their parents alone.

Her request was denied in court and the request to the governor did not pan out. Though some members remarked positively on Eva's abilities in the "workshops" and "education," they put greater value on the sanctions for her lack of discipline. The prisoners could lose benefits when they committed minor infractions and be confined to solitary cells for major infractions. Eva accumulated multiple infractions at the institutional level, such as the lack of silence in the dormitories, promoting indiscipline, defying the sisters' orders, and fighting with other prisoners. She also tried to escape, even though to jump over the wall she climbed the apiculture equipment and was seriously injured by bee stings.

Beyond punishment, the Olmos prison was also a space to receive medical treatments and undergo healing. Women convicted of the crime punished by article 202c—that is, for spreading a venereal disease—were forced to get treatment as the regulations indicated. In the records there are little notebooks in which physicians noted the evolution of a gonorrheal case, the medication administered, and the prisoner's behavior.

The Peronist transformation of the prison system also allowed women to use the new set of social policies to disrupt the daily monotony of the prison, practicing forms of leisure or obtaining small benefits. Eva took multiple opportunities to spend the money she earned to buy two pairs of glasses and clothes. For a decade she saved part of her earnings. In 1963, in preparation for her transfer to the San Nicolás prison, she noted she had saved 20,77.73 pesos, a small savings when considering that just for buying a new pair of glasses she had paid 500 pesos.

In addition to paid labor, Eva took advantage of new pedagogical initiatives introduced by the administration. In 1954 she submitted a request through the nuns for a scholarship to the Universidad Popular Sudamericana to take a course in dressmaking and sewing. While the Pitman Academies offered women the opportunity to enter the labor market as secretaries, the Universidad Popular Sudamericana offered a variety of correspondence courses that included drawing, commercial, industrial, domestic, and other training (Queirolo, 2018). The nuns supported her request to the provincial government and extended a letter in which they stated the prisoner had "talent." Once she finished the course, the nuns asked the Universidad Popular Sudamericana to grant her the certification for free, given that in that first year of work she had only been able to save thirty-three pesos in her account.

In sum, the experiences in the jails were not limited to the prison system but, for the prostitutes, were an opportunity to establish contingent social networks that functioned as knowledge networks. The small percentage who spent a lot of time behind bars took advantage of various activities to maintain their bonds and solicit benefits.

Negotiating Identity: Meanings of Selling Sex

The prosecution of women forced them to decide how to present themselves to public institutions; that is, it forced them to present their biography with fragments of their identities. Penitentiary staff, nuns, and police who created the prisoners' files were influenced by classist and sexist biases (Piscitelli and Lowenkron, 2015). Among the dozens of sections that included level of education, time spent in charity institutions, and parents' names, among others, one was dedicated to describing the woman's economic life: job (stated). Before this little box, repeated at least twice—in the record of

priors and in the prison intake form—the women invoked distinct categories before the state to define themselves in ways influenced by the possible expectations involved in the production of the document.

Among the pages of priors, penal files, and the form completed by the
prison administrators, the description could change. It is surprising to see
different responses, and it is difficult to determine the extent of consensus
that endured and to what extent an order of bureaucratic repetition was imposed. The decision whether to accept or deny it should not be presented in
contradictory terms. I prioritized the form completed in the prison, administered by the institution nuns as the prisoners completed this document
themselves.

These documents were not only descriptions of household economies.
The reciprocal expectations of the institution and prisoners possibly determined the categories the women used. Selling sex brought together
economic and intimate spheres, meaning that attempting to separate the
monetary aspect of sexuality was a mode of classification that concerned
moral precepts of class and gender (Zelizer, 2005). They possibly negotiated
with the police on minor details—at first glance irrelevant—about what they
would declare to the state regarding their work situation. Though the abolitionist law did not penalize the sale of sex done independently and auton-
omously, the imprisoned women worked with staff to define their work in
a way that generally did not include the concept of "prostitute." Though the
record of priors was part of the institutional profile, it is possible that
the use of other categories was associated with deeper meanings. Perhaps
notions about certain activities and the boundaries between the definitions of legitimate ways to make money were associated not only with the
fear of punishment but also with ideas of honor and morality the women
used to define a category that permeated their biographies.

With the polysemic nature they used to define the working world, prisoners valued terms like "domestic labor," referring to the work of housewives;
"servant" or "domestic service" when they worked as employees in domestic service; or "house servants" (*fámulas*) when they had been doing such
work since they were young. A significant number of women stated they
were unemployed or lacking any job, a choice they understood as more honorable or less risky than that of prostitute before the state (graph 3.2).

Angélica Mendoza wrote that the majority of women were workers,
which is in line with the data shown in the 1929 prison census (O'Connor,
1931). As illustrated in graph 3.2, the women detained for selling sex defined
themselves as dressmakers, cooks, seamstresses, laundrywomen, embroi-

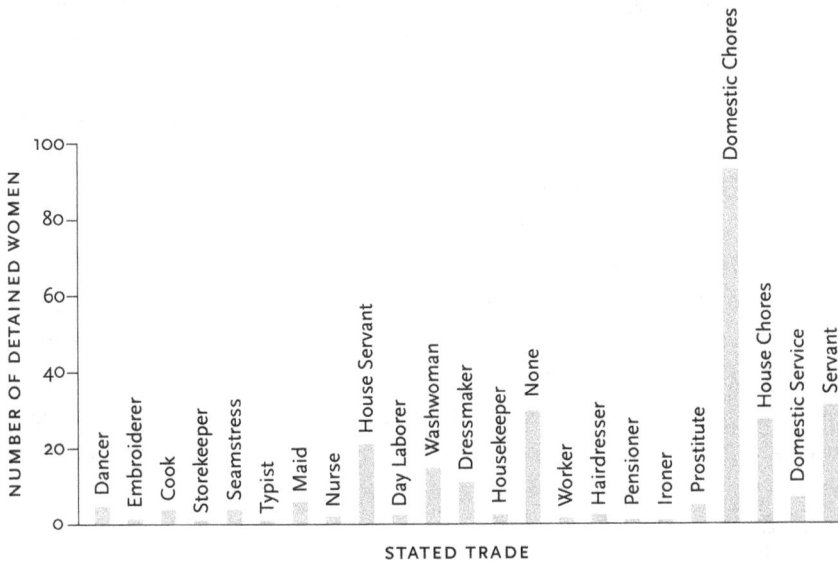

GRAPH 3.2 Trades stated by women detained in the Olmos prison (1936–71). Source: Compiled from the database of records from the Olmos women's prison of the SPB.

derers, hairdressers, nurses, pensioners, or ironers, positions and jobs that they held along with other work, as verified by the statements from neighbors in judicial files.

A question emerges from this map of meanings: Why did the women not refer to themselves as prostitutes? Was there a sense that prostitute was an identity? Did they understand it as a job or did they adjust to the parameters imposed by the state, which considered it a trade or sometimes a profession (when referred to as the "world's oldest profession")? Was the concept capable of articulating an identity associated with servicing clients? The selection of another identity functioned in part as a shield to avoid stigma (Lamas, 2017; Morcillo, 2010), a choice that could be a symptom of a morality shared by many social sectors as well as a decision with which the women believed they could minimize their punishment.

The meaning of "prostitute" was available as a way of organizing the experience of selling sex. It was a notion that, though with a negative connotation, was widely used. Among the prisoners themselves, the term "whore" functioned to classify groups (Mendoza, 1933). It was a bastardized and lambasted term, and it is possible that this stigma structured and blocked its semantic resignification, making it an identity. In the last decade, historians have recovered the interactionist perspective to analyze how different actors adjusted personal information in front of others to deal with a stigmatized attribute (Plumauzille and Rossigneux-Méheust, 2014). As such, some historians have signaled the limitations of utilizing these categories in written documents as those texts are incapable of recording social interactions (Hofman, 2017).

The meaning of "prostitute" was available to name the experience of selling sex, but it was a popular negative notion with which the prisoners discredited themselves (Mendoza, 1933). It was a lambasted sign that, though with the limitations of written documents, suggests it was administered by actors to manage a negative attribute (Plumauzille and Rossigneux-Méheust, 2014). The prisoners negotiated their biographies under the influence of various moralities and staff expectations accustomed to putting erratic lives in static boxes. The 2 percent who stated their work as prostitutes were older women who had registered in licensed brothels and possibly, due to their age, did not mind negotiating with the public agencies an identity that had given them stability and meaning throughout their lives.

We do not know with certainty if the women understood selling sex as work, but hypothetically it is possible to confirm that their choices did not form part of the habitual code that made sense of the working world. Social constructs of work decreasingly included unpaid domestic work. Thus, the women articulated notions associated with other work to define an identity before the state and thus gave value to the productive or reproductive work they did. In sum, negotiating an identity did not mean these women were lying, but they were only selectively reporting their biographies to construct their own identities. Leaning on economic activities beyond selling sex allowed them to divide their life to thus sustain an image they believed more acceptable for judicial officials or more in line with bureaucratic routines.

Profiles, Experiences, Trajectories, and Practices

Suspended in time and tattered by routine bureaucracy, the prison files offer incomplete details about the lives of women who sold sex. Though I believe these women negotiated with the staff in the construction of their files, the voice of the public agencies is amplified and inundates the documents' narratives. Indeed, even if I naively view these documents as transparent, it is important to consider that the arrest patterns depended in large part on the local needs of police as well as on the replication of preconceptions founded on classist and androcentric notions. Despite this deficiency,

I believe much of the information in these files can provide clues about the lives of these women.

Much of the sample is young: 4.7 percent of the women were underage; 69.5 percent were between nineteen and thirty years old; 16.1 percent were between thirty-one and forty years old; 6.5 percent were between forty-one and fifty years old; and 2.9 percent were older than fifty. The age records also describe the cycles of selling sex as well as the trajectories of the women. According to the database used for this study, the low number of underage women detained is because they were typically sent to charity institutions also administered by nuns and that had functioned as separate institutions since 1935. The court cases, as well as some of the cases resolved by the Supreme Court of Buenos Aires Province, indicate that the sale of sex could begin between the ages of thirteen and sixteen.

The figures on numbers of arrests are explained by the cycles of selling sex. Between the ages of nineteen and thirty, these women were potentially at the peak of their economic sexual life. In contrast, women older than forty were processed for corruption—that is, for the administration of a brothel or the management of other women; it is possible that they were restructuring their work by transforming their social capital, client networks, or workplaces to move from being a prostitute to a mediator or procurer. Though there was no specific age to mark this transition, it began when they could stop servicing clients and make money off of other girls.

Angélica Mendoza (1933: 40) noted that in the prison social structures, some women stood out for having personal capital tied to their clientele, when that group included elite men capable of providing benefits, but also associated with their age and the number of contacts in the "circle." Between 1940 and 1960, the social capital of many of the older women was due to the networks established during the era of licensed brothels, which allowed them to collaborate with those women who moved from establishment to establishment in search of clients: they connected with owners of bars or guesthouses where they could sleep and service men, or they knew women in other geographic areas as well as clients they could work as an access point to groups of men.

Regarding their relationship with men, 49.5 percent were single, 21.5 percent married, 19.7 percent in domestic partnerships, 4.7 percent separated, and 4.3 percent were widows. The prevalence of single women suggests that they would have had less leverage to negotiate with the police, that they could be protecting their boyfriends and domestic partners from a report of sexual exploitation, or the information suggests that it was difficult for a woman who sold sex to maintain a stable relationship. Mendoza (1933: 30) emphasized that the occasional boyfriends could operate as mediators between clients and the police. On the other hand, the separated women and widows would have had to look for ways to sustain themselves without relying on a man's income.

Their education level was key to understanding the perpetuated cycle of these women's subaltern societal positions when it came to gender and class. Among those with criminal records, the fact that seven of every ten women had not completed primary school suggests that, during their lifetime, families prioritized learning how to read and write as something necessary for employment. As such, 82.1 percent knew how to read and write. But this percentage also suggests that, by being women, most of whom were pushed toward domestic labor, they were excluded from continuing their studies. In the rural parts of the country, public policies valued learning a family trade and emphasized its role in support of a productive model, which potentially further restricted women's access to education (Gutiérrez, 2007).

This information aligns with public statistics. The 1929 prison census revealed similar rates of illiteracy and dropping out of school between first and third grade (O'Connor, 1931). In 1960, though the gaps decreased, women continued to occupy a lower position than men. The national census shows that while there was a significant drop in illiteracy rates, women from marginal or rural areas continued to represent the greatest percentage. In this sense, the 1931 school census revealed that 32 percent of children in Buenos Aires between the ages of five and thirteen did not attend high school or dropped out early. Halfway through the century, the country progressively increased access to education through higher numbers of institutions and attendance rates, especially in the capital and urban centers, but secondary education continued to be a privilege of a growing middle class and skilled laborers (Cammarota, 2014). While enrollment grew, the 1960 national census shows that of the 12 million children who accessed primary education, only a third reached sixth grade, and fewer went on to secondary education. This suggests that the educational experiences of these women were in line with other working-class and poorer families. Their lack of cultural capital was limiting, narrowing their options for how to earn a living.

Intrafamilial relations, being sent to a charity institution, and access to a first job were distinctive steps in the construction of the subalternity of the women who sold sex. A first step was associated with orphanhood, charity institutions, and job placement. Two of every ten women in the sample were orphans, and two of every ten women (though not necessarily the same two) passed through different charity or juvenile institutions where they were educated in domestic labor and then were assigned to homes where they could work (Allemandi, 2017).

The narrative construction of "prostitutes" as foreigners during the first decades of the twentieth century contrasts with the data that 94.3 percent of them were Argentine. Only four of every ten were daughters of foreigners, especially Spaniards and Italians. This situation varied throughout the twentieth century with the gradual replacement of transatlantic migration with the national movement as well as the increased presence of migrants from bordering countries such as Paraguay.

The presence of women born in other provinces is indicative of the migration to Buenos Aires in search of better opportunities that took place starting in the 1940s: 5 percent from Santa Fe, 5 percent from Entre Ríos, 4.3 percent from Tucumán, 3.9 percent from Córdoba, 3.2 percent from Corrientes, 2.2 percent from La Rioja, 1.8 percent from Chaco, 1.4 percent from Misiones, 1.4 percent from Santiago del Estero, 1.1 percent from Formosa, 1.1 percent from Mendoza, 0.8 percent from Catamarca, 0.7 percent from Río Negro, 0.4 percent from Salta, and 0.4 percent from La Pampa, while 5.3 percent of women migrated from other countries such as Brazil, Paraguay, Romania, Italy, Poland, Germany, and France. That is, more than half were born outside of the province of Buenos Aires. Possibly the arrival to new territory forced them, just like the foreigners, to activate social networks to settle in, as well as, in the case of selling sex, to negotiate with local actors, especially the police.

The disparity in the information regarding place of detention, residence, and birth—that is, the minimal correspondence between each of these things—is revealing of the mobile and dynamic nature of sex work. There are many women in these files born in places distinct from where they lived, for example, those who moved from the interior to the center of the Buenos Aires Province or to its surrounding cities, as well as women detained considerable distances from their residence. As I explore in the following three chapters, the women who sold sex in zones outside of Buenos Aires (rural and peri-urban spaces) used distinct tactics of movement to avoid police negotiation and find new clients among social groups that also showed markers of mobility between jobs and zones, like the day laborers. Therefore, I believe the social networks created—some in prison and others inherited from the licensed brothels—were essential to the development of this practice. Thus, it is possible to argue that this changed over time, marked by the mobility that implied the development of routes beginning in the middle of the twentieth century and the transportation of travelers that accelerated this process (Piglia, 2014).

Women were seen as the foci of venereal infections. Because of this, the Prophylaxis Law articulated the abolition of regulated prostitution through an array of measures with health care objectives, which assumed an androcentric interpretation of health (Biernat, 2013; Miranda, 2012). As I said, some detentions were also a way of forcing women to get treatment to eliminate the risk of infection. In contrast with the representations of the period, only 25.1 percent of the women were sick at the time of detention. From this small group, only 11.3 percent had sexually transmitted infections. Similar data were compared in the 1929 prison census, which indicated that only 0.25 percent of the detained people had venereal diseases. It is possible that the socialization and transmission of knowledge between individuals included the development of skills to prevent these illnesses, even though these methods, such as the use of douches, were not always effective, which was reiterated in the judicial files. It is possible to think that, because of the task they carried out in the constant attention to clients (some of whom perhaps attempted to prevent some infection), and in the conversations with friends or at the time of being detained, women circulated knowledge that curbed illnesses or allowed the women to hide their symptoms. At the same time, access to medication (some of which was effective) and the later development of penicillin gave women the ability to treat themselves (Biernat and Simonetto, 2017).

In sum, the data offers a glimpse of the experiences, practices, and social profiles of the women detained by the police in the Olmos prison for selling sex. Additionally, it is possible to compare patterns of dispossession that structured their trajectories and influenced their social position from which they managed their own lives.

· · · · · ·

The examination of the enforcement of abolitionist policy in Argentina can be thought of on two levels. On one level, police officers structured a punitive interpretation supported by the representation developed in other social groups as a part of everyday resources. These tactics were in apparent conflict with judicial organizations and functioned as part of the rituals of consolidating territorial power. On another, this interpretation constitutes a continuity. It is possible to mark two periods of the law: first, the creation of loopholes in abolitionism and regional neoregulationism (1937–55) corresponded with high rates of detention with the goal of disciplining "free prostitutes" of the previous administrative regime. Second, the punitive consolidation of abolitionism established a series of measures that broadened police power and made the punitive interpretation a core structure of state policy regarding sex work.

The experiences of women in prison were more than disciplinary. These institutions produced contingent networks that functioned as knowledge networks. This allowed me to deepen some knowledge involved in the labor of attracting clients and maintaining them. I also explored how the small percentage that spent a long time behind bars articulated distinct practices to sustain a network for relationships and profit.

In the third section I addressed the negotiated meanings with which women defined, before the state, the boundaries between the domestic economy and sexuality to inscribe the crime into their biographies. Along these lines, I demonstrated that the majority chose other economic activities to describe themselves, which means they did not ascribe to just one identity.

Finally, I explored how the information of my sample allowed me to trace the distinct dispossessions that acted as conditions of possibility that limited or developed the practices of these women. This description produces a social map that introduces the narrative of the practices studied in the following chapters.

4 Selling Sex

Experiences, Practices, and Social Meanings (1936–1960)

In 1948, in Ramón Santamarina, Buenos Aires Province, fourteen-year-old Catalina reported her husband for pimping.[1] She had a black eye and bruises and testified that her partner subjected her to physical punishment to force her to turn over the money she earned servicing clients. She stated she was hit with barbed wire while forced to be on all fours naked on a dirt floor in the middle of winter. A previous report indicates that Catalina had a similar experience when her first partner, ten years her senior, hit her to force her to have sexual relations with neighbors (DHJS, folder 657, file 218, 1948).

In 1959, Mónica was detained in Chascomús while servicing three boys in a ranch close to downtown.[2] She was a thirty-five-year-old single mother who lived with her father and washed clothes to earn money. She did not sell sex on the street to avoid the social stigma and potential conflicts with the police. As such, she had an agreement with an eighteen-year-old boy to give him a percentage in exchange for him finding her clients among the city's youth. After a time, Mónica reported the boy to end the agreement and be free to date a bricklayer (DHJS, folder 799, file 227, 1959).

The clear dissonance between these two stories demonstrates just how diverse the experience of buying and selling sex was. The objective of this chapter is to study the wide variety of relationships between men and women when it came to sexual services in the southern part of the Buenos Aires Province between 1937 and 1960. I examine the various degrees of coercion and the agreements that governed each, the meanings that were negotiated, and the practices that formed and reproduced these connections.

I understand that the social meanings and practices used in selling sex provide insight into local social dynamics. The connections between how money and sex circulated are illustrative of the borders between the public, the private, and the domestic in the lives of poor women from working-class families in peripheral zones. Furthermore, they provide information about the initial capabilities and available resources, among which some of the women made the sale of sex out to be a valid option (or not) to family members, friends, and neighbors. Therefore, this chapter addresses how specific ways of selling sex were intertwined with situated contexts, and as such, it offers some insight into life in the region's lower-income sectors (Pastoriza, 2008; Pérez and Garazi, 2014).

This chapter expands the geographic and temporal frameworks previously used. First, my scale includes small towns (focused on agrarian production), medium-sized cities (which include those with port access), and important cities of the region, such as Mar del Plata. They were part of the agricultural and social cycles that governed the patterns of movement and activity in the zone. Migrating for harvests, shipping, or seasonal work in Mar del Plata—which included the endless filet work in the fishing circuit, proto-industry, and the summer work opportunities created by tourism (hotels and businesses) (Pastoriza, 2008; Pérez and Garazi, 2014)—guide the spatial framework and make movement an explanatory factor in the practices of sexual services. Therefore, the root of this analysis in rural and urban zones outside of the capital reaffirms the relationship between the forms of buying and selling sex and economic, cultural, and social dynamics.

Second, while studies tend to focus on the regulation period, in this chapter I examine the practices, experiences, and meanings constructed around the sale of sex during the first period following the abolition of regulated prostitution. That is, I start with the passage of the Prophylaxis Law in 1936 and the transformations of regulations that created loopholes in the law's scope (such as approval for installing brothels in barracks), up to the cancellation of these provisions and the increase in the police's punitive power in 1960, which changed the relational dynamic between the state and the sale of sex.

While the period was marked by significant regulatory changes, the courts do not encapsulate sex-trade relations but do act as a framework for this study. I therefore understand that the practices of offering sex transgressed the temporal framework of the regulation period.

The examination of these women's life paths reveals how the intersection of age, gender, and class constituted experiences with the state (through their appeal or participation). I argue that seasonal patterns, such as the trend of women having been placed in other people's homes when underage, solidified their subaltern condition in relation to families and partners. Women's ancillary positions created a unique relationship with their bodies, intimacy, and sexuality, which contributed to how they were able to consider the sale of sex for income.

In this chapter I focus on testimonies from women involved in judicial proceedings for violating law 12.331, article 202c of the penal code, or the crime of corruption. I examine the testimonies of sixty-seven women, 140 clients, and sixty-three witnesses based on forty judicial files from the DHJS.

While the archivist's influence is always present when it comes to which of these documents are preserved from the totality, I also address some standard parameters when it comes to the living conditions, social profiles, and experiences of both men and women. To do so, my primary data points included cause of arrest, place of residence, year of birth and of arrest, age, marital status, level of education, degree of literacy, stated profession, number of priors, orphanhood, nationality of father and mother, time spent or not in the Sociedad de Beneficencia (Society of Beneficence) and other institutions with similar goals, the rate offered, the sale of sex during the regulation period, and whether or not there were signs of illness.

To meet these objectives, this chapter is organized in five parts. In the first section, I describe the sample studied to define the profiles and paths of the women prosecuted by the justice system of the Buenos Aires Province of the Departamento Sur (Southern Department) (headquartered in Dolores).[3] In the second section, I describe the intersection of class, gender, and age and how a cross section of people was influenced by a subaltern sense of body, intimacy, and sexuality. In the third section, I review a type of pimping in which husbands used violence as a form of control and operated outside of networks. In the fourth section, I reconstruct the precarious deals some women struck with men to define their sexual supply and negotiate their intimacy and earnings. Finally, I explore the role of mobility in the construction of the sexual supply and the use of social networks that were a legacy of the regulation period.

Social Profiles and Possible Paths to Selling Sex

With the abolition of regulated prostitution, recordkeeping on prostitution shifted from municipal records to legal departments and police stations. However, given the nature of the bureaucratic judicial process, civil servants were able to gather testimonies about events that otherwise would have been unlikely to leave behind a written record.

Though rare, the files from the first three decades of the twentieth century indicate that the state sanctioned the sale of sex outside the licensed brothel system. Doctors and public employees considered clandestine sexual services—that is, those that did not fit in the regulation model—to be the flaw in the system (Biernat, 2013; Múgica, 2014). Sexual services continued to be offered in private homes, and unlicensed establishments continued past the end of regulation, demonstrating the difficulty of adapting periodizations to legal changes.

The people taken to court in these files were detained for their limited ability to negotiate with the police. The officers tended to wait outside the place where women serviced clients to guarantee a witness in the raid. For example, in 1948 a thirty-one-year-old carpenter stated before the judge that when he was detained an officer told him, "You're going to have problems because of your woman, but you can fix that for fifty pesos." This was twenty pesos higher than the thirty pesos he paid a month for an apartment in Mar del Plata, while his wife charged five pesos per client, meaning she would have to service ten men to satisfy the police (DHJS, folder 650, file 278, 1948). Sometimes payments went beyond money: in 1953 Lucía, thirty-nine years old, reported that the police detained her because she refused to have sex with the commissioner (DHJS, folder 739, file 25, 1953).

These reports did not go far nor were they new: during the regulation period, there were many complaints about officers going too far with wards and madams. With these acts, the police commissioners tried to increase their direct claims to control, which were lost following the abolition of the licensed brothel system that was in place between 1875 and 1936 (Grammático, 2002; Múgica, 2014). During the regulation period in the Departamento Sur the police received numerous off-the-books payments from brothels (Linares, 2016).

The new, indirect state ties prompted territorial conflicts the police used to resist losing the power developed in a declining regulatory culture and strengthened informal punitive practices. The abolition of prostitution was paradoxical: in the 1930s, facing a crisis of liberalism, the state imposed policies that legitimized their intervention in the definition of "the private" as a mechanism in the construction of order (i.e., through abolition); through abolishing regulated prostitution there was a tendency to deregularize forms of control around paid sex that was legitimized in international policies. As such, the explicit regulation of the female body fomented by the nineteenth-century state system shifted the punishment of certain specific practices—that is, to the definition of possible limits of action regarding payment for sex as an outgrowth of the heterosexual culture guided by an ambiguous notion of "public morality."

Judicial agencies created administrative mechanisms that included physician and neighborhood interventions in order to present a moral judgment of women. Having physicians participate in trials was a way to link two fields to create a legal intention: victims and ideal perpetrators, as well as consensus regarding moral, classist, and gendered prescriptions (Ledesma Prietto and Ramacciotti, 2014; Riva, 2011).

The institutional appeal to the category of "neighbor" used institutional hierarchies to moderate women. The sixty-three witnesses who were convened to determine the morality of those accused legitimized traditional precepts of the edict. They were almost all married men (69.78 percent) between the ages of twenty-five and seventy-five, though the majority were between the ages of thirty-five and sixty-five (60.3 percent). Also taken into consideration as criteria were class and social status: they worked as landowners (20.63 percent) or businessmen (31.74 percent), but the group also included factory workers (1.58 percent), foremen (1.58 percent), and captains (1.58 percent). Meanwhile the accused were rural workers, operators, or sailors, and to a lesser extent bricklayers (1.58 percent), day laborers (14.28 percent), truck drivers (1.58 percent), drivers (4.76 percent), dockworkers (1.58 percent), self-employed (6.34 percent), police (1.58 percent), or fisherman (1.58 percent). It is clear from these occupations that class played a role in who had the ethical and moral authority to comment on the lives of people examined by the state through a classist and ageist lens.

Many of the women detained were young, minors or adults between the ages of thirteen and thirty-five, though the age range spanned thirteen to sixty-five. The number of priors included in the trials progressively grew with age, which indicates that during their lives these women continued selling sex and were harassed by policies that limited their paths.

The marital status of the women varied from single (44.67 percent) to married (7.37 percent), in domestic partnership (25.37), separated (4.69 percent), or widowed (1.34 percent), conditions that implied ties controlled by men with whom they did or did not share a home and with whom they negotiated the use of the money they earned for their labor. In the case of married women or domestic partnerships, the existence of children and a partner who did not have stable employment made the sale of sex out to be a possible way to earn an income to sustain the home. On the other hand, the separated and widowed women had to look for ways to survive without relying on a man's income.

Women's occupation and search for how to make a living provided information on both domestic economies and the meanings placed on their labor. Because of the characteristics of the legal proceedings, the women were forced to declare a job recognized by the justice system. The choice of terms such as laundrywoman, servant, or housewife therefore corresponds with two dimensions: the supplementary activities with which the women managed to earn a living and the biographical information they considered to establish how they presented themselves. That is, the selection of one activity over another gives insight into the negotiated meanings that the women gave to the act of selling sex. As discussed in the previous chapter, the women rarely recognized prostitution as credible employment; therefore, they avoided defining selling sex as a job (perhaps out of fear of the state being punitive or following their own moral standards).

Their lives were shaped by the contemporary economic trends of central, southern, and northern Buenos Aires. Poverty was characterized by the precarity of supplies that made it difficult to access sustainable conditions for survival in local markets associated primarily with agricultural production and, in some cases, proto-industry. Halfway through the 1930s, the shrinkage of the growth cycle in the pampa zone, the technification, and the concentration of property reduced opportunities for stable employment in the ranches, estates, and farms (Balsa, 2006). The volatility of job opportunities associated with agricultural cycles offered different employment opportunities for men and women, which accentuated the fragile living conditions and cyclical movement of those at the margins.

The employment volatility in the export economies was ongoing, and though Peronism accelerated the consumption capacity of workers in these cities, the observance of their rights was minimized in sectors with low union rates (Ribeiro, 2008). Between 1937 and 1960 there was a massive congregation of seasonal workers in charge of farming vegetables, threshing grains, and bundling grains from March to June and November to January (Villulla, 2014). The work that could be done in the port was not that far from paid domestic labor for women, if payments were made regularly. The transfer of income from the field to the city that took place during the Perón period was strained by the drop in prices of raw materials in the following decades and the decrease in exports following the war. Between 1949 and 1952, grain production slowed, causing a significant economic contraction (Ribeiro, 2008).

These trends further limited the possibilities women had to enter the workforce as they tended to work in domestic service or, for those living in Mar del Plata, as shopkeepers or seasonal or domestic workers in hotels, boarding houses, or summer houses (Garazi, 2016). Entering the workforce early was decisive in determining class subalternity. The placement of girls as domestic employees was a privileged access point (Allemandi, 2017;

Villalta, 2012). As seen in the testimonies from mothers and daughters recorded in the court files, the process was reproduced intergenerationally: according to my database, 39 percent of the cases were placed in the homes of others by the state or welfare charities.

If the family acted as a social construct, a field that distributed various types of capital among its members (Bourdieu, 1997), the generational regularity of the time poor young women spent as servants returns us to an act of serfdom characteristic of the social reproduction of classes. As seen in the next section, these women's families participated as agents of social reproduction in that they confirmed their daughters' positions in society and made them endure through time.

The defendants worked in the various jobs they declared to hold in the court. Offering to do laundry for unaccompanied men in the fields was as much a way to subsist as was earning extra income if they serviced their own clients. When they lived with men, this work allowed women to supplement the periods of unemployment their partners experienced outside the shipping and harvesting seasons. In contrast to the information produced in Buenos Aires by the National Institute of Nutrition, which indicated that 96 percent of husbands covered most of the family budget (Escudero, 1939b), women from poor families were driven to try different ways of supplementing their partner's income.

The women defined their experience using categories that did not align with available representations of prostitution. Assessing their personal biography through the lens of work associated with the domestic world was a part of a female performance before the justice system—that is, as the embodiment of certain virtues and aptitudes that establish a performance that sets up a process of reading both what belongs to the body and what does not. The women who sold sex chose representations equipped with symbolic capital to negotiate, as much with the state as with their neighbors, the legitimate framework of their actions.

Their performative plea to define their state classification as domestic workers or housewives expresses a commitment to values of classification associated with a semiotics of honor. The performance the women adopted demanded a lot of energy to sustain the folds that allowed them to cover vast parts of their social lives: domestic work, partners, buyers of sex, and families.

On the other hand, beyond the penalties or attributes that these choices entailed, the commitment to the dominant code perhaps made it so that these women did not experience selling sex as work. This would mean they would represent this activity as something ancillary, a contingent situation that did not define their lives as a whole and they would reject the activity as the cultural core of their identity.

The lack of education limited women's ability to obtain other kinds of jobs: more than half of the interrogated women stated they were illiterate. According to the 1947 census, among urban populations, 9.4 percent of women did not know how to read or write, while in rural zones 13.4 percent could not. This allows us to think about the marginal position women occupied in the working world and about the profound inequality they faced in police proceedings. Often, perhaps inspired by the advice of their lawyer, they rejected their initial statement in which they generally acknowledged some presumed crime by affirming that they had been read a different testimony or that they had not signed the document because they did not know how to do so.

The economic cycles characterized the sale of sex as a mobile activity. More than half of the detained women were arrested in a city other than their city of birth or residence, and a third of them had more than one prior in police stations in other precincts. By living in communities with lower demographic density in which the close relationships between community members were of utmost importance, moving was a way to evade some restrictions and make money to survive. The rapid recognition by neighbors, which could mobilize a rumor quick enough to bestow a woman with the status of prostitute as well as gather a group of clients, and the pressure from local police officers, who forced the women to pay some fee with money or sex, limited the permanent sale of sex in a single establishment.

The women who offered sex also depended on clients earning money to spend with them. For this reason, following the harvests, where men gathered after work or went to bars, was a useful way to obtain clients where they worked. Seasonal work was part of a pattern of circulation for the male workforce. The role of these women in offering adequate sexual services for their clients involved seasonal movement tied to the circulation of the male workforce.

Following this introduction, in the following section I go more in depth into the life paths, social meanings, and practices of selling sex.

The Domestic Construction of the Subaltern Sexuality

In 1942 in Balcarce, a mother went to the police station to report the corruption of her fifteen-year-old daughter Andrea.[4] The girl did not live with her parents; like other poor girls of her age, she was "placed" as a servant in a home with higher income. A thirty-nine-year-old Spanish baker gave her room and board in exchange for her work. Andrea's father was a rural day laborer with a meager salary with which he could barely sustain his five daughters and wife. As such, Andrea was "placed" and for eight days cleaned in the business and home of the family until she left them.

Andrea moved in with José, a twenty-nine-year-old day laborer she considered to be her boyfriend and whom her mother indicated as a corruptor who forced her daughter to have sexual relations with neighbors. When the judge inquired about her loss of virginity, interpreted by the authorities as the indicator of corruption, the girl stated that her first sexual relationship was with the baker's son in exchange for two pesos, money she later gave to her mother. After considering this situation, with an eye toward cutting off the girl's ties with both her partner and her family, the judge sent her to a juvenile institution in La Plata (Olmos) until she came of age, separating her from a family the justice system considered incompetent. Six years later, Andrea left the institution under the guardianship of a civil servant who helped her get a job in domestic service (DHJS, folder 508, file 22, 1942).

These reports were also a reaction to the expectations of a new generation (Cahn, 2007; Freidenraij, 2016). Controlling children's departure from the home and their potential flight showed the tensions between what was normative and anchored in familial reproduction and rebellion driven by the youthful fantasy of independence. We could argue that Andrea was a symptom of new generational expectations to construct independent lives, like getting together with José, and the structural effects that shaped their life path aided by state agencies.

Because of the precarity of their subsistence, poor working families were open to moving daughters and sons through other homes, often aided by state or welfare agencies (Allemandi, 2017; Stagno and Giovagnetti, 2010; Villalta, 2012). Law 19.903, Patronage of Minors, passed in 1919, redefined notions of custody attributed in the civil code and granted the state the ability to regulate the tutelage of children and adolescents considered "delinquent minors . . . materially or morally abandoned." The law allowed judicial officers and private actors (welfare societies and families) to relocate minors in jobs to guarantee their subsistence in order to reform their behavior. This change was accompanied by successive reforms that altered custody, such as the law that in 1926 gave greater legal authority to single mothers. In 1931, by decree, the National Patronage of Juveniles was reorganized, and in 1937 law 4664 created the juvenile courts, though in zones in which this study focuses, youth, both boys and girls, continued to be under correctional, criminal, or civil courts (Guy, 2008; Zapiola, 2008).

The intersection of age, class, and gender was decisive in the negotiations that Andrea could establish between the public, private, and domestic and constitutive of her subaltern sexual experience. The placement was a deciding factor when it came to these women's paths both in terms of class and sexual experiences. Those classified as minors struggled with public interventions that intensified their subaltern conditions. The girls sought alternative forms of subsistence, activities with which they tried to sustain their existence outside of their origin group: the search for employment in another city, exchange of sex for money, consolidation or breakup of the marital unit, or domestic partnership. Far from transforming the female body into an object of control, the state participated in a system in which, through civil servant interventions and private appeals, boundaries of women's domestic experiences were disputed.

María's complaint about her daughter's supposed perversion legitimized that a judicial agency would decide how and where Andrea should develop a life beyond her family. The civil servants measured what in the new environment was not healthy for the young woman's development. The relationship with José, which she later ended, was considered problematic. The Argentine laws created a world of male silence around patriarchal violence in which heterosexual sex was considered naturally consensual, so it was generally poor women who had to prove their moral value associated with virginity to be considered an "ideal victim" (Guy, 2003).

It is possible the mother appealed to the police to return her daughter to the home where she had been "placed," a measure that would help her feed her family when her husband was absent with the harvest, which involved his movement to farms or ranches far from their home for several full days, or workdays from morning to night (Villula, 2014). Her aspirations did not pan out and ended with the girl's being sent to an institution. When the claimants resorted to the justice system, they generally did so with limited information and without full understanding of the physical and material consequences of their actions. The claimants tended to simplify the causal mechanisms they considered relevant to consciously use the inconsistencies of the rules and sanctions system. They made use of a selective logic that explains the individual behaviors between the subjectively desired and socially required behaviors (Levi, 1990). It is possible that the rumors and advice from partners functioned to circulate popular knowledge. This kind of decision brought together erratic and pragmatic practices associated with quotidian needs and desires. It is possible that in rural zones, like those where Andrea lived, in which fathers could be gone for long periods of time, mothers would administer domestic discipline and, therefore, were also the ones who could resort to state agencies to ask for help to punish children.

The corruption complaint indicates a questionable sexual link between a minor and an adult and required a "deflowering" exam, a procedure conducted by the police doctor to determine the state of the victim's body. The physician would inspect the minor's vagina to certify the hymen's condition. The female genitalia became a symbol for the woman's moral condition and was also the safeguard of personal intimacy. It is likely that the hands-on procedure was an invasive practice that violated the personhood of the examined woman. The police doctor determined in the examination whether the woman was a virgin and, in the case of not being one, how long before and in what way she had lost her virginity. He then interviewed the patient to write a report about the girl's moral aptitudes and then recommended judicial actions. For the physician, the internal scars were the mark of an "abandoned minor" and "minimal family care" (DHJS, folder 508, file 22, 1942), words that held a privileged place in the ruling that separated Andrea from her parents.

Medical and judicial discourse came together to confirm a model of motherhood that blamed those who did not comply with the abilities assigned as natural due to their condition as women: the care and rearing of their children (Calandria, 2015; Nari, 2004). The broadening of this kind of state attribution and intervention was inscribed in new social policies that sought to construct maternal models with protection and tutelage (Biernat and Ramacciotti, 2013).

The institutional violence of examining the female body was legitimized in the dual statutory nature of Andrea's gender and age. In a gendered dimension, the centrality of this examination in the definition of the trial and the selection of the genital state as the precept to measure individual purity affirmed the naturalization of sexual difference (Scott, 2016). Therefore, the control, measurement, and hands-on procedure comprised a system of medical acts that infiltrated the minor's body.

Public discourse constructed the woman as a passive object, a depository for the masculine libido (Valobra, 2015). For Nerio Rojas (1943), a recognized physician specialized in legal medicine and a national legislator of the Unión Cívica Radical (UCR), the certification of the "total rupture of the hymen" was the necessary condition to determine the purity of a woman and was indicative of her moral condition.[5] Certifying genitalia, representing it as something able to be transformed or using this symptom as evidence, was the opposite of what was done with male genitalia (generally not examined). In the male reproductive apparatus, they could not indicate possible marks of a corrupted natural state given it would not be a potentially defiled entity. It is not by chance that the figure of the *uranista*, or gay man, was conceived by sexology as the inverse of a man through anal penetration. The figure of the minor, pure as that which is not penetrated, affirmed an ontological representation of the female being that, in its correct development, could only abandon this condition preferably through nuptial union.

Calling Andrea a minor indicated an age in which the normative prescriptions fed the intersection of gender, class, and age and constitutive elements of her domestic experience. From the beginning of the century, the term minor was used by political elites and intellectuals to describe children and adolescents considered unaware of appropriate behavior, spatial localization, education, work, sexuality, and relationships with adults acceptable for their age (Zapiola, 2008).

Legal limits converged in the lives of young women like Andrea—due to their age and gender—with borders of class because the difficulties the women faced to guarantee their sustenance defined their range of possible decisions. These diverse intersections allow us to concretely address the women and girls at the intersection of the complex, irreducible, and variable effects—economic, political, cultural, psychological, subjective, and experiential—that are derived when multiple acts of differentiation intersect in historically specific contexts to demonstrate that the different corners of social life cannot be separated in discreet, pure forms (Brah and Phoenix, 2004). That is, the active formation of class was structured in relation to gender as an element that structurally defined the symbolic place of the subjects and the generation as a variable entity associated with socially anticipated prescriptions and the access to legal status.

In Andrea's biography, these lines were blurred. Her ancillary position with her family members and the state was constructed in the intersection of a contingent status like age with her position of gender and class. As young women, minors occupied a liminal position in the judicial system: they were old enough to be employed but did not have total autonomy from their parents or, once united, from their partners or husbands. Since 1907, law 5291 used a special system to regulate the employment of children over the age of ten and women. In 1924 law 11.317 divided the standards into rural and urban work, raised the minimum working age to twelve, and prohibited minors under the age of fourteen to work in domestic service (Pagani and Alcaraz, 1991). It is in this context that, like other poor, young girls, Andrea was "placed" as a servant in someone else's house. By leaving home, the girl directly contributed to her parents and sisters (giving them some income) or indirectly (eliminating a mouth to feed) did so (Panter-Brick and Smith, 2000). As adults, women also occupied an ancillary position in relation to older men in the division of domestic labor. In a time of flux, Andrea formed her experience and in the face of immediate conflict activated mechanisms that, without knowing it, mobilized these complex systems.

The entrance into her boss's home was a constitutive "step" in the consolidation of her class position. Though women participated in fluid employment, the access to work associated with a low status of gender and age cemented in just one season their future in terms of class (Milanich, 2010). Poor, young girls experienced unequal conditions compared to families with higher incomes (though not necessarily excessive) to subvert the possibility of hunger.

A third of women recorded in this sample were employed as servants at the time of detention while almost half had been servants before coming of age and getting married or moving in with a boyfriend to dedicate themselves to domestic chores. Many of the mothers of these young women stated they were also "placed" in their youth. The placement of minors in others' homes was not a practice unique to rural spaces: some studies have shown that between 1900 and 1940, there was a high demand for girls and boys in Buenos Aires for domestic service (Pagani and Alcaraz, 1991).

This multifaceted ancillary position marked a unique experience with the body, intimacy, and sexuality that made the boundaries between domestic employment and the sale of sex more porous as forms of survival. Andrea provided sexual services to the baker's son for two pesos, a sexual experience that can happen in patriarchal customs such as the "droit du seigneur" for which the boss or his son had a right to the first night of the young women on his ranch. She gave the money to her mother and sisters so they could buy food. Beyond these apparent exaltations of patriarchal classism, among the young women of working families, extramarital sex was common even though it had later consequences (Barrancos, 2012). At the same time, though the baker's son was not part of the local elite, in families of high birth and perhaps among the middle class of provincial towns or cities was rooted the idea that domestic service girls guaranteed access to a first sexual experience without the risk of venereal disease (Losada, 2009).

Andrea emphasized this sexual tie with the expectation of gaining her sought-after independence. Perhaps she hoped that by pointing out that this act was meant to help her mother, she could avoid being entered into the judicial records for prostitution; she hoped to connect economics and intimacy to avoid moral stigma (DHJD, folder 508, file 22, 1942).

To be "placed" was an experience unique to poor girls. It implied uprooting them from the group they initially belonged to and forcing them to be part of homes in a liminal condition between what was work and what was family (Pérez, Cutuli, and Garazi, 2018). For the receiving families, the placement was seen as a favor to the minor's domestic group of origin and also as an act that gave them status in the local social hierarchy. The hosts had various arguments to legitimize this situation. Giménez, the Spanish baker, explained hosting Andrea as a favor to her mother. Just like other neighbors—men and businessmen brought together to give their opinion on the minor's moral behavior—this indicated that the girl worked in his home to save herself from unseemly behavior (DHJS, folder 508, file 22, 1942).

The cohabitation placed this relationship at the intersection among labor, friendship, the affective, and the domestic, which blurred the employment relationships, working connections in which the definition of the paid or unpaid nature of the employment was negotiated (Pérez and Canavaro, 2016). Andrea's payment was composed of lodging, a small amount of money, and food meant for her family. The mother found out that Andrea was no longer in the baker's house when one of her daughters went to get "the cookies and bread" they received in exchange for her work (DHJS, folder 508, file 22, 1942).

Andrea left Giménez's house to live with José without him guaranteeing her subsistence. She opted for the illegitimate relationship that would end with being sent to an institution and the complete loss of her rights until she came of age (DHJS, folder 508, file 22, 1942), a risk that did not correspond with a strategy that makes sense in the present day, but that expressed the desires and expectations of overcoming her living conditions with the structural restrictions that made up for it. To make a decision that was not within her attributes due to being a minor activated the family mechanisms to return her to an auxiliary position where it would be possible for her mother to combine her moral beliefs on the anticipated destiny of her children with the family's material needs. The judicial agency intervened to restore model family ties it considered had been disturbed. To do so, the authorities tended to bring the parents together as a framework of the canonical domestic place that cared for the children. It brought together a group of neighbors and asked them about the moral conduct of the parents, which was condemned by the majority, who indicated that due to the extreme poverty and "lack of attention" the couple had four daughters "with questionable morality." The judge's decision to move Andrea to the juvenile division of the Olmos prison in La Plata rectified an intervention that condemned family attitudes. The suspension of parental custody was the state mark of a decision that attempted to create a new life and therefore a new privacy.

When she was later sent to an institution, it involved a transfer of 371 kilometers from her place of residence, which—we can imagine— completely cut her off from her parents and sisters. In 1944, at eighteen years old, Andrea wrote to the judge to ask him to consider de-institutionalizing her. To write a letter, selecting the exact arguments to convince the judge, demonstrates that even in situations in which women ceded their rights to the state, they tried to forge their destinies. Though she was given permission to leave thanks to a report of good conduct, the opportunity was delayed a year because of the scarlet fever epidemic that affected the ward. In 1945, Andrea left under the tutelage of a civil servant who would monitor her behavior until she turned twenty-one and would help her get a job in domestic service (DHJS, folder 508, file 22, 1942).

In sum, I argue that the intersection of a woman's identities was constitutive of the construction of an experience of domesticity, the body, and sexuality that, governed by the state, shaped the margins of negotiation of poor, young women. These are stories that shine a light on the personhood and the material experiences of those who sold sex.

Male Appropriations: Marriages, Money, and Violence

Various relationships with men were possible routes for young, poor women to create a life separate from their parents. It was an anticipated change in their lives that meant they would occupy a new place in the home. As mentioned in the beginning of this chapter, in 1947, in Ramón Santamarina, Catalina moved in with a bricklayer ten years older than her, then later left because he hit her, and joined an illegal brothel. Then she married Roberto, a day laborer who packaged seasonal products in the port and was the son of the prostitute who ran the bar where she sold sex for the first time. In 1948 Catalina reported her partner because he hit her to take her money that she earned by offering sexual services to workers in the area. She made her statement with Ana, a sixteen-year-old orphaned friend who mere days before had run away from the house where she was living with her partner for having been subjected to similar violence. According to the commissioner's notes, Catalina was sobbing as she begged the court to free her from her pain (DHJS, folder 657, file 7, 1948).

Because of the volatile and minimal income their partners earned, the poor women in the region sought their own income to sustain themselves, such as working as laundrywomen, seamstresses, domestic servants, informal employment, or sex workers, among others. Because of the seasonal nature of the region's workforce, many men had to move for work, establishing periods of relative autonomy in which women were required to maintain their homes and became the head of the family. This circuit of looking for work in the haciendas, barracks, and ports defined the movement of clients who required sexual services in the different locations. In contrast, in low seasons in which husbands or partners were not employed, some women sold sex to satisfy the economic needs of their families.

In 1948 Catalina arrived at the police station with a black eye. In his statement, Roberto confirmed that he had hit her because she had left the house and had not left him any food for when he got home from work. The public defender, Roberto's lawyer, rationalized this act as did some of the witnesses who pointed to Catalina's questionable morality. Perhaps Roberto resorted to this argument convinced his peers would agree, though possibly his beating—like the others—formed part of the resolution in Catalina's favor.

The marital unit was a space of state intervention founded on judicial, social, and cultural norms that reinforced the unequal distribution of domestic duties. The consensus between the lawyer and Roberto about the justified nature of the blow expresses a historically situated meaning in horizontal (male) and vertical (against the woman) terms about the forms of control in the home (Tinsman, 1995). Until the 1960s, a matrimonial model was promoted in which the woman was the subject of male tutelage (Giordano, 2012). Marriage was the formalization in which the domestic space was financed, though some also chose living with a partner and not marrying to attain the same results.

Ana, who accompanied Catalina to the police, described her situation as similar to her friend's. As an orphan, since the age of four she had been "placed" in a home where she was abused. When she ran away, she had sexual relations with men in exchange for food and shelter. Like Catalina— or perhaps in an effort to align their stories to strengthen their report— Ana stated that she moved in with a municipal employee who forced her to have sexual relations with neighbors through torture (DHJS, folder 657, file 7, 1948).

Women saw in these unions with men the possibility for a change in their living situations and lives. When Catalina first asked for permission to get married, she did so because being "single and not having family support, I thought I'd be treated better" (DHJS, folder 657, file 7, 1948). In the judicial files, the women did not spare praise when referring to unions with concepts associated with "love" and emphasized that they were trying to "alleviate" their families. These affirmations were part of a female performance that calibrated their sensibilities to qualities the state considered positive; their narratives contained a dual dimensionality: establishing their identity before the justice system as honorable women and a legitimate feeling toward a relationship they had taken a chance on.

Violence was used as a mechanism to affirm male control over the home. The blows Roberto used to guarantee he would receive the money the girl earned were built on a shared male consensus, but they went beyond what was permissible. To avoid violence, Catalina had to hand over all her money. Her rates were seven pesos per coitus in her home or fifty pesos to spend the night with the client. Without a schedule, the encounters could be in the morning or at night and did not last more than half an hour, which allowed her to earn more than when she was "placed" as a servant (forty pesos).

In both cases, daily violence in the domestic space provoked a debate about the legitimate use of money. On the one hand, the appeal to male violence reinforced his power over the income, even though it was the woman who bought provisions. On the other hand, the naturalized position of the female body meant that the woman was the one capable of exchanging sex for money to earn an income in the home. Following this argument, if we understand by the domestic the dedication of female time to the care of another, there are multiple ways these men resorted to violence to take the money and time the women invested in the work.

In the arguments in the police report and from the witnesses, including Ana—Catalina's friend—they agreed that the sexual exploitation of the young woman was explained by the fact that she was white and blond, which they believed guaranteed a good number of clients. These notes are an example of how whiteness persisted as a driving force of Argentine beauty standards. As I explained in chapter 1, whiteness usually remained a present but unspoken force in Argentine public documents due to the elites' obsession with producing a homogeneous, raceless society; in that sense, medical and judicial body measurements became a second language to measure the production of racialized social hierarchies. This notion coincided with the nationalist narrative from Manuel Gálvez (1905), for whom Argentine men focused their libido on foreign prostitutes given they considered white skin attractive. Along with these ideas, subcommissioner Ernesto Pareja (1937) also emphasized that Argentines were more attracted to white women and that physical features such as the size of their ears or cranial characteristics defined the potential for prostitution.

The metonymic construction of trafficking women with the goal of sexual exploitation as an unambiguous image of sex work made it difficult to record other kinds of daily violence and exploitation in which existed a particular form of pimping (not in a network) that implied the monetary appropriation by the domestic partner or spouse.

The male understanding of the appropriation of money as an expression of his domestic control contrasted with some of the images of the period. In urban centers throughout the 1940s, companies appealed to women as consumers in charge of the home in their role as "middle class" housewives (Pite, 2016). Poor women living in nonmetropolitan areas likely did not directly identify with the discourses of the publicity strategy, but the absence of men associated with work left women in control of and responsible for the home. This triggered conflicts in which men, women, and children established their roles, the distribution of tasks, and attributions.

Though abolitionism meant that the state eliminated the sale of sex that took place in the system of licensed brothels, women struggled with local circumstances. In this representation of violent male control, women were the protagonists in police reports. To get away from their spouses, the women making reports narrated in detail the symptoms of the violence with which their husbands had appropriated their money. Marriage was binding before the first divorce laws were enacted between 1954 and 1955 and were finally installed in 1989 (Giordano, Ramacciotti, and Valobra, 2015).

The fact that more than half of the defendants had priors suggests that through multiple experiences they could develop a rudimentary knowledge of the law. Therefore, influenced by the public defenders, the narrative tactics the women presented in court constituted a flexible and customary use of rules. Judicial interventions in defining the domestic sphere were recurrent in Catalina's life. One year before accusing her husband, as victim of a corruption report, Catalina had managed to get the state to support her in getting married because she was an orphan (DHJS, folder 657, file 218, 1948). With what she knew about the law, she gathered her courage when in 1948 she explained to the police that her husband violated law 12.331 that penalized sexual exploitation. This decision meant she had to undergo the deflowering exam, which meant she was subjected to state and marital violence.

Catalina's experience encouraged Ana to make a report, indicating intuitive and scattered knowledge secretly circulating. Catalina helped Ana, letting her sleep on her floor when she left her husband. Though, as Catalina stated, her husband did not allow her to buy food, she took money to share food with the woman, who was already malnourished, information that was confirmed by the medical exam (DHJS, folder 657, file 7, 1948). There were also conflicts between the two women; in the last court appearance, perhaps to save the husband Catalina had already left, Ana changed her statement, saying the man treated her well and bought her "everything she asked for," which shows that the relationships between women involved in violent domestic partnerships were multifaceted and dynamic.

In sum, the overlap between normative interventions and domestic violence limited the use of the income earned by poor women. At the same time, in the face of situations of extreme violence, the women found ways to create new domestic spaces and experiences.

Negotiating Intimacy and Money

Selling sex involved encounters with public agencies, pimps, local authorities, domestic partners, and neighbors. As such, the women had to repeatedly negotiate the conditions of these exchanges, using such tools as flirting, pooling income, negotiating with mediators to find clients, protecting personal image and honor, sharing a room and "going halfsies," and mutual agreements.

Women were careful to maintain their affective and economic ties, separating money and intimacy—that is, boyfriends and johns. In 1939 in Tres Arroyos, fourteen-year-old Mirta married an older bricklayer with the consent of her fifty-year-old widowed mother.[6] The relationship was short lived, and the mother later stated that her daughter could no longer withstand the husband's abuse. Mirta left after a few months and moved in with Carlos, a twenty-year-old baker with whom she moved to Mar del Plata. They shared a room with another couple, Alicia and Pablo, a nineteen-year-old servant and a twenty-six-year-old day laborer. In 1940 Mirta reported Carlos for committing domestic violence in order to take the money she earned selling sex (DHJS, folder 525, file 28, 1940).

In a letter to her mother, Mirta wrote that getting together with Carlos would alleviate the widow and her three daughters of their economic problems. The expectations of this union were shared by her mother, who told the judge that "she was hopeful he would give her a better life." It is possible that in the combination of these exchanges, in the act of writing and reporting, the women organized their domestic experiences and gave a coherent posterior meaning to their decisions (DHJS, folder 525, file 28, 1940).

These statements complicate the interpretations that considered that the public servants constructed the subjects of their policies and express that, though the state defined the parameters of what was socially admissible, these notions transcended social boundaries. In the judicial files, many witnesses expressed dominant notions about unions with men. The tie with Carlos allowed Mirta to rationally organize her experience as different from other sexual encounters, and though with her boyfriend the economic and sexual overlapped, the romantic perspective seemed to be at the heart of her narratives. The women also negotiated their domestic futures; Mirta went from the status of married to living with another man whom she later reported to the justice system for taking her money (DHJS, folder 525, file 28, 1940).

Even though there was a marked difference between clients and boyfriends, the sale of sex was not reduced to an economic matter. There were also exchanges with clients of material, monetary, and affective goods. Mirta and Alicia walked the city in search of boys with whom they could "spend some time" and "earn some pesos." The street was more attractive than the bedroom in which both couples lived together and where there was essentially no place for intimacy (DHJS, folder 525, file 28, 1940). For workers, the street was a space of socialization where they established private lives (Gayol, 2000). They also had limits for enjoying their money; like other girls they had to give it to family members or partners to maintain the home, which means that the creation of nonmonetary ties with clients allowed women to access a world of leisure that was off limits to them.

Courtship was an erotic mechanism that blurred the border between the amorous and economic and broadened the options to access dates and gifts in addition to money. In the sale of sex, these boundaries were not clear: the high exposure of the body was a strong emotional arrangement, a dramatic game between the people buying and selling that enabled courtship, a masculine performance in which romance and luxury created links among sex, money, and objects that gave the women privileges in terms of their intimacy and earnings. It was the access to a world of consumption reserved for urban, middle-class couples, such as meals in restaurants, visits to the movies, and gifts, an aspiration for many that grew starting in the 1940s among sectors of the population not reached by the growth of purchasing power (Pérez, 2016).

Mirta and Alicia went out with two young men who gave them stockings, invited them to the movies, and bought them pastries. At night they went out to eat and had sex in a hotel downtown. The clients testified that they defined the payment as ten pesos to each as a gift, an attractive sum when considering that the room where the women lived cost twenty pesos a month. Cataloging money as a gift negated the status of client and allowed the women to earn more by inserting it in a fragile balance between the economic and affective. The courtship was a game of multiple talents, a complex sexual service that allowed the men to present themselves as winners in an amorous conquest. Thus, the two girls experienced similar warm receptions in the city, such as being invited to private parties or car rides.

Before reporting Matías, Mirta got a job canning sardines in a factory. Access to this job gave her the confidence to redefine the pact with her boyfriend given her new salary allowed her to rent a room, and she turned to the police to draw the line with Matías. Consulted by the judge, Mirta confirmed she could sustain herself with her pay, though various clients testified that she continued seeing them. Perhaps Mirta decided to foster the relationship with her clients to complement her low wages given women filled 80 percent of the jobs in fishing companies in shifts of twelve to fourteen hours for 2.70 pesos, two pesos less than the men (Rucco, 2008).

A second practice implied precarious alliances with men to negotiate the use of the street. This situation allowed women to administer multiple identities, protect their honor before their families or neighbors, and thus define legitimate lifestyles. Mediated by greater or lesser degrees of violence, some women established precarious agreements with men to define the offer of paid sex.

At the beginning of this chapter, I mentioned Mónica, a separated thirty-five-year-old woman who lived with her father in Chascomús. She had made an agreement with eighteen-year-old Lucas that he would get her clients for a commission. Though he was looked down on by his neighbors for having spent time in juvenile correction, he was a key informant for all those who sought entertainments considered "marginal," such as prostitution. Lucas found a room close to a social club that organized nighttime dancing and gathered at the gates of the establishment three young men between the ages of sixteen and eighteen whom he offered the opportunity to "spend a little time" with a woman who *"changaba,"* or worked odd jobs. For the three sessions Mónica received thirty pesos and Lucas twenty; they could not earn more than the three employees would earn in the field and construction (DHJS, folder 799, file 227, 1959).

The arrangements did not go on forever: the deal with Lucas went into crisis when "Pelado," a bricklayer who migrated for work, returned and proposed a "serious life" to Mónica. She reported her business partner with the argument that he wanted to force her to maintain relations with more men than she wanted. She thus twice avoided appearing at private houses where the boy tried to get her to serve her clients. In a later statement, she clarified that with the judicial appeal she wanted to scare the young man and thus organize her new life.

These agreements did not always conflict with amorous relations. Like Mirta, Mónica had a sexual and affective life that overlapped with sex work. In front of the justice system, she distinguished encounters with clients and boyfriends, a division she used to differentiate relationships and inscribe them in the romantic ideal in which intimacy and economics were considered separate spheres. Inspired by romantic scripts, the separation between economics and emotions was essential for classifying in front of others the relationships of those selling sex (Morcillo, 2010; Sanders, 2017; Zelizer, 2005). It is possible that the borders between pleasure, sexuality, and love were more porous than the stagnant images Mónica presented in her testimony; it is difficult to know when a client could achieve the status of boyfriend or if on another occasion, she maintained a compatible romantic relationship with her work. Through these distances, Mónica managed certain attributes and capitals in front of neighbors, lovers, and family members as she sustained a precarious identity; she also presented this separation to the court to validate certain moral parameters that she believed could be measured.

The money earned by selling sex was not always enough. There could be good or bad stints; it could be a daily activity or an occasional means to supplement income. To her neighbors, Mónica was a laundrywoman who washed their garments. It was possibly when unaccompanied men brought her clothes to wash that she offered sex in exchange for money. Therefore, these activities were supplementary and porous; the interpersonal interaction defined the borders.

Historian Lara Putnam (2013) has shown the role of disputes for honor about sex workers and working-class women in general in her study about migration, sexuality, and labor in Costa Rica. As emphasized in chapter 3, the defendants did not call themselves prostitutes before the justice system; they defined themselves with other jobs associated with the domestic world. Mónica begged the judge not to get a statement from her elderly father because it put at risk the reputation of both and would force her to explain to her father how she made money. In contrast to the binary representations with which the doctors and civil servants differentiated honorable women (associated with the domestic) and illegitimate women (public), the defendants were concerned with their reputation and honor. This invites us to think about how the care of one's image made visible the circulation of values associated with the bourgeois puritan discourse in the plural languages of the poorer sectors.

Mónica turned to Lucas as a means for protecting her father's reputation and getting clients, which was associated with how difficult it was to be discreet in a city where the low demographic density prioritized mechanisms of interpersonal control. Her neighbors preferred to define her as a "poor laundry woman" whom they considered a "good woman." Her friend Ursula, a nineteen-year-old domestic employee, testified that she put some distance between herself and Mónica to "protect her honor." She confirmed that the two of them had fought because Mónica, after separating from a man who "did not contribute economically and was a cheater," "gave herself over to a life with other men." For Ursula, it was a dishonest act that would drive away Mónica's laundry clients, those who would consider her immoral. Though in some situations of poverty the commercialization of sexuality was a valid option to guarantee subsistence, there was no social "consensus" about it. The legitimate nature of this type of sale was always at odds with the interpretations of other peers of the same class, given that the various moralities of the working classes allowed a certain degree of flexibility even though in sexual practices they had narrow moral judgments, especially regarding female sexuality (Acha, 2014; Barrancos, 2012).

The defendants resorted to a unique performance to negotiate the social stigma that resulted from the sale of sex, a form of differentiation that varied according to the interlocutor. Before the court, Mónica's testimonial construction as a laundrywoman, the choice of information associated with motherhood, and the framework that emphasized her honorable character sought to evade the stigma of public servants. The attempts to avoid her father learning that she sold sex and perhaps the manipulation of this information to some laundry clients (or revealing it to acquire a client) would have to do with the virtues she could obtain by being recognized as an honorable woman.

Another extensive practice was the use of the family home for selling sex. In sharp contrast with the legal complains of pimping made by women, some partners were tried for having made offers "of mutual agreement." For example, the police detained Alfredo and Guadalupe, a couple aged twenty-one and twenty-two, respectively, in two instances between 1952 and 1954. He worked as a day laborer in the port and in the grain warehouses, which meant they moved back and forth between Quequén and Necochea, two cities with a lot of prostitutes looking for clients among dockworkers, soldiers, and sailors in the summer when they loaded and piled wheat for export (DHJS, folder 34,601, file 145, 1952–54).[7]

The 1954 dockworker agreement stipulated a daily wage of 56.52 pesos, though possibly in the region it was not quite that high and was closer to forty-five or fifty pesos (Sindicato Unidos Portuarios Argentinos, no. 1, 1954: 35). Earning opportunities in this job depended as much on the harvest season as on the physical state of the worker, which would allow him to work extra hours or night shifts. In the low season they could earn 400 pesos or up to a maximum of 1,500, which then declined in periods of unemployment. Guadalupe explained to the judge that in this situation she decided to "practice prostitution." The woman had five clients per city among soldiers and day laborers whom she serviced for rates between fifteen and twenty pesos; even though each took half an hour, on rare occasions she met with three clients a day to surpass her partner's wage.

In 1954, Alfredo came to the justice system after a knife fight with a client who refused to pay his wife for her services. The stabbed man argued that he had loaned money to the woman, for which he took the sexual act as a form of payment. Her husband intervened with violence to resolve the conflict, which caught the attention of neighbors and the police (DHJS, folder 34,601, file 145, 1952–54). Indeed, the use of force was conceived of as a male attribute to resolve domestic disputes. That women asked men for help to resolve disputes confirmed the binary roles in which violence was accepted as a natural masculine aptitude but, at the same time, indicated a flexible use of relationships to negotiate with other men.

Guadalupe also showed she was able to manage what information was given to the judicial institutions to influence the outcome of her cases, though perhaps she was not fully aware she was doing so. The two times she was questioned, she confirmed that a month earlier she had sold sex, and she was the only one who used the home. This affirmation reduced the punitive capacity of a law whose focus of proof was the male appropriation of a woman's money, a prescription that allowed her and her partner to evade the legal sanctions. This testimony also reaffirms how jobs acted as complements for survival.

The acknowledgment of trading female sex for some kind of payment was based on the difficulties these women faced to survive. In 1944, Marcos and Leandra, twenty-seven and twenty-four years old, respectively, and parents of a ten-year-old son, were detained by the police and accused of pimping. When the judicial employee interrogated the woman, she argued that her husband's income as a bricklayer was insufficient to feed her son. Though she was given a municipal violation, the police waited a year to return to search her home, possibly looking for some benefit. Residing in a suburban part of Necochea in a house with one bedroom on a lot where another family lived, this young, illiterate woman received more than ten men (DHJS, folder 558, file 442, 1944).

Leandra emphasized her son's needs to appeal to compassion and reduce the potential penalties she expected the justice system would give her. In the case that the justice system did not take such information as an extenuating circumstance, it would fine her partner 1,000 pesos that he could not pay, which would mean prison for six months for him, the primary breadwinner of the house. The woman earned a low two pesos per encounter. Finally, two years later, the case expired, letting the two go free without a fine.

At the same time, domestic agreements problematized the geographic imagination of the sale of sex. There were many reasons women used private homes to sell sex. First, the abolition of regulated prostitution dissolved the licensed brothel, increasing new spaces to sell sex. Perhaps the private homes were more discreet than the bars and allowed people to avoid police attention for a while. Second, during the regulation period, unlike in other zones, in the studied region the cities approved the use of homes as licensed brothels (Linares, 2016).

In sum, the women used many practices to negotiate their intimacy and money with the state and their partners (when they had them). Courtship, the use of one's own home, the choice of arguments before the justice system, or complementary jobs were available tactics to survive in an adverse world.

Traveling to Sell

The sale of sexual services was characterized by the movement tied to local and regional socioeconomic dynamics defined by the circulation of a male workforce, police harassment, and the lack of private spaces. It is worth clarifying that the journeys the prostitute made transcended normative changes; in the municipal records of Departamento Sur abolished in 1936, there is mention of girls from rural towns in the interior of the province who moved according to planting and harvesting periods, but once the licensed brothels were abolished, state restrictions were reduced, increasing travel. There were more than a few reasons for women to move. Though before the abolition of regulated prostitution women moved from one brothel to another, the annulment of the regulatory control encouraged this process. A look at the priors indicates that women avoided constant negotiation with the local police, to whom they frequently lost part of their money, by moving.

In 1944 Ignacio, a thirty-seven-year-old rural day laborer, traveled with his wife Carolina 100 kilometers from Necochea to Miramar to work picking and packaging potatoes.[8] She was detained while servicing a rural day laborer in a ranch where she lived with Ignacio. Ignacio told the police that he knew nothing about his wife's activity, an argument that could help him not be accused of pimping; in his second statement, he justified his lack of knowledge with his long shifts and confirmed that because of his low salary he could not support "my wife and two children" (DHJS, folder 578, file 75, 1944). The fact that they left their children in the care of friends is a sign of an agreement between the couple for her to sell sex to the day laborers gathered for the harvest. As such, they inserted themselves in a mobile labor market; the same year Carolina and her husband were detained in Mar del Plata, where they had migrated for work (DHJS, folder 578, file 13, 1944).

Every week, Carolina and her friend Violeta traveled to Miramar to attend to the sexual demand of a group of construction workers. As such, Carolina established an agreement with an ex-client whom she had serviced in Santamarina and now worked in the city. He and his friend were in charge of gathering their coworkers and giving a place of residence to the girls in exchange for a portion of what they were paid. Violeta, a domestic employee who had met Carolina in Necochea, accepted her friend's proposal to "earn a few pesos" (DHJS, folder 578, file 13, 1944).

This circulation of contacts through different cities presents a landscape of movement of men, women, and families as women turned to acquaintances to construct the sexual supply. Sharing information by word of mouth was also important. A seventeen-year-old waiter approached the house where the women were to ask if it was true "what the whole town was saying." After confirming it, he paid some money to have sexual relations with Marta (DHJS, folder 578, file 13, 1944).

They called "going halfsies" the practice of equitably redistributing the money collected from various clients. Carolina was in charge of managing the money and the relationship with the men; thus, she negotiated to reduce the percentage of the total obtained by her colleagues from thirty to twenty pesos in exchange for spending the night with them. In two days, they slept with fifteen men total and earned forty-eight pesos from clients who earned ten pesos a day, and though Carolina serviced more men, they distributed the money equitably. This technique also allowed them to sexually service groups of men by combining courtship, sensuality, and control. Gathering fifteen men and sexually servicing them could be transformed into a ritual of courtship, sensuality, and control that involved two women. In the partnership there was mutual protection, a negotiation that as a pair became simpler.

The movement from the peripheral cities contrasted with the sale of sex in the city. The anonymity of the fragmentation of the metropolis was condensed in the *giro*, a public performance of street prowling through specific zones in search of clients. As previously mentioned, in 1952 in Buenos Aires, the taxi driver union asked the Ministry of the Interior to reinstate the vehicle of a driver accused by the police of pimping. The driver served as an intermediary between men and the girls who walked the street, picking up women and taking them from one place to another, in a practice the guild's secretary general referred to as a *giro* (AGN, Ministry of the Interior [secret], box 502, document 504).

The contrast between these forms of movement—one with greater distances in search of pockets of sexual demand and the other more protected but involving a performance to acquire a client—concerns the many forms used to construct a sexual supply in relation to space, understood as a network of social relationships. Take the case of Lucrecia, who in 1950 was detained in her home located 200 meters from the Necochea port. The woman was walking around the area in search of sailors or dockworkers to whom she could sell sex, until the dispute with a Spanish crewman brought conflicts with the police in the area (DHJS, folder 566, file 12, 1951).

The travel routes were marked in that period by the socialization constructed during the years of licensed brothels. The networks inherited by the regulation culture functioned as pockets of social capital useful in the search for locations and clients. Around 20 percent of those who appear in the corpus compiled for this project had some experience in a licensed brothel, which is more than a third of the women older than twenty-five and almost half the women older than thirty-five.

Archival documents show the afterlives of networks crafted during times of regulation. In Dolores, in 1940, the police shut down an establishment selling clandestine alcoholic beverages that was operating in the establishment of the National Democratic Party in which Magdalena, wife of the bar owner Inocencio, "serviced her clients."[9] It was a party with conservative leanings that was in operation from 1938 to 1958 and that was a continuation of the National Autonomist Party. The bar allowed direct contact between the space of male leisure and the offer of sex. The police arrived at the establishment because of the report from the owner, who confirmed that he had allowed the location to be used for political meetings. The party leaders sublet it to Inocencio for him to set up his business. Inocencio was seized to satisfy the 1,000 pesos fine that the law stipulated for pimping and obtained conditional freedom. Though his savings were not enough to pay what was required by the judge, without a doubt they were greater than those recorded in other cases in which the payment of the penalty was impossible (DHJS, folder 509, file 171, 1959).

At the age of eighteen, Magdalena entered a brothel in Bahía Blanca. In 1932, when she was twenty-two, she met Inocencio, a pharmacy employee who visited her as a client and quickly became her partner. In 1934 they returned to Magdalena's family house in Guatraché.[10] The return was full of conflict. Juan decided to marry her "to save her from the dishonor of the life she led." The local climate of that community could have pressured them to make the relationship official. Inhabited by a community of Mennonites, it was a more permeable town to the principles of religiosity and communal control. But the family's rejection made this couple move through towns such as Tres Arroyos, Tandil, Juárez, Olavarría, Azul, Necochea, and Mar del Plata. The implementation of the Prophylaxis Law marked a split in both of their narratives. It was no longer possible for Magdalena to work in local brothels, or at least it was more complicated, which is why she looked for other ways to attract clients. The use of social networks made it easier to find space and clients. It was a social universe comprising actors impacted by the regulation culture and who allowed the temporary installation of women in bars or establishments in their movement through Buenos Aires Province.

When the police detained Inocencio, Magdalena's old acquaintances arrived, who, according to them, had shared periods of time with her in brothels during the regulation period. Some showed solidarity and tried to help the couple, while others spoke freely about the sexual favors this woman offered in the bar.

The stories about migration circuits increased in the archive. By traveling around the province, women shared knowledge and shaped local sex markets. In that sense, travel for sex commerce articulated lateral strategies to complement low incomes using old networks from times of regulation and to avoid risking one social profile in local scenarios. They also show how moving was always a chance to start new lives by avoiding potential moral sanctions. In 1941, in Santamarina, Lucía spent a few months in Leoncio and Mercedes's bar. The three were detained when Lucía charged a twenty-five-year-old day laborer who had a few drinks at the bar two pesos. For the police and witnesses, Lucía was a prostitute with knowledge of the trade given that among her belongings she had disinfectant and toilet paper (DHJS, folder 540, file 139, 1941). In other cases of the period, the discovery of latex prophylactics, rouge, or disinfectants constituted material proof of an act that, at the end of the day, was not penalized by the law. Police and clients shared a notion of the feminine in which knowledge of sex and self-care was the symptom of nontraditional femininity. Lucía told the judge that she decided to stay at Mercedes and her husband's bar for a few weeks while she "made a few pesos" to be able to continue her travels to Mar del Plata. She negotiated her stay with the wife, whom she met when she managed a local brothel that was formally dismantled in 1936 and later replaced by the bar. She stated that her intention was to find shelter and food as well as support a marriage that was not in its best moment (DHJS, folder 540, file 139, 1941).

In 1947 Silvia, who was from Balcarce, stopped for a few days in Mar del Plata in the home of Elena, twenty-seven years old, and Ricardo, a twenty-eight-year-old bricklayer.[11] Elena met Silvia in a shuttered brothel where they had lived together. Though the city offered clients, the police had detained her three times. Ricardo stated that he accepted Silvia because his wife "was round" (pregnant), they had a younger daughter, and his work was not stable. Silvia and Ricardo argued that the income from the girl allowed them to feed the household (DHJS, folder 610, file 13, 1947). Silvia's objective was to gather enough money to leave for Punta Alta, a port city close to Bahía Blanca, for which she needed to receive clients for three days. "I've done this work before," she told the judge when she tried to explain that it was an infrequent practice to make "a few pesos."

The rule changes were decisive to a greater or lesser extent in the lives of women depending on their previous statutory condition. Milena was twenty-two years old when in 1935 in Adolfo Gonzales Chaves she met Miguel, who was her client in a licensed brothel in a small rural community close to Tres Arroyos.[12] After the brothel was closed, both moved to Lobería.[13] Miguel rented a car in Necochea to be a taxi driver and worked as a day laborer. Their lives became mobile as they moved from one peripheral town to another. Some of the clients questioned by the police said they could not provide information because they were only there for the harvest. Milena argued that the only reason she committed this act was because she was trying to minimize their home's deficit during a bad period, especially because of the difficulties her partner faced renting a car to drive as a taxi. The partner was detained for six months because they were unable to pay the fine.

The relationships described thus far show that the obstacles of regulation culture acted as support of economic and affective ties. At some point, the networks of this culture brought together an array of possible modes of economic survival with emotional criteria in which the common experience of the old relationships of co-living in the licensed brothel rooms were appreciated. As a byproduct of this obstacle, we can think about how the periodization of these actors was not tied to the general political courts or to those of the law who intervened in their activity. The imposition of the abolitionist policy in the 1960s was not the decisive piece in the lives and relationships of these women who, at least with certain limitations, could move and find clients amid fluctuations in which the contraction and retraction of the margins shrunk or grew the field of possible actions.

· · · · · ·

Throughout this chapter I investigated the profiles, practices, meanings, and paths of the women who sold sex in Buenos Aires Province between 1936 and 1960. Examining the court files, I reconstructed the available options for a group of women who, impacted by distinct state, economic, and cultural influences, offered sexual services to make money.

In the first section I outlined a combined perspective of the women, their clients, and witnesses of the justice system. The search for representative regularities allowed me to sketch out some profiles associated with their life paths. These profiles allow a demarcation of a variety of situations in which, controlled by their family or husbands, with greater or lesser autonomy, subjected to state or marital violence or with greater agency, the women supported themselves at the time by selling sex, coexisting, and navigating rule changes.

From statements made by the women and witnesses, it is also conceivable that the women organized this experience through porous identities and activities. The women's supplementary work—such as washing clothes or cleaning houses—with the sale of sex demonstrates that these women managed unstable social identities that were not tied to the relationship between intimacy and economics. Perhaps guided by certain notions associated with honor, they defined themselves by excluding stigmatized categories without denying having accepted money for maintaining sexual relations with men.

Second, the paths of a small sample representative of the rest of the cases allows us to connect the worlds of paid and unpaid domestic labor and the sale of sex. I consider that, throughout their lives, the intersection of gender, class, and age was constitutive of notions about women's bodies, intimacy, and privacy. I thus understand that, governed by the state or their families, these conditions constituted the margins of negotiations and their experience of selling sex.

Third, I examined a profile in which the formulation of the offer was influenced by high rates of marital and institutional violence. Thus, the overlapping of various legal forms that marked the lives of a significant group of poor women was characteristic given that many of them wielded various forms of historic agency to go about their daily activities and negotiate the right to and use of their income.

Fourth, I described the varied practices with which the women who sold sex negotiated their intimacy and the use of their money with the state, their partners (when they had them), and their clients. Courtship, the use of one's own home, the choice of arguments before the justice system, and the combination of jobs and sex work were available tools to survive.

Fifth, I explored the profiles and kinds of offers with which the women turned to men as mediators to obtain clients or a physical location to service them. In these cases, in contrast to those impacted by physical violence, the division of money implied a tacit contract on both parts in which, though inequities took precedence, the women had a greater opportunity to use their money.

Finally, I explored women's mobility as it relates to selling sex. On the one hand, I observed that this matter connects their need to obtain money with the cyclical nature that marked society and the regional economy in which the need to move geographically or occupationally was a distinctive fact. Thus, I underscored the journeys some women took to places of work, harvest areas, or other locations in search of clients. On the other hand, I noted that the survival of regulation-era "networks" during regulation changes was used to relocate and thus access clients.

5 Paying to Be a Man

Sex Consumers, Workers, and Male Performances (1936–1960)

Let's revisit, from a different perspective, Mónica's case, which I discussed in the previous chapter. In 1959 in Chascomús, an eighteen-year-old shoe polisher, a seventeen-year-old rural laborer, and a sixteen-year-old brick-layer got together at a dance. There they met up with Lucas, a young man who "led a bad life," who told them he had "brought a girl to work." For one of the boys, it was valuable information; it was his opportunity "to debut." The verb "to debut" designates the first performance of a theatrical work and, in this instance, describes the first dramatic act at the heart of the male performance. It was the general term at that time used to describe the man's new role and introduction into a world of peers. Lucas brought them to a nearby ranch where they paid Mónica to have sex. According to their testimony, they waited in line outside of the room where the "woman to nail" was located. When the police arrived, they detained Lucas and Mónica and brought in the young men as witnesses (DHJS, folder 799, file 227, 1959).

The purpose of this chapter is to analyze the practices and meanings of sexual consumption in the testimonies given by workers in peri-urban and rural zones in the southern and central departments of Buenos Aires Province from 1937 to 1960. I restore the languages and rituals men used before the justice system to give meaning to their experiences that were inscribed in male socialization in order to examine the forms of consumption (who, how, when, where, and why) and the role of paying for sex in the construction of plebeian male cultures.

While historians have observed the interest of physicians and civil servants in the role of male sexuality (Biernat, 2007; Guy, 1991; Milanesio, 2005; Miranda, 2012; Quirolo, 2014), they have paid little attention to those who consumed sexual services. This stagnation may be explained by the scarcity of documents and the difficulty in sketching out the practices of slippery actors as well as the historiographic limitations in restoring the role of this consumption in male daily life.

This chapter also dialogues with labor history. The focus on working-class cultures, the languages of class, and their moral codes (Jones, 1983; Thompson, 1989) encouraged the study of the daily lives of workers, broadened the notion of work, went beyond unions, and empowered a new agenda, which considered leisure as part of class community building (Lobato, 2008; Loyola and Camarero, 2016). The focus on this intersection of gender and class fostered questions about virility rituals and the construction of a common culture (Klubock, 1998). Observing the historicity of sexual consumption allows us to examine the social networks between men in the reification of a popular masculinity mediated by class and sustained in the use of free time. I ask why historians have considered in their descriptions of leisure, union sporting events and socializing in bars above visits to the brothel. I understand the act of paying for a sexual service as an activity around which class identities are articulated.

This chapter is organized in four sections. First, I reconstruct the possible meanings of paying for sex. To do so, I examine the testimonies of 140 clients brought together by the justice system as witnesses for the police and included in forty criminal trials held by the DHJS and the DHJC. The men were cited to verify they paid for sex in an attempt to accuse women and men of pimping. To accomplish this, the police waited outside the place where the woman was selling sex and detained the client when he turned up so they could collect evidence. Unlike the women who alleged they did not remember their clients when intimidated by the police so as not to lose them, the men spoke openly about their sexual adventures. The trial created an opportunity for these men to use offensive terms that would not otherwise be stated (Farge, 2013). The consumers were obligated to explain a situation they considered natural: the male prerogative to have access to paid intercourse. In the context of a judicial mechanism composed of police and civil servants, which I understand here to be a space of male socialization, the men used expressions that both disrupted the dull narrative of the files and resisted translation. In their tales, they exalted symptoms of heterosexual male performance, embellishing their narratives with crude language and virile gestures. These were expressions of a corporality that gave them prestige in front of the men who recorded their testimonies (Barclay, 2014).

This chapter examines the sexual consumption of the working class and acknowledges that the elite and urban middle classes also consumed sex. While the men of the elite typically went to brothels with separate spaces for their consumption of sex, the clients called to testify had less room to make excuses to the commissioners. Therefore, although their participation in the trial did not imply that they were being prosecuted, how state agencies used these men to testify formed part of a mechanism through which they affirmed precepts of class that defined who was more able to pay for sex and who less. This situation invites us to historicize a particular male experience: the convergence of virility and plebeian culture, expressed in specific languages and uses of the body. Furthermore, in their later work constructing judicial archives, it was the workers in the repositories who chose (with unknown criteria) cases they considered representative.

Paying for sex with friends activated a heterogenous cultural system in which men also confirmed their hierarchical status before women and that, in the intersection of gender and class, placed them in dissimilar positions. This explains how the conditions of being a man, worker, and heterosexual intersected in their daily lives.

In this chapter I use four levels of analysis. First, I construct a narrative about the men who consumed sex with the arguments made through the perspective of unions and the scientific and political fields. Second, using court cases, I reconstruct the universe of who, how, when, where, and the cost involved in these transactions. Third, I focus primarily on the daily rituals, objects, and materiality of male cultures in specific contexts—that is, on the ways in which a subject creates a two-pronged process by participating in the sex market as both a consumer and an individual perpetuator of a wide-ranging culture of masculinity. Finally, I address the male plebeian language used to narrate, rank everyday relationships, and make sense of practices of sexual consumption.

Biologically Male, Socially Disorganized, and Naturally Consumers

In chapter 2 I introduced the head of FATLYF, José Quevedo (1951), who in 1949 stated in a speech that paying for sex demonstrated the difficulties workers faced to get married, which he attributed to low salaries. He went on to specify that working-class men could not "avoid going to a brothel to satisfy their physiological needs." As the sexology manuals stated and soldiers wrote from their barracks, the union leaders agreed that men were sexually uncontrollable by nature. They acknowledged that their base paid for sex as entertainment, and on various occasions the union media demanded their affiliates dedicate more time to labor organizing than to brothels: "Where do your most sacred interests lie? In the café, in the broth-els, in public pastimes, or in the union?" asked the candy workers guild (*Unión Confiteros*, 4, 1917: 1).

The communist teacher Angélica Mendoza also emphasized the role of those buying sexual services. To her, women were aware of the "ease of their earnings and know that the market is always open" (Mendoza, 1933: 44). She believed the need to copulate was natural for men and was protected by what she called "bourgeois morality."

In leaflets and statements, representations of sexual consumption de-picted men as incapable of controlling their natural, physiologically het-erosexual, and impulsive instincts with a woman who, lacking morality that would protect her, gave in to the pressures and offered sex in exchange for money. Quevedo, like some literati of the cultural elite, emphasized the sup-posed uncontrolled sexual spirit of the workers that made them natural consumers.

The Justicialist union leader's worry was in line with the anxiety about the volatility of the male body, which emphasized the reproductive nature of his body and his responsibility to maintain the family and nation in the time of crisis in liberal Argentina. At that time, the model of masculinity was undergoing a transformation: the figure of President Juan Domingo Perón and his public behavior functioned as catalysts of a profound social angst and modernization of the male ideal, presenting it as attractive, do-mestic, and elegant (Milanesio, 2014). This process involved representations and renewals of language that brought together the anxieties of new gen-erations to exercise this new model of masculinity as the continuation of rituals and practices of revalidating virility tied to class.

Paradoxically, the many representations of paying for sex articulated an ambiguous celebratory image of the act that understood payment was a di-rect result of male biology as well as a growing concern for regulating the actions of the male body to protect his reproductive capabilities, a context in which there was an increase in the private offering of products meant to pro-tect the consumer's virility. In the magazine *Caras y Caretas*, widely available throughout the city, products were advertised to reduce "male nerves" that caused couples to fight (*Caras y Caretas*, 1685, 17 January 1931: 95), popular science books on how to be manly (1782, 7 February 1932: 131), products to be good heads of households (1512, 13 December 1930: 42), braces to main-tain a virile posture (1502, 4 November 1930: 55), and oils made with ani-mal hormones that promised to bring out a man's sexual capacities (1701, 5 April 1931: 24), among others products.

What terms were available for experiencing their own sex? Or what were the possible images to make sexuality real? The physicians, lawyers, and statesmen concerned with intervening in this field developed explanations similar to those of the unions, but it is unclear how much of those explanations got through to the workers. *Archivos de Medicina Legal* laid the groundwork that prostitution was society's collective response to addressing men's "sexual hunger." In a speech, representatives of the publication lamented that boys from high society had to satisfy themselves with women from a lower class who lacked intelligence and were emotionally unstable (Eiris and Cerini, 1939b).

In the sexology manuals used in local clinics to diagnose and treat sexual illnesses, prostitution was explained as a direct result of the male "being." The man's urgency to ejaculate naturally made him a consumer. The manuals constructed a notion of masculine sexuality as a metaphor of instinct: animal, irrational, and boundless, a notion that was also filtered through the prescriptive meanings of class. The places where sex was sold were described as "unpleasant, where you are at risk for sexual diseases" and provoked "depression due to the prophylactic measures taken before or after copulation." The pleasure that took place there was considered "mediocre" and for "men of lower classes." Thus, they argued that, according to the Kinsey Report, 74 percent of male workers regularly visited brothels, while in the university environment only 28 percent had done so (Pellegrini, 1950).

Specialists were especially interested in the sexual consumption of workers. Scientists inspired by gradients of social reform suggested a man's desire for healthy offspring and sparked panic regarding the correct function of virile sexuality. They emphasized that low salaries motivated workers' daughters to exchange sex for money. They understood that in one class, in which they saw a decline of love and morality, these women filled the roles of relaxation and satisfaction, meaning the debate was connected to the productive capacities of the country (Eiris and Cerini, 1939b). In parliamentary speeches, the nation's representatives argued that the health of men who paid for sex should be cared for because they were the economic future of the nation (Diario de Sesiones de la Cámara de Diputados, 6 June 1920).

Until the 1960s, public organizations did not talk directly about sex consumers. Pedro Baliña (1962), one of the local specialists with the greatest influence in the drafting of policies for social prophylaxis and the abolition of prostitution, echoed the UN's demands by suggesting policies that attacked the demand for prostitution. This implied looking for educational methods so that men would control their uncontrollable sexual impulses.

Though the medical field seemed divided between those in favor of the regulation regime and those in favor of the abolition of prostitution through the Prophylaxis Law, no one questioned the biological and natural concept from which they constructed models of gendered behavior: supplying and demanding sex were naturally complementary.

For the deputy commissioner of the Buenos Aires Police, Ernesto Pareja (1937), the sex drive was at the center of male anatomy and was responsible for men's physical and spiritual health. People of all ages and class standings experienced this, but it was the low-earning workers who, frustrated by not being able to start a marriage, became those who most fed the demand for prostitution. If they could not provide a house and maintain a family, they were incapable of reproducing with dignity and exercising their sexuality.

In one of the dozens of letters sent by representatives of the army to the Ministry of the Interior to advocate for loopholes in the prohibition of licensed brothels in barracks, Matías Gobatto, a doctor in a military camp in Comodoro Rivadavia, asked for the law to be changed for the workers as well. From his perspective, the groups of YPF workers, isolated to drill sites and without access to women, risked inverting their natural condition and becoming homosexual.

The notion of *being* a man anchored in an uncontrollable libido that could only be satisfied through intercourse produced an ideology of corporal use in which the consumption of sexual services became legitimate. The man was thus the universal symbol of the consumption of prostitution. It was his active ability, sometimes associated with glandular secretions, that legitimized uses of the body.

In sum, the trajectory of these discourses rationalized natural differences in the sex-trade relationships between men and women. The former were consumers possessing an uncontrollable will to buy, which at the same time assumed the flip side of masculine ideology as an economic provider and, therefore, with the power to carry out said transaction. The women, as those who were offering sex, associated with reproduction, were the only ones capable of supplying the care that the men naturally needed to continue their productive work. At the same time, specialists saw workers as the focus of said activity. While some talked about paid sex to emphasize the supposed immorality of the lower class, others used the subject to make an argument about the social inequity that limited certain individuals to having a "moral" life in marriage.

Working, Paying, and "Nailing": Sex as Entertainment

In 1940 in the city of Dolores, twenty-year-old Juan went to dinner with his friends: Armando, a thirty-five-year-old rural day laborer, Ismael, a forty-eight-year-old day laborer, and Danilo, a twenty-seven-year-old shopkeeper. After dinner they decided to go to Marta's house as she hosted women "passing through" to "receive visitors." Male socialization took place in neighborhoods, clubs, and bars that supported a camaraderie beyond working relationships. Their social world took place among work, fistfights, games, food, drinking, and women, including as a subject of conversation. In these spaces and through these chats, men defined participating together—but not simultaneously—the virile ritual of paying for a sexual service. These activities, along with others, were part of the network with which these men assumed dominant male heterosexuality from a subaltern position. What role did paying for sexual services play in this network?

In their police interrogations, men had different responses to describe an event they considered natural. Though law 12.331 did not penalize women who independently practiced prostitution but did penalize pimping, the police interpreted the regulation in punitive terms to maintain some control over the activity. Officers waited for a woman to service a client to bust into the establishment and arrest her in front of a witness. Thus, rural day laborers, dockworkers, soldiers, and sailors filled the police stations to testify, unlike the men of the local elite, who had social capital that helped them avoid these situations.

Therefore, with this complex landscape of masculinity accepted as universal but reintroduced as unique to the working classes, it is worth analyzing how aspects of masculinity influenced by sexual demand and money were constructed and jeopardized. Even though in societies with low demographic density the hierarchical differentiation was more stratified than in the city, it is difficult to define the borders and confirm differences between dominant and subaltern cultures. The physical proximity made those class experiences more polarized and more porous; the volatile and precarious existence that displaced young men from their towns due to the harvest, packing, or military service complicated those channels used to codify the differentiation and subjectification of plebeian masculinity.

Who were the men who spent part of their salary on buying ephemeral pleasure and how did they live? The documents indicate they were between the ages of fifteen and seventy-three. The element of cross-generational relationships was a key part of understanding how peers saw each other as part of this network of masculine culture. They worked diverse jobs associated with agriculture, construction, ports, barracks, and, to a lesser extent, factories. The youngest men, single and without a family to support, moved more easily in search of employment. At the same time, it is possible that the young men were featured the most in the records as a result of prejudices that guided police action. In this sense, the segregation of paying for sex that distinguished plebeian and rich bodies was measured not only by state decisions but also by a set of permeable practices: the son of a wealthy family would have his first sexual experience with a girl "placed" as a servant in his home and thus avoid visiting a brothel where he could contract a venereal disease, or was brought by his uncles or parents to a brothel considered apt for men of good standing (Losada, 2009).

By living in zones dedicated to the export of raw materials, men's lives were precarious and frequently swung between different jobs. As such, the files feature bricklayers (20 percent), rural day laborers (22.85 percent), and dockworkers (12.14 percent); there are also employees of businesses (8.57 percent), bakers (3.57 percent), truck drivers (2.85 percent), waiters (2.85 percent), carpenters (2.85 percent), drivers (2.14 percent), fisherman (2.14 percent), farmers (1.42 percent), sailors (1.42 percent), soldiers (1.42 percent), factory workers (0.71 percent), ranchers (0.71 percent), and police (0.71 percent). Later in the 1930s, technological advances and land rentals tended to reduce the stable workforce, both creating a free workforce and contributing to its spread (Balsa, 2006). Working life encouraged men to come together and socialize outside of the workplace.

Paying for sex was embedded in leisure time, which is why the variety of notions and uses distinguished the forms of sexual consumption. As Edward P. Thompson (1989) pointed out, there were obstacles between the precapitalist seasonal cycles and the new homogenizing discipline of industrial labor. The rural day laborers testified that their work was tied to cycles, and though in some situations they worked from morning to night, in the off-season they had open windows of free time while they looked for other jobs. Even for those working on ranches, it is feasible that, between herding cattle and fencing tasks, there were periods of time to drink *maté*, chat with a friend, or escape to have sex—activities that require little time.

According to their testimonies, the clients said that the sexual services took between ten and thirty minutes. Lodged in private homes in the peripheries of the urban centers, some close to the roads, the women were at accessible distances. It is possible that these downtimes varied throughout the year: during harvest periods the work could be more grueling than during other times. Something similar happened to the dockworkers who packed produce for export. They could earn high wages in short working periods that they would have to live off of for the rest of the year without a permanent job, so their "free time" was not as stable as it was for workers in businesses with fixed schedules. That leisure time was valuable, and entertainment was precious in small towns where life could be monotonous for young, single men. Paying for sex was an option along with card games, long drunken spells, fights, horse racing, and other diversions. In this sense, it is possible that, unlike the practices in Mar del Plata where going to the movies, eating in a restaurant, and walking the boardwalk were important additions to forms of socialization and friendship, the low population defined other uses of free time.

The time in the porous borders between work and unemployment converged with the quotidian experience of towns or small cities. As I have noted, some women moved to towns with lower demographic density to take advantage of the unoccupied clientele. In 1940 the Mar del Plata police detained Lucrecia, a woman from Santamarina who came to the city several times a month to service her clients. Norberto (worker, twenty-one years old), Pablo (carpenter, twenty-three), Matías (bricklayer, twenty-seven), and Pablo (bricklayer, twenty-six) ate dinner and drank in a bar. The four had decided to find a woman they had heard about in the club. When the police arrived at her home, located in the outskirts of the city, they found her with the four men (DHJS, folder 506, file 27, 1940).

Lucrecia was living with an unemployed baker with whom she shared her money with the goal of moving to Córdoba to treat her pulmonary tuberculosis. It is likely that the woman hid these characteristics from clients, given this illness did carry a social and sexual stigma (DHJS, folder 506, file 27, 1940). People with tuberculosis were presented as sexual maniacs addicted to masturbation and onanism, an illness tied to the "tuberculosis cabaret" environment, and it was believed that their kisses were contagious (Armus, 2007).

To find Lucrecia, the four friends took a taxi. The drivers often mediated between women and their clients. Contact with various passengers and conversations in the car gave taxi drivers unusual social capital. The driver was in charge of making the meeting happen by taking the men to the home. He was the first to get out of the car and agree on a price and service with Lucrecia, from whom he might receive a commission. Finally, the girl had sex with the four men until the police arrived and took her money (DHJS, folder 506, file 27, 1940).

Among the evidence the police confiscated from Lucrecia were the cards that belonged to her "special" clients. They were men with incomes higher than her regular clients, were between thirty and fifty years old, were married, and possibly paid more. They were the owner of a bar, a store-keeper, the owner of a small steel plant (an exceptional case as he was the only one with such high income found in the judicial files), owner of a factory, and a welder (DHJS, folder 506, file 27, 1940). During her time in the Buen Pastor prison in Buenos Aires, Angélica Mendoza (1933: 28) explained that the prostitutes with "better clientele" and who received better payments were considered more elite.

The marital status of Lucrecia's clientele gives insights into the framework of legitimate activities for men. Among the clients there were many men who were married or living with a girlfriend. Adultery in Argentina was one of the few grounds for divorce, provided one party took the initiative and pursued legal action. A recent analysis showed that during the 1940s, 70 percent of the lawsuits for this crime were filed by men. Indeed, the civil code and the commercial code had different definitions and penalties for female and male adultery, thus expressing the institutionalization of the double moral standards for men (Giordano, Ramacciotti, and Valobra, 2015).

Many wives tolerated infidelity by considering it natural, which is why in these cases the men faced no legal consequences. The marital union was conceived by doctors and lawyers as a union in which sexuality should be used for procreation. Recreational sexuality was seen as a male attribute, and men were the ones who could seek it outside marriage (Ledesma Prietto and Ramacciotti, 2014). The permissive discourse did not keep men from hiding the situation for fear of exposure. Being brought in as witnesses for being clients of a prostitute could expose their partners to loss of prestige with their neighbors. The men denied their contact with Lucrecia and said the cards could have been found in their businesses (DHJS, folder 506, file 27, 1940). This indicates that the consumers managed a fragile balance among legitimate sexual practices, prestige with their male counterparts, marital relations, and the honor of their partners in their neighborhood communities. We do not know whether the police call was hidden from their wives, if this brought some kind of consequence, or if the men were able to minimize it, but we can note that the male sexual practices involved unequal agreements between various actors.

Because of the informality of the practices, the agreements between those who bought and sold sex were informal and involved a negotiation of prices, time dedicated, and type of service. Of the four young men, Lucrecia decided not to have sex with Norberto. Though he tried to pay for the service, the woman did not like the way he looked. Perhaps based on the passive representations of women, the witness thought Lucrecia was rude and disrespectful; he did not understand why "she did not let me sexually possess her" (DHJS, folder 506, file 27, 1940).

Norberto was frustrated. The situation exposed his virility to his peers—friends and the police. If the notion of uncontrollability given to male sexuality legitimized the practices of sexual consumption, it also regulated how one should use his or her own body. Rejection or approval could be subjects of conversation among men in their meeting places, where the organization of identities was measured in the intersection of self-perception and how others perceived them.

Informality made prices variable. It is difficult to establish a reliable rate for sex, given the transaction was always negotiable and depended on whether it was a visit or involved an overnight stay. Some witnesses described how much work this kind of entertainment cost. For Ignacio, a twenty-seven-year-old bricklayer, the half hour visit with Silvia cost three pesos, a quarter of his daily wage that was 12.5 pesos (DHJS, folder 610, file 13, 1947). In Lobería, in 1948, Ana charged five pesos for the same service, while an underage pair in Mar Chiquita received no more than two pesos (DHJS, folder 656, file 268, 1948).[1] The prices the women were able to negotiate never went beyond a quarter of the workers' wages, which was significant for low-wage earners but still possible for them to pay. José, from Necochea, paid a sixth (five pesos) of what he paid for the one-room ranch where he slept for thirty pesos. It is likely that the ability to manage their household economy allowed them to pay these expenses without their status as single or married being relevant when making the decision (DHJS, folder 650, file 208, 1948). In other cases, agreements could be more flexible: Ana, an illegitimate daughter and orphan who from the age of fifteen roamed Quequén in search of a source of subsistence, slept with men in exchange for food and a bed (DHJS, folder 657, file 15, 1948). It was not all that different from the statement made by the widower Marcos, a seventy-two-year-old Spanish immigrant who had relations with

Clotilde, an impoverished thirty-nine-year-old widow, in exchange for food (DHJS, folder 512, file 27, 1940).

The negotiations were not always peaceful. In 1940, in the Necochea port, Oscar, a dockworker employed to load grains on a Danish ship, went to a bar. He ordered a beer and paid ninety cents for it and then had sexual relations with the cook, Mariela. After the act, Oscar testified that he refused to pay her and was going to give her a "better tip." The woman took money from his pocket, 100 pesos he had earned the day before. Oscar went to the police to report a right he felt was violated. The woman had taken from his pants a quantity of money higher than what he considered the act was worth (DHJS, folder 592, file 151, 1940).

It is impossible to define the limit between "tips" and payments for sexual services. The negotiation between clients and prostitutes condensed deeply gendered norms, moral interpretations of being, and notions of economic fairness. For the police, Maríela's act had been theft, given the man's money was taken without his consent. But the cook denied the theft; she did not present herself as a prostitute and argued that she had not stolen anything. These gray areas in the definition of the condition of that money were symptoms of the disputes for the definition of a price considered fair for the sexual service.

The how and whom of sexual consumption involved friendships and co-workers. Ezequiel, a twenty-five-year-old bricklayer, was on a project in Miramar, and he and another bricklayer invited two women, Jazmín and Mercedes, to "service" their fifteen friends. The arrested man knew Jazmín from a service he solicited when he was in Mar del Plata. Though the arrival of the girls was also an opportunity to earn a commission from what the other bricklayers paid, once the day ended, he preferred to exchange a large portion of the earnings for a night with the women (DHJS, folder 578, file 13, 1944).

The group of seventeen bricklayers decided to invite and have sexual relations with Jazmín and Mercedes during a cookout. Talking about and deciding on nonsimultaneous sexual relations was an option supported in the trust developed during hours of work and nourished at the bar. There were tacit agreements about conversation topics and other possible uses of the workspace. This situation establishes a porous condition between the supposed solid borders between the workplace as a disciplined foundation and the free dedication to leisure. Having relations in the company of colleagues was a challenge to labor regulations, a two-pronged action that affirmed a masculine position that regulated the body and a metaphor that subverted the disciplinary order of employment. Workers employed different tactics to appropriate the workspace; that is, they developed activities unique to the domestic sphere with which they disrupted the meanings jumbled in a particular workplace, such as in construction, in which the produced merchandise and the workplace completely overlapped.

This group decision also had a generational aspect to it. Marcos, thirty-nine and the oldest of this group of bricklayers, proposed his house to host the women over two days so that "the participants could relieve their desires and I can make a few pesos." The age difference between the nineteen-year-old workers and the older ones was not an obstacle in the overarching notion of plebeian masculinity. The fact that the generations were spending time together meant that the group was cohesive, in that they relied on impartial and supervisory notions and cultivated status changes by exalting the masculinity observed from one generation to another. In subsequent visits, the women also serviced younger men for whom, as many emphasize in their testimonies, the arrival of these women was an opportunity to "debut"—that is, to acquire a new status in the eyes of the older men (DHJS, folder 578, file 13, 1944).

The intersection among gender, age, and class shaped the forms of sexual consumption. The variation between precarious conditions of existence and differentiated socialization among the metropolis, medium-sized cities, and towns was characteristic of how the men demanded sexual services. When the fifteen-year-old girl introduced in chapter 4, Catalina from Santamarina, testified to the police about the variety of services offered, she explained that the service was from morning to night. The girl's informal openness of schedule is explained by the presence of truck drivers who wanted to spend the night with her and "country people" who preferred the day (DHJS, folder 657, file 7, 1948).

These cases suggest that the relationships among marital status, age, occupation, and place of residence shaped the forms of paying for sex. The times a rural worker would have in harvest periods, when he had sufficient capital to pay for a visit, were not similar to the truck driver's availability. Neither was the relationship between a resident of the same town, who possibly knew the girl, the same as that of a hauler who drove on the highways and for whom, perhaps, the night schedule was his leisure time. The same could be said about married men. For example, for the businessmen, visiting in the morning or afternoon or during their lunch break allowed them to maintain a legitimate life in the parameter of a double standard. This shows how the tensions mentioned before between an imaginary universal masculinity and a contextualized individual manifestation of masculinity can also be seen in this diverse group of men.

In sum, there was tension between the dominant ideals of male sexuality and its specific embodiments. Social status, marital status, and whether someone was a seasonal worker specifically conditioned how the concept of masculinity interacted with the consumption of paid sex. The absence of a shared, unified market was reflected in the price differences, precarious agreements, and access to service. At the same time, the diversity in uses of time and spaces (homes or workplaces) offers insight into the forms of male socialization and entertainment.

Rituals of Manhood

The end of the workday was a perfect time for coworkers to find a girl to pay for sex. In 1954 in the rural part of Mercedes, Alejandro, a forty-nine-year-old day laborer, went with his coworkers to a house where once a week Josefa came to service her clients.[2] Josefa, forty years old from San Antonio de Giles, was visited by men of all ages, generally truck drivers and day laborers who waited outside the lodging until they were called. This is why the police detained her multiple times (DHJC, folder 516, file 1470, 1959). It was a widespread practice to stand in a group outside while waiting to be serviced.

The consumption of sexual services frequently involved a group search. There is no shortage of stories in which men verified the group decision to "spend some time with a woman" and stated they went "by mutual agreement," such as the one shared by seventeen-year-old Mónica's client in the Chascomús police station (DHJS, folder 799, file 227, 1959) (see chapter 4). Going with a friend to look for sexual encounters in exchange for money was an act with deep symbolic significance that involved embodied virile notions through erotic rituals. Deciding to pay for sex with friends entailed talking among peers, tracking down information about where to go, non-simultaneously sharing a woman's body, waiting outside a room while the other had sex, and later, exchanging stories about the experience. It thus formed a disorganized but efficient chain that brought together interpretations of masculinity.

At the risk of anachronism, Robert Darnton and David Roche's notes about the glazier Jacques-Louis Ménétra's diary are a historiographic contribution for thinking about the relationship among masculinity, subalternity, and daily life (Ménétra, Darnton, and Goldhammer, 1986). First, this narrative disrupts the idea of a harmonious, organized masculine experience. Sharing a woman nonsimultaneously was an origin of friendship as much as conflict, two variables organized around the desired female object through which the insecure side of masculinity is expressed. Buenos Aires men established connections with one another in relation to the women in disorganized networks that could either prioritize the harmony of going together to pay for sex or the conflict with others when honor was at play. Second, it is possible that friendship was built as much in the working world as in spaces of group recreation.

Following Robert Darnton's exploration of working-class masculinities, we can consider the "brothel" an antidisciplinary space for men, in contrast to work or time spent in institutions. In the Buenos Aires suburbs, the brothel coexisted with irregular uses of private houses, bars, and workplaces. Entertainment areas that supported consumption were spaces that resulted in the unification (friendship) or conflict (confrontation) that defined masculinity. The daily nature of that consumption or competition was in relation to the perpetuation of a fragile male identity.

The expressive capacity of masculinity as a vertical and horizontal code (Segato, 2017) makes tangible some of the possible meanings and relationships that begin with the object of consumption: in this case, the woman as soon as she offers the ephemeral good of pleasure. This relationship was ambiguous, full of various factors ranging from setting a price for a service to practices such as flirting, which the man also attempted to use to define and give meaning to his role in the sexual act. Moreover, there was a horizontal code because the time invested in going as a group to that space, the dialogues shared about deciding together to request a sexual service, or waiting while a friend "had a visit" also established channels in which each man circulated a foundational message about his place as a man in relation to others.

Group payment for sex was also a theme in literature. In his novel *Los siete locos* (2009 [1929]) (*The Seven Madmen* in Nick Caistor's translation), Roberto Arlt had one of his perceptive fictional characters articulate the emotions at play: "Waiting in a brothel like that fills you with shame, believe me. There's nothing sadder than to be there, surrounded by pale faces trying to hide their dreadful lust beneath false, evasive smiles. And there's something even more humiliating . . . it's hard to say what it is . . . but time rushes through your ears, and you can't help hearing a bed creaking inside, then a silence, and later, the sound of the washbasin" (Arlt, 2015: 195). When the clients were asked to explain this act that they considered normal, they described it as a natural act and described the wait as a part of the time involved in requesting a sexual service. But literary fiction provides a useful vehicle for the historical imagination about some of the perceptions of that wait: that game of mutual gazes, the sounds of the environment, and the network that brought together perceptions of how and with what criteria that act produced a group measurement of masculinity. During the time while each group member waited to pay for intercourse, there were likely ironic remarks and conversations.

In their testimonies, the consumers emphasized how long they each spent having sex, and they always thought it lasted longer. For example, in 1946 León, a nineteen-year-old fisherman, bragged to the police about how much time he spent having sex with a girl to whom he "gifted a few pesos" for having sex with him and whom he defined as his ex-girlfriend: "I went to a hotel where I spent three hours with Catalina, during which time we had carnal relations several times" (DHJS, folder 596, file 178, 1946).

The ritual of demanding a sexual service in a group defined some things that did and did not change in a man's status. Martín, a seventeen-year-old rural day laborer, went to Azucena's in the town of Mercedes following a recommendation from his coworkers to "debut with the woman." After this act took place, the rest of his coworkers paid for the same service (DHJS, folder 516, file 1470, 1959).

The reciprocity with older men in workplaces was one way to measure a young man's sexuality. The loss of virginity was a turning point in the transition from neophyte in a vassal world to being a "man." The symbolic significance of the masculine performance refers to the theatricality of a new status with which a man announced a status to his peers. It was the passage from vassalage to a new relationship in the male community in which exaggeration, jokes, and narratives gave meaning to sexual development.

Visiting a prostitute to take this step was generally accepted as a natural part of male sexual development before marriage, an act considered fundamental for his sexuality. As Germán García emphasized in his novel *Nanina* (1968), which recounts the classic memories of a working-class young man from the north-central part of Buenos Aires Province (Junín), the relationships among peers and with an older friend are essential to the interpretation of the first sexual experiences. When the protagonist has symptoms of crabs in the dressing room, his coworkers celebrate it as for them this fact means he has become a sexual adult: the loss of virginity and the reification of male heterosexuality as the confirmation of the projection of his desire toward the opposite sex. In both cases, heterosexual intercourse is exalted as a step from liminal subject with a man's body and with adult functions (work) to the symbolic status that consecrates that activity: having had sexual relations with a woman.

The acquisition of the body's virility depended on the expression of group rituals. The men stated that during their youth they made use of various practices with which they negotiated belonging in an imaginary male community. The public hospital sexologists recorded them. The physician José Opizzo (1963) explained the erectile dysfunction of a twenty-four-year-old man as a result of sexual practices he engaged in as a teenager with a "group of friends" that included collective masturbation and penetration. Ironically, the exaltation of the "active" ability to penetrate another woman or man, among other abilities, were ways to delineate belonging. Group masturbation was a practice discussed on numerous occasions in these doctor's offices and constituted a ritual to confirm their virility. Even though the men shared a sexual space, they challenged one another to show off their ability to expound on their object of heterosexual desire as central to their masculinity.

Friend groups maintained an imaginary community in which the decision to have nonsimultaneous sexual relations with the same woman implied a common language, shared notions of male heterosexual desire, and forms of exercising it. It involved daily conversations that took place in recreational spaces such as bars.

Beginning at the close of the nineteenth century, the consumption of alcohol was considered a social problem that limited the construction of a stable work discipline that was detrimental to the country's growth (Armus, 2007). Sandra Gayol (2000) noted that in the framework of masculine socialization in Buenos Aires bars, especially during the period of intense immigration that decreased in the 1940s, buying someone's drink was an excuse to initiate a conversation, look for company, and broaden friend networks. Drinking rituals demanded reciprocity in which the notions of masculinity and honor in the knowledge of how to drink took precedence over social differences.

At some point sharing drinks, talking about women, and organizing group consumption were procedures that articulated notions of masculinity and honor. Beyond the shared analogies, the consumption of alcoholic drinks was a stimulant that influenced the exaltation of competition as part of masculine culture. Men in groups, frequently tired and drunk, created tense environments. Defendants' prior records reveal that the violence was physical entertainment that ended in arrests for minor damages. In 1944

José was detained after, totally inebriated, he confronted another man at a bar for not wanting to give him ten cents for an Argentine cockade; the police officer did not seem surprised and identified the port day laborer from Necochea as responsible for five previous confrontations. He had also fought with his nephew over the result of a horse race that ended with both men being hospitalized after ingesting excessive amounts of gin (DHJS, folder 34,601, file 145, 1952–1954). While it was generally resolved with fists, there were opportunities for confrontations that involved knives. In these fights, the physical rivalry with which the body was judged was characteristic of plebeian masculine culture. It was the test of knowledge, that of fighting well, and of an attitude in defense of virile honor.

Plebeian notions of the male body were far from those of the middle class or elite, as was their representation of honor. Like the women who offered to have sex in exchange for money, due to their limited wealth, these men had nothing more to offer than their own body, the same body they used to sell their labor. Their experiences with the excessive use of physical force, different diets, and low cost of their labor implied a complex articulation of virile gestures that regulated their performances.

The bar could also be a space of sexual demand. For example, as seen in the previous chapter, in Leoncio and Mercedes's bar that was in operation in Ramón Santamarina in 1941, a couple who had previously managed a brothel was visited by various boys because of the news that a girl was temporarily staying there. The police found a double bed in the back where the woman serviced her clients, along with disinfectant products such as alcohol and toilet paper (DHJS, folder 540, file 139, 1941).

Certain objects were indicative of the practice of sexual consumption: alcoholic drinks, beds, and toilets. In other raids, the police found latex condoms, which they pointed to as proof because those items were considered popular among clients and prostitutes. The police noted that they "found a latex condom with rouge marks . . . possibly used to practice fellatio" (DHJS, folder 650, file 278, 1948). The witnesses described that on site they generally drank and played betting games, which were also prohibited, but the arrival of a woman to the city sent several day laborers into a frenzy when they looked for the opportunity to "visit" her.

Bars could become a viable location but were less common as many of the trials revealed that the use of homes took precedence in a transitional moment when the traditional place of the brothel tended to disband given the policies to abolish regulated prostitution. In 1940, in Balcarce, Pedro (worker, twenty-seven) met up with his friends in a bar to have a few drinks.

Later they decided to find a woman who, "as everyone knows, has practiced prostitution there for a long time." They went to Ignacia's, a forty-two-year-old ex-madam of a brothel who received the boys in her house along with her twenty-four-year-old daughter. The house had a small room with chairs where the boys waited outside the room where the younger woman serviced them one by one (DHJS, folder 505, file 190, 1940). The fact that the boys did not hesitate to knock on the door even though it was eleven p.m. suggests the certainty those comments generated among the men and the knowledge that allowed them to map where to find a sexual service without the need of an apparent marker.

The access to private homes known by the male community questioned the traditional divisions between public and private presented by modern discourse. The concern among the medical community for the so-called clandestinity tended to mark the "secret" nature of the communities of women who, relegated from "public life," practiced prostitution on its margins. Contradictorily, the use of the concept of "public women" tended to emphasize the inversion of a cultural construct of the sexual difference in which the feminine was associated with the private. But as indicated by narrating approval as part of the pattern of double standard in the search for women outside of marriage by married men, the reaffirmation of the institution of monogamy through an external resource and the knowledge shared by the community of men about how and where to find this kind of service placed these spaces at the center of the public sphere. There they met and recognized one another as peers and talked about it.

In 1948 in Mar del Plata, Joaquin and Tomás, twenty-one-year-old and nineteen-year-old bricklayers, met up to drink in a bar. After chatting for a while, they decided to find a girl they "could nail for a while." The consultation with a taxi driver was a tool to complete their mission: the driver dropped them off at a house and spoke with Roberta, who let them into her room with the recommended payment (DHJS, folder 511, file 755, 1946). The boost in new spaces and participants where sex was offered, which continued after the abolition of the licensed brothel, complicated the connections between the world of male socialization and the offer of paid sex. The old brothel, even with rules that limited the consumption of alcohol, functioned as a space that allowed for direct contact between sexual and recreational forms of male leisure. Card games, conversations, and the consumption of alcohol shaped the purchase of sexual services.

Men also used their own homes as places to have sex. Setting special meetings among friends allowed the participation of others. In Ayacucho in 1940, a thirty-year-old day laborer arranged for three friends and two women to have a cookout at his home.[3] For this kind of gathering the women earned an additional thirty pesos, enough to pay a month's rent (DHJS, folder 512, file 27, 1940). The shared experience of consuming meat among men also implied an act of masculine "camaraderie," the only culinary preparation not associated with female practices and considered representative of national virility (Pite, 2016). This monetary bonus is explained by the extended day: they spent more time with the men than the time typically offered to a client for intercourse and acted as the man's companions in front of his friends. That same year, in Mar del Plata, the employees of a movie theater made a similar agreement with Alicia and Mirta (see chapter 4). Though other friends joined, the girls only shared a bed with their two hosts (DHJS, folder 525, file 28, 1940).

Men had broad access to spaces. As in the case of the bricklayers in Miramar, the use of homes or workplaces was an act with which they sexually appropriated spaces. In 1940 in Mar del Plata, a forty-one-year-old Greek pizza maker invited Mirta and Alicia to spend the night in the restaurant with him and his coworker. Though he did not know the women, the man observed that they always ate pizza at the restaurant with different men, which is why he thought they must be "women of the night." He and his colleague shared this belief given that, from their male understanding of sexuality, for a woman to go to a place like that accompanied by various men, she must be a prostitute. That is how they proposed to sleep with them in the pizza shop, where the next night they had sexual relations in exchange for money (DHJS, folder 525, file 28, 1940).

The relationship between the working world and sexual consumption had direct implications in the contextualized way this took place. Unlike a belief maintained in the popular imagination that this was mostly a nocturnal activity, the variability of leisure times in the judicial cases shows there was availability all day for these types of transactions. It also is not possible to say that the workplace (as a public sphere) appeared separate from the home (as a domestic, private unit). Many sexual acts took place without making space for conceptual differences of this kind, demonstrating that in situations in which intimacy could not be practiced in the spaces socially assigned, the borders between the public and private become permeable.

In sum, there were many spaces and ways of gathering with which the men requested the services of a prostitute. The places acted as a support as much of the sexual act as of the circulation of information to access it. The shared experience in workplaces was also complemented by those obtained in other spaces, such as bars. At the same time, the group request for access to a shared woman put in play a vertical and horizontal dimension. The men constructed their masculinity both in relation to the woman and with the common gaze of their colleagues, where the shared notion of masculinity and femininity was confirmed in the sexual act.

Talking Like Men: The Language and Embodiment of Virility

The agreements between men to have nonsimultaneous sex are explained in the public record. In bars or during downtime at work, men joked and talked about sports, problems at work, and, above all, women. Describing women as objects of their desire reinforced their status as men.

The fact that men from Mar del Plata gathered in a bar would decide together to contact Jazmín and openly talk with the taxi driver, who functioned as a mediator, indicates that the subject was a common topic of conversation among peers. If the history of sexualities entails a gradual changing of borders, the conversation about buying sex was deemed socially acceptable. The conversation did not transgress any social norm and was raw material that led the group to gather outside the door of a chalet to wait for each to finish having sex.

The conversations involved a ritual with specific settings: bars, cookouts, soccer matches, workplaces, and macho revelry and functioned as networks governed by hierarchies regarding how to understand the male domain and its margins of belonging. Being a man implied some knowledge in which schemes between the body and language intersected; the forms of speaking, gestures, and content of narratives made sense of a common experience. Talking about women meant both evaluating female beauty and deploying a language of intimacy, exposing one's sexual adventures and conquests to impress peers.

Recounting their experiences as consumers of sexual services also meant that information circulated about how to reach a woman who would offer sex. When the group of bricklayers from Miramar hosted the women in their home, a seventeen-year-old boy was flustered when he arrived at one of their houses with the news that he could "debut" with one of the girls. As previously argued, the horizontal circulation—the deployment of this message—reveals that masculine identity was founded in relation to others. It was the transversal record that made both the Greek pizzeria risk identifying a girl as a prostitute and others to ask for directions to find out where "to be serviced."

The safety men felt to talk openly and question some women was a substantial part of their performance. In 1940, León, a thirty-five-year-old Spaniard, and Javier, his twenty-year-old employee, stated that they had been talking in their car about "men's things" when they saw Mirta and Alicia pass by. They recognized that the women worked in "night life." For León, the catcalls they aimed at the women "did not upset them," which is how they quickly confirmed they were "women of the night" and invited them to get in their car (DHJS, folder 525, file 28, 1940). The catcall was a tool that responded to the patterns of people's behavior. The growing tendency toward anonymity allowed men to define the virile universe outward, signal their object of desire, and reaffirm it in front of their friends. It was also a means by which the public domain was made more masculine, reinforcing that the feminine belonged in the private sphere.

When they were called to appear before the police or the justice system, they found themselves in front of male civil servants before whom the witness-clients employed various metaphors to make their notions of masculinity tangible. The justice system was also a space of male socialization. The presence of men on both sides of the interrogation (in the police station or courtroom), where positions of status and class were articulated, created a setting in which masculinized languages of class were utilized and became performative of their masculine self-perception (Barclay, 2014). It was always a specific terminology, filtered by the confessional selection of the judicial discourse and its translations, but that in some opportunities—especially when the first testimonials were recorded by police—went beyond the aseptic positivist pretension of the legal discourse, for example, "a woman to nail"; "*mi bicho*" ("my animal," referring to genitals); "to possess" sexually; "*echar un polvo*" or "fuck"; "unload"; "give it to her"; "*ningun forro con el fusil*," or "no jacket on the gun" (not using a condom), among others.

Whether they are the vestiges of a masculine popular culture or the way state offices defined men, the language originates from the same place: the assumption of a naturalized sexual difference. The police and judicial employees certified in their narratives that men approached a brothel to satisfy a "physiological need." Therefore, it was a matter inscribed in their bodies according to which, for the state, the man was a being with urgent physiological needs that could only be satisfied through intercourse. It was not unusual for the judicial files to describe the witnesses as "[single men] in search of release" or describe their acts as the "fulfillment of needs" (DHJS, folder 550, file 320, 1940).

For their part, the men chatted among themselves in these situations about their experiences, their victories over their peers. In 1953 in Necochea, Roberto, a twenty-three-year-old day laborer, learned from his colleagues that one man's wife "*changaba*," or "worked." It was common for these men to judge a woman for her attitudes, implying she would go around alone or "dressed provocatively" as clues that she was "a woman of the night" and to sometimes harass her. One night the group of coworkers exchanged ideas about why their colleague Nico's partner obviously did this work. They did not wait even a week to contact her. This situation later ended with a complaint to the justice system for minor damages. When a dockworker went to the woman's home to pay her for her services, Nico attacked the client with the argument that he did not want to pay the correct fee or was perhaps motivated by the issues these practices caused for the couple (DHJS, folder 579, file 73, 1953).

The men's stories delivered before the justice system do not allow for a full comparison of the dominant and plebeian notions of masculinity, but it is possible that in their narratives some ideologies were affirmed. In some cases, the arrested women were brought before the justice system because of a report made by their own clients. The penalty in article 202c of the penal code that stated "he [or she] who spreads dangerous, contagious disease to other persons shall be reprimanded with isolation or prison for three to fifteen years" and was a reason for police action and reports by those who were infected. The justice system intervention in spheres reserved for individual health and intimacy forced men to talk about their own bodies (Farge, 2008). Describing their bodies allowed these men to extend the metaphors, selective expressions with which, influenced by pain, differentiated their body parts and considered genitalia as the core of their identities.

Matías, the fisherman previously mentioned in this chapter, went to the police station in 1946 to demand that the police bring in two women with whom he had sex in prior weeks. Though he was not sure which, Mabel or Julieta, he was convinced that one had given him gonorrhea, which according to his testimony gave him intense shame for "damaging his member" (DHJS, folder 596, file 178, 1946). In 1952 the health chief in a navy unit in Mar del Plata reported that various conscripts suffered from these diseases. Though Juan, a twenty-two-year-old farmer who had been fulfilling his military service the year before, described that he had a similar disease when he had been a kid in Córdoba, the police went directly to look for two women "known for practicing prostitution." The medical tests showed that the women did not have any diseases; perhaps, having done the work for several years, they knew it was best to demand the use of protection. From the story some military members told, it was deduced that they did not have sex with those women but with others whom they had met at a dance (DHJS, folder 733, file 9, 1952).

Many men, like some doctors, also had an androcentric notion of health. In their reports to the justice system, they accused women of infecting them and thus reinforced the understanding that they, the men, were passive recipients of the disease, perhaps because cleaning and health were work attributed to women by being associated with reproductive domestic tasks, at the center of which was the focus on men. For this reason, many men in their testimonies took time to detail whether the women had cleaned the penis as they hoped. Some complained if they only did so with a washbasin, alcohol, and a little toilet paper; even though some testimonials reveal the knowledge of access to condoms, their use was not highly valued (Biernat, 2018).

The language that workers used also relied on their bodies as metonymies of virility. In their testimonials they used different metaphors that can be grouped in two categories: their penis and the objectified woman. Both articulate a narrative that emphasized the active capacities of their bodies and the virulence with which they carried out the act. As Pablo Ben (2009) indicates, the metaphors plebeian culture generally used about masculine sexuality placed their genitalia at the center to signal that it was crystalized in the act of penetrating the other woman or man.

In 1954 Ricardo, a sixteen-year-old rural day laborer from Mercedes, Buenos Aires Province, went to the police to report being infected with a venereal disease. The minor, who went to the woman "La Gorda" to "debut," was accompanied by his father to make his statement. He said that several hours after paying seven pesos to conduct the act—his colleagues waiting for him at the ranch door—he felt something "significant swelling and a few small bumps on my dick's head." He told the police they did not use "a jacket" but did it "*a la criolla*," "fucking her just once." The man said he was ashamed of what was happening to his genitals. Norberto, twenty-seven years old—the oldest of the group of day laborers who went to that house—told the police he was not there more than "the necessary time to unload," and that he did not use a "jacket on his gun" (DHJS, folder 516, file 1470, 1954).

The metaphors the men used to talk about their genitals tended to present them as violent, untamed instruments. The lack of preventative measures was explained by the fact that they practiced their relations in a traditional way—that is, in accordance with nature. The idea of criollo was associated with the centrality of agriculture and nature in the idea of the nation, thus leading to bestial violence. The war-like description of the penis as an unprotected member used to penetrate a woman and the exaltation of that lack of protection had a lot of subtext: health anxieties were part of female delicacy and not an instinctive virility lacking a concern for venereal diseases or pregnancy.

The pleasure of skin-to-skin contact reinforced the violent imagery of the unquestionable centrality of male pleasure as well as the inability to take the time to put on a condom. That small decision and its enunciation were the apotheosis of a virile being according to which in intimacy it was the man who decided whether it was necessary to practice safe sex. The recognition of that act as critical to his manly virulence was motivated by a sexuality that could only be imagined in androcentric terms.

The clients used violent imperatives to explain their actions to the police. They selected active verbs that put them at the center of the story, and therefore, of the sex, situations in which they both exercised their biological right as men and were in control. They only lost control when they had to deal with circumstances of the female domain, such as cleaning and hygiene. The reason was not compatible with the great phallic sign in which they seemed to be captured when, in private moments, nature put them in their place, incapable of restraining an uncontainable sexuality. In their descriptions, female and male tasks were rapidly distributed in their valorization of the acts and the classifications of the spheres of belonging.

The references with which the men described the women tended to put them as the objects of the action. Even when their husbands agreed to precarious relationships so the women could offer a sexual service, those men quickly clarified that because of their economic situation they allowed their women to "submit their bodies" to a condition they considered shameful. The three young men who in 1959 met up at the door of a ranch after having met at a Chascomús club told the police they were thrilled to have a "woman to nail" (DHJS, folder 799, file 227, 1959).

Participating in a group in the consumption of sexual services, yelling a "catcall" at a girl on the street, or talking among friends in different situations, were part of the virile ritual. I propose reading these rituals as theatrical performances in which different forms of control are performed in contexts where certain signs and actions should take place to control images of power and authority. This conceptualization allows us to think about the dramatization of the metaphors used. This could be seen in the ways people chose to talk about being a man in relation to a female subalternity as a performative act. But we also know that these "public" signs are not homogenous nor stable texts (Levi, 1990). The choices these groups made to initiate these dramas, how to experience and agree on a performance with them, allows us to measure borders, reference points, and insert in the imaginary intersection as they perceived their male *being* with others.

In sum, in the virile language of the witnesses, women were depicted as depository objects of that libido. Before the law, men defined themselves as subjects standing before passive objects that in the moment of the sexual act would only be depositories of their instruments, objects of penetration of their bestial, natural needs. Their bodies shaped by language were defined thus as active and productive entities of a sexuality that had to be channeled.

· · · · · ·

Here I studied the consumption of sexual services as a phenomenon situated in space and time that articulated the embodiment of virile culture. Men participated in various forms of selling and buying sex, acquiring, offering, or mediating it.

I argue that there was a plebeian interpretation of dominant masculinity. Though this could be noted as a transversal code, it is in the individual gestures, the specific syntax, where it gained its ritualistic strength.

I identify two levels of the procedures. In one of them, the rituals, objects, situations, and subjects were activated and validated social status. I deconstruct the idea that meaning moved in two directions (horizontally and vertically). In these situations, for some men—those who debuted—it could be the step to access official masculinity: credentials with his peers. For others, it was a confirmation of a desire that, legitimized before the assumption of a natural belonging, validated his privileges as a man. On the other hand, these procedures were also a way to circulate a narrative of masculinity, a linguistic intervention, the intersection of the body and action. The men had various approaches to present before the law what happened, outlining what for them was fair and their notions about gender.

References to implicated women and metaphors with which they exalted the apotheosis of their virility through their genitals are not cultural interventions on an aseptic natural surface. My reference to the theatricality of seeking out services and my question about how and why these men arranged the consumption of sexual services (generally) in groups also raise questions about how sexual difference materialized (Butler, 2015), about how these bodies solidified the possible boundaries of their "sex." In this sinuous path, where experience is no longer a transparent entity that validates an ontological notion of identities (Scott, 2001), where being a man and heterosexual becomes a contingent intersection between structure(s) and agency, we also have to ask another question: How can we balance and choose one experience over another? Was the experience of work a public experience and that of sex a private one? These still-open questions pose the challenge of thinking about the dark map in which the subjects subtly act. This becomes even less clear to the eye when influenced by time.

6 Intimacy, Territories, and the Police

Selling and Buying Sex in the 1960s and 1970s

One morning in 1963 in Luján, Irma was detained by the police. At eighteen years old, she was arrested on the side of RN 7, which is a highway connecting the Argentine west, from Buenos Aires to Santa Fe, Córdoba, San Luis, and Mendoza, with Chile.[1] She was accused of violating article 43 of decree 24.333—making vagrancy a criminal offense, a regulation in effect since 1956 that penalized those who "being capable of working professionally dedicate themselves to begging or vagrancy." The police officer defined her as a "*rutera*" for selling sex to truck drivers and traveling with them in their vehicles. The girl reported that she had been beaten and raped by four police officers and defined the events as "police abuse"; that is, she identified the event as an act beyond the formal responsibilities of the officers. Nothing ever came of her complaint (DHJC, folder 348, file 574, 1963).

In this chapter, I analyze the various arrangements for exchanging sex for money in the northern and western zones of Buenos Aires Province during the 1960s and 1970s. I study modes of selling (the offer) and buying (the consumption) sex and their intersection with the conflicts that arose as space was redefined due to renewed police intervention, which began in 1960 when the state supported abolitionism and coercive policies. As such, in this chapter I integrate the dynamics of those who sold, bought, or mediated sex as a complete circuit marked by a new political period.

My periodization corresponds with two simultaneous processes. On the one hand, during the 1960s and '70s, public institutions ramped up practices that persecuted sexual-affective arrangements they considered inconsistent with "public morality." Though many of the regulations used were introduced in the first quarter of the twentieth century, the authorization to enforce them increased in the 1960s, thereby making the connection between sexual and political metaphors in moral ideology that solidified a sense of order. I decided to use 1984 as the cutoff for this study as it was the year the Raúl Alfonsín administration decreed that the original abolitionist meaning from 1936 be restored to law 12.331. Democratization paved the way for a group of individuals to question the provincial mechanisms of territorial control, an ongoing, present-day dispute in certain provinces. On the other hand, the periodization allows us to problematize the so-called sexual revolution as a descriptive category of the period as much as it is understood as the process by which blueprints for relationships were loosened without disrupting the patriarchal and heterosexual core (Cosse, 2010). Here I describe dissonant experiences that express the social and cultural transformations of the period as diverse and primarily urban.

The relationship between the regulation of prostitution and territorial control sparked questions by tapping into a concern about the social construction of space (Howell, 2004; Múgica, 2014; Schettini, 2016; Swedberg, 2017). Gender studies made it possible to think about how the mapping of a place is central to establishing symbolic and material positionality tied to the intersection of gender, class, race, and age. Understanding a site as a practiced place—that is, as a structure of routine practices—leads to thinking about how, over time, social, political, cultural, and economic borders are created and reproduced. That is, we can understand how the material aspect of a space impacts the relationship between subjects, but also how discourses come to be when they are negotiated sexually (Conlon, 2004).

I make three arguments. First, the abolition of regulated prostitution marked a new relationship among state agencies, sex workers, and clients. The growing emphasis on police power as a guarantor of "public morality" dramatized a territorialization of state power that conflicted with the practices of sex work. As such, the reforms and procedures that broadened the punitive powers of public agencies—supported by regulations such as misdemeanor codes and government directives—also reveal the margins of negotiation and dispute for the three roles being analyzed. Police officers took advantage of the misdemeanor codes that aligned with law 16.666 (1965) that definitively established the abolition of regulated prostitution. Lawmakers passed law 12.331 and executive order 11.925/57 and dissolved all special rules that had allowed loopholes, such as permission to install houses of tolerance close to military barracks located outside of urban zones (repealing decree 10.638/44 and law 12.912). At the same time, the regulation reforms in 1960 and 1976 targeted the role of *rufianismo*, or pimping, as a metonymic image of commercial-sex relations and promoted a punitive interpretation of the abolitionist policy. In this sense, I evaluate the tensions between state and popular notions of classist, sexual, and gendered uses of geography.

Second, I argue that during this period in the studied region, there was a revival of traditional locations for selling sex. The reappearance of some brothels and bars under classic systems that coexisted with less stable forms of movement shows that despite the growth in ways to commercialize sex, early-twentieth-century cultural obstacles were rearranged to satisfy the demands made by groups of men: in the case of highways, truck drivers and travelers; in the countryside, unaccompanied men (farmers, dairy farmers, tractor drivers), among others. Then again, the freshly minted punitive approach may have made previously impermeable spaces more visible through the negotiation of new arrangements seen in these cases.

Third, I study in greater detail how the dialectic interaction between selling and buying sex was critical, in this case those of the rural day laborers and truck drivers who bought services connected to the ruteras and "rural prostitution." That is, I ask how the specific forms of demand revitalized the creation of informal circuits of selling and buying, which shapes the diverse experiences of exchanging sex for money. Along these lines, I believe that the meaning of territory tied to the state dispute for control of space, the persistence of traditional places, and the formation of practices that connected clients with women who offered services, can be read through regional and local dynamics in relation to national phenomena. In this sense, I consider the changes, if there were any, in how women, police, and clients understood these interactions. At the same time, my scale, by responding to nonurban spaces in Buenos Aires Province, allows for thinking about these figures as agents of change who could have a certain strength among the median layers of Buenos Aires and were unstable among poor workers and the popular sectors of the peripheral zones. As such, I examine judicial documents extracted from DHJC, which allow me to study a wide regional scale that covers the north and west of Buenos Aires Province.

The chapter is divided into four sections. In the first, I briefly describe the sample. In the second, I study the conflicts among those who sell sex, consume sex, and the police. In the third, I analyze the sexual supply on the highways, the travel practices, and the truck drivers' and travelers' purchasing of sex. In the final section, I examine various forms of buying and selling sex in agrarian zones with low demographic densities and their relationship with the sexual notions and practices of individuals in nonmetropolitan zones.

Buying and Selling Sex in the 1960s and 1970s

As I addressed in chapter 3, the 1960s was a decade marked by changes in state interventions brought about by the strengthening of restrictive policies. In 1957 Argentina aligned with the UN treaty to suppress the trafficking of persons. In 1965 Arturuo Umberto Illia's administration made it law using a punitive interpretation. The resulting regulation looked primarily at third-party appropriation of money as a focal point for the state's legal involvement; that is, the criminalization of pimping was established as the state's primary involvement with those who sold sex. At the same time, the new regulations punished anyone who offered a space to carry out or facilitate this activity (law 16.666).

In criminal matters, once the UN convention was in force, Argentina rolled out an array of policies that further restricted acknowledgment of multiple ways of selling sex and developed categories that contributed to the advancement of the agenda on "trafficking women." In 1968, the de facto government's law 17.567, later repealed, added article 127 of the penal code, a sentencing for pimping that states that those who "promoted or facilitated the entrance into or exit from the country of a woman or minor to practice prostitution would be repressed with confinement or prison for three to six years. The sentence will be extended to eight years if any of the following circumstances enumerated in article 126 bis concur (concretely referred to as the means—deception, violence, abuse of authority, or any other means of intimidation or coercion—and to the relationships—ascendent, descendent, spouse, brother, tutor, or in charge of the education or guardianship, or custodian of the victim)." Ironically, while these dispositions tended to be tools to punish practices of sexual exploitation, police officers made use of them to increase their territorial powers over the selling and buying of sexual services.

Beyond these changes, the practices and trajectories of those who bought or sold sex stayed the same or underwent minor transformations. The sex trade faced a new landscape in which conflicts with the police increased. The new police initiative reignited an old dispute about the extent of state influence on commercial sex relations, which revealed a latent conflict because of the negotiations between participants around the structure of informal circuits of the sex markets.

For this section, I worked with twenty-five trials to reconstruct the lives of seventy-five women who sold sex, 168 clients, and twenty-eight witnesses, all residents of cities or towns in the western and northern zones of Buenos Aires Province. This scale includes places in Greater Buenos Aires, department capitals, such as Mercedes, and villages such as 12 de Octubre, a place with only 300 inhabitants. The violent reinstitutionalization of state morality increased the number of defendants in each judicial file. The judicial records of defendants were gradually shifted to imprisonment note-books in police stations, increased by the police's new punitive privileges.

Though studies have revealed the paradoxes of social mobility among the urban working class, women of working-class families had jobs that were limited to the service industry (Dalle, 2016). Daughters of poor, working-class families in rural zones were reluctant to take part in this process and preferred to preserve their habitual life cycles. Women arrested for selling sex were thirteen to sixty-nine years old, though the majority were between thirteen and twenty-seven (62.66 percent). Perhaps the presence of girls in the sample is because they resorted to public spaces to sell sex more of-ten than the adult women, while the older women became mediators.

The early age for starting to sell sex can be seen from multiple angles: the early entrance into the world of paid or unpaid labor and notions rooted in the poor, working-class people. Many women were "placed" in homes where they developed a distinct understanding of their body, inti-macy, and sexuality that marked their life paths in the zigzagging step from one activity to another.

Some of the detained women came from provinces like Santa Fe, Chaco, or Salta and had been "placed" as servants in family homes since girlhood. Seventy percent were orphans who had nothing but their ability to work. To leave these homes, many of them resorted to selling sex as a legal access to mobility and privacy. Unlike previous decades, there are records of women from bordering countries like Paraguay who roamed through Bue-nos Aires Province in search of work and gained a presence among the do-mestic workers.

The life paths of the detained women stood in contrast with the increas-ing number of minors and young women entering the labor market due to an increase in school attendance. They were women from poor families who, through the sale of sex, encountered the salaried world of male adults. Though in 1960 the high rates of female employment were noted as a pro-gressive symbol of development in Latin American markets, participation was unequal and focused on women who entered offices and businesses. At the same time, once the policies of the military dictatorship initiated in 1966 were established, the number of women working in manufacturing and a monoproductive model of raw materials intensified (De Fanelli, 1991).

Perhaps the transformations of the urban centers modified how the women who sold sex perceived their activity. Many of them defined them-selves as "prostitutes," or "ruteras," in the presence of the police, recogniz-ing the activity as legitimate labor, even if the police defined them as "unemployed," given they did not fit in predictable categories to fill out a form. Though the information ran counter to that recorded in the SPB, where there does not seem to be a gradual change in the words people chose to define themselves, it is conceivable that the new police attitudes would force women to reformulate the way they represented themselves in their relationship with the state.

There were years of economic expansion and real wage increases for workers, which is why it is conceivable that there was more money for leisure than in previous decades. Though women suffered virulent police persecution, it is feasible that their earnings increased.

Professional discourse around prostitution also changed. Public health doctors associated with the World Health Organization began to focus on those who consumed sexual services (Baliña, 1962). Statements from the consortium of Catholic doctors expressed a new consensus among physicians to abandon congenital explanations to instead lean toward studies of society. That consensus was summarized in the definition that "no woman is born a prostitute, but any woman can become one" (Riesco, 1963).

The abandonment of biological explanations led to social explanations of prostitution accompanied by a damning narrative stressing that the sexual commerce was explained by disorganized families, undervalued mothers, self-destructive feelings, yearnings to dominate men, coldness, and rebelliousness. Clients gained relevance in the analysis, and among the abolitionists' slogans emerged describing practices of paying for sex as "without a price there is no prostitution" (Queirel, 1978).

Certain social studies carried out by doctors emphasized that some women from the Córdoba Province recognized prostitution as a form of work in different censuses, though this was a notable minority (Riesco, 1963). According to the information found in my sample, the women who sold sex continued appealing to supplementary activities to survive. Some worked as seamstresses (4 percent), domestic employees (9.75 percent), servants (12 percent), waitresses (4 percent), dressmakers (10.60 percent), hairdressers (2.66 percent), washerwomen (5.33 percent), barkeeps (8 percent), or domestic workers (21.33 percent).

The defendants were mostly illiterate. Eight of every ten women stated they did not know how to read or write. In twentieth-century Argentina, rates of illiteracy were low, which means this information is indicative of the positionality of these women in relation to other workers. The lack of reading and writing skills could have limited their avenues for negotiation with the police when the women had to confirm that their statement had been taken correctly or they had to sign a legal document. Some of them associated their illiteracy with their placement in homes as servants or with the fact that their parents moved around, meaning most had not finished primary school. At the same time, the combination of school data and markers of poverty brings us to the profiles and life paths of those who sold sex. The increasing rates of school attendance among the Argentine workforce structurally changed the volume of available capital to differentiate within the ranks of the working world (Cammarota, 2014).

Among the women in my sample, 80 percent were single, 10.66 percent married, 4 percent separated, 4 percent living with a partner, and 2.66 percent widowed. The single women may have had greater agency to sell sex and avoid any kind of intermediary. Many of them traveled along the highways and did not always live in a fixed place. Rooms in bars or pension houses allowed them to rent places and then move with certain ease, avoiding the constant threat of the police. It is also possible that they avoided naming their partners to prevent them from being accused of sexual exploitation.

The social research conducted by physicians revealed common experiences among the prostitutes. Though the health care employees compiled information and explained the lives of these women using a filter of moralist precepts, they emphasized low literacy rates; poor farming, laborer, or worker families; and the number of orphans who had been "placed" as domestic employees when young. In 1961 Dr. Rafael Garzón, a dermatologist professor in Piel del Hospital in Córdoba, surveyed 216 women who practiced prostitution, among whom 144 were daughters of "workers and farmers" and entered the labor market at an average age of fourteen. In 1962 a survey developed in "emergency villages" or shanty towns in Córdoba Province, from the Institute for Hygiene and Social Medicine at the National University of Córdoba, corroborated that out of 212 surveyed women, 52 percent were illiterate, 20 percent had left the home where they had been "placed" when they got pregnant, 31 percent were orphans, and 62.8 percent had been selling sex since before the age of sixteen. The studies presented by the consortium of Catholic doctors also reaffirmed the presence of "orphaned women" and "young women coming from domestic service" (Garzón, 1961).

Belonging to the poorest fringes of society marked the women's potential paths and influenced their senses of intimacy and their own bodies. In 1968 in San Nicolás, Juan, the twenty-eight-year-old owner of a bar, was imprisoned for facilitating the prostitution of fourteen-year-old Lucía, an orphaned girl who was begging. The medical experts and witnesses had a hard time confirming the minor's true age as they deemed her "body had been damaged by her work making her look older" (Suprema Corte de Justicia de la Provincia de Buenos Aires, Ac. 13.354: Ramírez, Juan Bautista. Corrupción. 1968, t. 1, pp. 865–75). The image gathered by the civil servants emphasized the social distances that solidified the edges of a class. On the one hand, it is possible that the expansion of youth as a parameter would conflict with the aesthetic of a girl who roamed the streets in search of food and shelter, for which she had been a victim of repeated abuses.

Though the doctors continued fighting against venereal diseases and insisted on recording a new outbreak between 1960 and 1963 that was associated with prostitution, they also emphasized that the introduction of penicillin and its adoption in Argentina in 1946 reduced the number of people affected. In my sample, the number of sick women was drastically reduced compared to previous decades. Though the use of prophylactic technologies expanded, some people continued to suffer from infections because they used rudimentary cleaning methods like wash basins, hot water, or alcohol. To a lesser extent, the limited use of latex condoms could be associated as much with the high price of the product as with men's refusal to use them as they considered it a threat to their masculinity.

Clients who testified were primarily young. Though there are records of consumers from the age of fourteen to seventy-five, seven of every ten were between fourteen and thirty-five years old, and most were single (six of every ten). They had various jobs, though the most common were wage-earning workers who, according to the material conditions of their activity, established distinct patterns of consumption and helped create forms of selling sexual services.

Travelers, truck drivers, and drivers bought sex on the sides of highways or in their vehicles, which were used as a space for consumption. Drivers paid for something more than sexual services; they sought company during their long, solitary workdays. In contrast, farmers, small shopkeepers, dairy farmers, and day laborers used their homes and built client-seller connections that became durable over time, as I will outline in the last section of this chapter.

Men's participation was not always as consumers. Between 1960 and 1970 there was a greater presence of men who offered sex for money. The growing consolidation of urban homosexual socialization allowed men from the country's interior, from working-class families, or poor young men to sell sex in urban centers in an increasingly visible market: the so-called taxi boys (Perlongher, 1999). The term marked a difference from what women in the same condition were called: they were not "male prostitutes," nor did they have the same stigma. Many of them were migrants from underresourced provinces in Argentina who, when they came to Buenos Aires, had to spend time searching for housing and stable income.

The magazine *Somos* (no. 2, 1973), a publication of the Frente de Liberación Homosexual (the Gay Liberation Front), told some of their stories. Carlos, twenty-three, and Nelson, seventeen, offered different services that included "letting down your flag" (fellatio) and "taking it from behind" (penetrating the client). Business relationships were not only shaped by money. Andrés was twenty-three and came from Tucumán Province. He did not ask for only money from his clients but rather worked as an escort to cafés expecting to receive food, sometimes clothing, and shelter for the night. Some others were workers, apprentices of a pleasure they were said to look down on and that they justified by receiving money that legitimized an act they felt degrading of their heterosexual status. Thus, for example, Norberto, a twenty-year-old metalworker, told his interviewer, "I always charge them, so they can't say I'm like those fags" (*Somos*, no. 2, 1973).

In 1983 the magazine *¡Esto!* sounded the alarm about "the peril of the taxi boys'" related to the "alarming statistics of murders of homosexuals." It explained that these men walked the streets of Santa Fe, Pueyrredón, and Rodríguez Peña to get into their clients' cars. In contrast to *Somos*, which presented them as virile men, *¡Esto!* presented ambiguous images of the men as effeminate individuals who walked in groups holding hands and published photographs that showed androgynous body language. News items with headlines such as "The Taxi Boys in Disgrace" emphasized the existence of gangs of men who mugged their clients once they established trust (*Crónica*, 26 February 1983). Some of these characters carried out robberies in which the opportunity to have sex with men made it possible to earn a different kind of money, a situation that frequently ended in murder. *Chongos* were violent toward gay men as a mechanism through which the man who sold sex or participated in a sexual act be considered part of a heterosexual performance, thus clarifying sexual boundaries (Insausti, 2011; Simonetto, 2018).

The accelerating transformations of sexual identity during the second half of the twentieth century also influenced the diverse ways in which sex was sold. In 1949 a group of physicians presented the interview of M, a twenty-year-old *travesti* maid who spent time in brothels to establish friendships with prostitutes and thus also obtain potential sexual and emotional encounters with men (Belvey, 1939). Though as a political identity *travestismo* or cross-dressing was not established until the 1960s, trans femininities were made visible in carnival parades, revues, and hair salons as well as in the sale of sex on the street (Cutuli, 2013). *Travestismo* was recognized by the state, which penalized it with ambiguous regulations that condemned both the "*amanerados*," or "effeminate," and the travestis. In 1966, the reform of the Buenos Aires Province law 8031 classified as "exploitation of public credulity" the activity of those who "in their daily lives dress and pass themselves off as a person of the opposite sex." This is a symptom of the growing visibility of practices that fit that definition. The argument focused on credibility, as a consensus of truth, referring to the biological anchoring of the sense of reality. It accused these figures of a lack of truth (related to the body) for blurring that imaginary gendered citizenship: man or woman.

The press reported on the growing urban presence and the cohabitation of feminine travestis in spaces for selling sex. In 1971 in a raid in the outskirts of Retiro, Buenos Aires, eighty citizens were detained, including "travestis, prostitutes, and homosexuals" (*Crónica*, 12 July 1971). As I have previously studied with Marce Joan Butierrez, many travestis sold sex along the Pan American, a national highway that connects Buenos Aires with the whole hemisphere. Travestis and cisgender sex workers offered sexual services, and because of the visible presence of travestis, it was called *travestilandia*. The press reported the cruel life of those travestis working on the highway; this was a space of conflict where cisgender and travesti sex workers fought to coexist in these commercial zones (*Fin de siglo* 13, 1 July 1988.) During the 1980s, news about the violence against travestis caught the media's attention: many drivers deliberately hit travestis with their cars. Due to police repression, these crimes usually went unpunished. It was this cruel violence that sparked the first travesti demonstrations in Plaza de Mayo in 1987 (Butierrez and Simonetto, 2020). In the provincial cities, the police also prepared to restrict these forms of socialization associated with the sale of sex. Thus, for example, in Bahía Blanca the press recounted in a burlesque tone that some prostitutes detained by the police "were not ladies but common homosexuals" who wore "high heels and notable slits in their skirts" (*Crónica*, 7 May 1973).

In sum, this sample presents a varied landscape in which class, age, and gender played a role in how sex was bought and sold. The women who sold sex belonged to a fringe of poor, working-class families who shared specific experiences that influenced an interpretation of their sexuality and body. I also believe that the transformations in sexual identities that took place in the second half of the twentieth century played a role in the visibility of commercial sex relations that went against heterosexual norms. As we will see in the following sections, the variables among consumers make it possible to capture the connections between the consumption and offer of sex. That is, the action of the consumers was essential to defining the possibility of an offer.

The Police: Morality as a Form of Territorial Power

In 1966 the Mercedes police raided a *parrilla*, or steakhouse, on RN 5, which connects the provinces of Buenos Aires and La Pampa. Alfonso, forty-four and the owner of the establishment, resisted the operation and claimed that the police had "broken their agreement." He also exclaimed, "They'll regret it." As he told them, he was a friend of the commissioner (DHJC, folder 360, file 1733, 1966). Leandro, a twenty-one-year-old enlisted soldier, went to the parrilla to visit a woman who was living in a back room where she serviced clients for 500 pesos. The woman had been there for four days and managed to flee as soon as she heard the police. The soldier said she was wearing a robe, waiting for him on the bed where they regularly had sex. As the report details, the operative acted "in accordance with the directives sent down by superiors and separation of morality related to the punishment of the illegal practice of prostitution" (DHJC, folder 360, file 1733, 1966).

These phrases regularly appear in the first reports of these incidents. The 1960s were the start of a new period; abolitionism with loopholes ended with the passing of a set of laws that again made pimping the state's central focus while there was also a growing demand to exert moralizing control on the territory. The state's punitive initiative displaced the accusations filed by civilians and increased the attempts to institutionalize the negotiation with establishments that offered paid sex and room rentals.

Alfonso's surprise seems to correspond with an informal agreement that the police broke. The new attitude commanded by the "superiority and separation of morality" initiated a cycle of renegotiation of tacit local contracts. The police's growing administrative privileges gave the agents mechanisms to institute routine checks to broaden their social and economic power over the sex market. The fact that four years later the same bar would be raided due to a report of minor damages and promotion of prostitution suggests that over time the limitation of judicial intervention was a tool for the police to negotiate their place in the sex market.

The arrival of Juan Carlos Onganía to power in 1966 accelerated changes in the police's territorial authority. The government pushed through police reform that put the focus on educating officers and underscored the idea that society was in a moral crisis that could only be saved with an intervention that would safeguard the conceptual divisions between the public and private and that would also restore a corrupted social structure (Eidelman, 2015).

The reinterpretation of "public morality" created a structure in which sexuality and politics acted as complementary metaphors of a sense of order. In the judicial cases analyzed, the proceedings based on the misdemeanor code displaced the Prophylaxis Law. It was a more dynamic kind of punishment that required fewer proceedings. These notions were not new and corresponded with a tendency that persisted in the Argentine state during the swings between civil and military governments.

The landscape was a product of the convergence and redefinition of medium-duration processes. First, the modern misdemeanor codes passed in the provinces starting in the 1930s interpreted public morality as the articulation of androcentric, classist, prescriptive policies that solidified the state's projection of the legitimate uses of the space. These regulations were policies meant to control movement insomuch as they attempted to restrict the free travel of the population, defined prescriptions on the uses of cities, and established criteria about what was acceptable for society (Barrenche, 2010). The objective of these codes was to limit action and socialization opportunities for "leftists," "the amoral" (gay men), "prostitutes," and "the disorderly" (poor urbanites).

These codes imprinted in the "public morality" discourse the us/them dichotomy as the primary source of social ties. Criminalization separated out dissidents who were alarming people about the loss of any kind of barrier around what it means to be a part of an imagined community (Sabsay, 2011).

In 1945 the governor of Buenos Aires Province, Juan Atilio Bramuglia, created a commission to write a provincial misdemeanor code (decree 378). As Ranaan Rein (1999) points out, Bramuglia had been designated as the interventor for Edelmiro Farrel and his vice president Juan Domingo Perón's military government. He was a man of socialist tradition who had been legal counsel to the workers associations of the Telephone Union, Tramway Union, and Railway Union, as well as legal counsel to the General Confederation of Labor during the 1920s and 1930s. Bramuglia used as references the 1932 Buenos Aires city code from president José Félix Uriburu and the 1940 Santa

Fe city code from the radical Manuel María de Iriondo, which demonstrated how widespread consensus was on these policies. Both codes punished selling sex in public in order to condemn gay men and prostitutes by alluding to the notion of "scandal."

During Perón's second presidency, raids were used to crack down on "*patoteros*," or "thugs," and the "amoral" (Acha, 2014). In 1950, the chief of the Buenos Aires police was given the status of misdemeanor judge, which allowed him to make accusations and apply the nascent regulations (decree 873). Despite notable departures from the 1955 regime, the initiatives of sexual and social control in the territory continued. In 1956, under Emilio Bonnecarrére's government, interventor of Buenos Aires Province, the first code was passed, which specified the punishable infractions (provincial law 5571).

The 1966 regime reform expanded police authority. In 1973 the dictator Alejandro Agustín Lanusse enacted law 8031 through his provincial interventor, and it furthered this expansion. Under the precept of reconstructing conservative systems, establishing a link between state coercion and community control, which they considered corrupted, it allowed subjects older than sixteen to report offenders and notify the family—as a unifying unit of society—in the case a minor was detained (law 8031). Between 1976 and 1980, fines and punishments were increased. Updating the fines was a way of rectifying and evaluating the role this regulation played in the provincial state. In 1973 punishment was extended to obscene acts, words or drawings, immoral spectacles, or public drunkenness (decrees 22/66, 8571/76, 8730/77; laws 9039/80, 9493/80).

The misdemeanor codes allowed police to accuse individuals and directly apply the law. In 1965 the government also reinstated through executive order 16.666 the full return of the law passed in 1936 and dissolved all the neoregulatory palliative measures. At the same time, article 126 of the penal code, which criminalized the facilitation of prostitution, was another way for the police to get involved because it specifically punished the tenants of places where women practiced prostitution, such as parrillas, bars, and motels.

Building on the precedent of the 1936 Prophylaxis Law, pimps were punished with fines of 200 to 2,000 pesos. The 1955 code punished men with "bad habits" who were accompanied by a minor or offered themselves in public. Under this legal vagueness, police had more prerogatives that allowed them to reinforce the heterosexual-homosexual dichotomy. As I pointed out in chapter 3, from 1966 on, there was a significant increase in the regulations used to punish the socialization of sexual dissidents.

To mark this continuity does not imply a homogenous reading of the process but allows us to examine how these informal practices within the state confirmed political and discursive approaches amplified by the new framework of an authoritarian government. It had to do with a new policy that fostered a range of possible actions in which the police, by being both judge and party, capable of jailing and fining, could use quotidian proceedings to discourage the sale of sex. The raids, which gained notoriety during Onganía's regime, were celebrated by the national press, which stated that "morality does not go out of style" and warned the government that it was necessary to concentrate on "certain persons, for whom morality and good customs are subject to personal interpretation" because "under the false argument that times change, the function of parks and plazas is being altered, allowing for unpleasant situations, even for the straightlaced" (*Clarín*, 12 May 1966). *Crónica* published in the police section a daily report of the implications in Buenos Aires Province. All the news where moral standards appeared to be broken was destined for that section, thus creating narrow margins where homosexuality, crime, and prostitution were implicitly related worlds.

By reading the criminal section of *Crónica* between 1966 and 1967, I calculated that just this newspaper reported that in Buenos Aires the police detained 4,752 people out of a larger group of people submitted to frisks, roadside checks, and background checks. A total of 2,900 police officers were used in the zones of Arrecife, Azul, Bahía Blanca, Bragado, Berazategui, Dock Sud, Lanús, La Plata, Mar del Plata, Morón, and San Martín. It is worth noting that this sample does not include political arrests. Within the complex map of people accused, including homosexuals, poor urbanites, drunks, and the "disorderly," the infractions associated with prostitution reached 5 percent. While 1 percent were for pimping, the other 4 percent were women accused of "scandal" for offering sex in public.

The increase in the legitimacy of action protected police officers so they could reassert a punitive interpretation of the law. In 1973, at kilometer fifty-six on Route 7 in the *partido* General Rodríguez, the police raided a parrilla and took 270 pesos.[2] They accused the owner of making the facility available so that Daniela, a twenty-two-year-old from Chaco, could offer sex for money. The police noted in the report that they took as proof "a wash basin and a towel" as well as the money in the register (DHJC, folder 540, file 1238, 1973). Daniela had worked in a house in Buenos Aires as a domestic employee. She testified that because of the low wages of her job, in a bus trip to Luján she saw an advertisement for a kitchen helper in exchange for food, lodging, and twenty pesos a day, so she showed up to work. She also noted that the elements gathered as evidence were found in different places and that the police had carried out the search without any witnesses (DHJC, folder 540, file 1238, 1973).

It is not possible to discern whether Daniela was simply an employee and the police used that case, as the owner said, to extort a little money or, as the police stated, she changed her testimony to defend the parrilla owner. The dilemma allows us to speculate on the logic of police action. The construction of proof—that is, the definition of the factual legitimacy of the crime—established a relationship among objects: a bed, money, a wash basin, and a towel revealed the logic with which the police administered the classification of individuals and attempted to present them before the justice system.

On the one hand, in the police's general proceedings against women accused of prostitution, there was an argument about the legitimate use of money and the implications of the monetary exchange between men and women. Following Zelizer's (2005) notes, one could argue that the state was guided under the premise of hostile spheres in which the commercial and the intimate are presumed separate. To avoid being officially recorded as a prostitute, some women stated that the money they earned had been given to them by a "friend." These distinctions between the use of money show gray areas in which emotions, sexuality, and economics conjure simultaneous and apparently dissimilar relations. On the other hand, the grouping and selection of hygienic objects as evidence suggests that female knowledge of prophylactic methods was associated per se with the sale of sex. These belongings suggested a woman's indecorum at not having monogamous sex.

The moralizing policies did not have consistent results. In July 1966, in Ramos Mejía, some neighbors lodged a complaint with the education department for the presence of prostitutes in a hotel located half a block from the school.[3] Gathered in the fire station, they wrote a letter in which they noted, "Our children are the most harmed. . . . It gives lodging to couples who never spend more than twelve hours." As an intelligence agent of the Buenos Aires police detailed, the residential Hotel Lido was rented by the hour by couples to have sex, and men frequently went there with "prostitutes." The establishment had been shut down in 1961 for violating the Prophylaxis Law, even though the city later returned it to the owner (DIPBA, folder 3, file 137, 1966). Furthermore, civil participation in complaints is an indication of the porous borders between the state and the construction of a notion of public morality. The circulation of prescriptive sexual knowledge and the generational adhesion of margins of the population to a way of experiencing their gender that seemed threatened created a sense of order.

The women who sold sex also had to develop tactics to avoid police mobilization. The new legal authority inherited by the misdemeanor codes and provincial laws allowed them to punish women with fines or imprison them. In 1967, in the city of Morón, the police raided a bar where ten women spent time in search of clients.[4] The women were between eighteen and thirty years old, came from Paraguay, Salta, and Buenos Aires, and were submitted to the proceedings for misdemeanors. According to their statements, the ten repeated exactly the same testimony in which they stated they were going to Merlo Auto Club to dance and drink with some friends with whom "they go out and meet up at inns in the area." The women did not deny that they exchanged sex for money and decided to approach a lawyer to appeal the fine imposed by the police. In their defense, the lawyer questioned the punitive interpretation of the Prophylaxis Law and confirmed that the simple practice of prostitution as an independent individual did not constitute a crime, rejecting the "true anarchy of the interpretation." The judge who presided over the case ruled in favor of the women, who were freed from the fine, and opened a summary of police misconduct investigation (DHJC, folder 386, file 1233, 1967).

The attempts at intransigence in the face of these punitive versions of the regulation corresponded to disparate practices and not to a coordinated approach. These women did not fully identify with a hermetic figure from which they sought to erase their stigma or reject the consequences of coercive state actions, but with daily practices of survival, they attempted to safeguard themselves in cracks that seemed to get narrower. This file is an unusual case because it reveals the connection between sex and money as a subjective experience intersected by some displacement. In this sense, when the women were asked about their occupation, some stated they were dressmakers or domestic employees, but the majority did not have any shame defining themselves as prostitutes. It could be that, because of the direct experience with a brutal version of the state from groups of women who shared spaces of common sexual attention, other available meanings about their daily labor were established. The ambiguity of these semantic fields was perhaps the start of a process that led to future discussions. The scattered, quotidian actions to subvert the law demonstrated that the women who sold sex were not a direct emanation of legal control but were also constructed by transgressing and using the space in search of clients.

In sum, police action cemented a long state tendency that, amplified by authoritarian governments, gave the police greater authority in the search for moral control over the territory. In the face of this situation, the women who offered sex for money sustained their scattered practices with which they attempted to subvert the law and negotiate with the police.

Ruteras: Sexual Supply and Demand on the Move

In 1970 the band Almendra recorded the song "Rutas Argentinas" with the lyrics, "Tengo los dedos ateridos / de tanto esperar / a ese hombre que me lleve por las rutas argentinas" ("My fingers are frozen stiff / from waiting so long / for that man who will take me on the Argentine highways"). The rock song thematized the rich social life that thrived along the concrete strips uniting the country and its inhabitants. The world of paved veins extended the threads connecting towns, thus changing the opportunities for leisure travel for inhabitants.

Arteries were created—driven by the state to promote the transport of goods or tourism—that created a new geographic experience. Between 1920 and 1930, Argentina became the Latin American country with the highest number of cars and the fourth-highest country in the world. Between 1930 and 1960, the state paved more than 10,000 kilometers. The cars and trucks on the road made up an intermediary landscape between the urban and rural, which further problematized the country's borders and promoted a hybrid historic experience (Piglia, 2014).

The highways supported the increase of contingent relationships in which different subjects experienced intermittent social interactions. It stimulated the circulation of large and small amounts of money through the movement of goods and spending by truckers or travelers in search of entertainment. While the country's primary form of transportation continued to be the railroad, new forms of transportation allowed for the circulation of individuals without a fixed job in a space but who earned money in the transit from one point to another. This situation also fostered a leisure agenda in the world of work. For the sale of sex, the highways were a setting in which the game of chance, of the passage of travelers and truck drivers, presented a constant renewal of the sexual demand seen in available roadside stops in parrillas, restaurants, and motels.

Irma, eighteen, was defined by the police as a "rutera," a local term used to refer to "someone who, practicing prostitution in various places, travels and sleeps with truck drivers along the highways" (DHJC, folder 348, file 574, 1963). The concept emerged in the trials, establishing more and more what was happening at police stations. In a magazine for the ultra-right-wing Catholic organization *Tacuara* (no. 2, 1969), there is a piece about the "ruteras" in an insert next to prostitution, Coca-Cola, and homosexuality as foreign threats of imperialism. This publication indicates the widespread circulation of the term.

Irma was an orphan, which is why she lived with her aunt in Mercedes. She would stand in front of a tire repair shop close to a service station, two regular stops for drivers, and there she would agree upon the services offered to the truck drivers: sex and company during the journey. She would ride with drivers from Mercedes to General Rodríguez (49.5 km), Navarro (50.9 km), Suipacha (29.5 km), Chivilcoy (65.4 km), and Luján (35.5 km). For the short distances, it was possible for her to go and return on the same day. According to Jorge, an enlisted soldier who identified himself as her ex-boyfriend, the girl traveled around, disappearing for several days from her aunt's home (DHJC, folder 348, file 574, 1963).

This service went beyond intercourse and implied companionship in the vehicle. For the truck drivers, the encounters with the girls for short distances could function as negotiated opportunities to reduce the loneliness of the long workdays driving, which is why I think the consumption of sex and the rutera's company defined for the drivers the uses of free time within the workday. As such, I argue that the conditions of consumption were central to the patterns of the availability of sexual services.

The truck drivers' work both forced them to be alone and offered them an intimate space on the move. In contrast to other paid workers, the fixed capital moved with them, which allowed women to negotiate the difficulty of finding a place to service them. The relative autonomy of the drivers to work without the immediate oversight of superiors also limited the disciplinary nature of the working space. Furthermore, the fluidity of the travel allowed the girls to go from one place to another, renewing their clientele with greater speed. Unlike the farmers located in a fixed place, the ruteras' clients had fewer opportunities to face oversight from the community or their wives.

Moving along the shoulders of the roads always implied a certain degree of vulnerability when it came to the police. This is proven in Irma's case, as she was raped by police officers. Territorial mobility and limited opportunities for the girl to establish a local community exposed her to an empowered, virulent institution as well as to men whose travel in the area was circumstantial.

While the women's mobility allowed them to fulfill their clients' needs, women occasionally opted for fixed places. It is difficult to imagine that the sale of sex was always mobile; women maintained social lives anchored in places with established ties to family and friends. To do their work, they depended on businesses built along the highways where they could rent a room to sleep, find clientele, or service them: parrillas, restaurants, and motels.

In 1972 on RN 7, the San Andres de Giles police detained Marcos, a sixty-year-old man from San Juan with a wife and two children and owner of a parrilla where ruteras would stop.[5] Behind Marcos's business, some ruteras rented a room for 500 pesos a day. It was an accessible price. Josefa, twenty-five, came from Buenos Aires, where she had worked as a domestic employee. She had spent three months traveling the highways to maintain relations with drivers who were going toward Mendoza, until she reached Luján (36.1 km) and San Antonio de Areco (26.8 km) (DHJC, folder 548, file 50, 1972). Lía, who was sharing the room with Josefa, said that she charged 3,000 pesos per service for the truck drivers. For a first-class driver, the price was a little under a seventh of his weekly wages, given that on top of his salary he received between 3,565 and 5,000 pesos a day for food and lodging outside his home (depending on whether he did extra hours and how far he was from home).[6] The women came from all over: Úrsula, thirty-five, came from Quilmes (125 km), where she lived with her aunt; Leticia, sixty-four, a widowed hairdresser, came from the city of San Juan in Santa Fe Province (224 km).

The police raided the parrilla when Josefa was in her room with Ramón, a dairy farmer. They stated that there was no money being exchanged between them and defined themselves as friends who had sex. This statement could have come out of a desperate attempt to avoid problems with the police or the growing flexibility of romantic relationships, demonstrating that, beyond having the ability to travel, the ruteras were women who also fostered an affective space where they obtained circumstantial pleasure or solidarity (DHJC, folder 548, file 50, 1972).

The diverse origin of the ruteras was distinctive of their practices. Among the ten women detained in the Merlo Auto Club who would go to a lawyer to appeal, there were women from the western part of Buenos Aires, two from Salta, and one from Paraguay (DHJC, folder 386, file 1233,

1967). Women gathered on the sides of the highways had more varied origins and were attracted by the constant movement of the clients. These women's origins were no longer those seen at the beginning of the century, such as Jewish, Polish, or French, as the transatlantic migratory cycle no longer existed; they came from the north of Argentina, bordering countries, or zones on the outskirts of Buenos Aires.

The movement of these women demanded they have knowledge and social capital to decipher how and when to find a place to sleep. As such, the knowledge of recreational places and resorting to social networks were two central elements. In 1972, in the outskirts of San Justo, the police raided the restaurant La Rueda, run by Miranda.[7] Lucía, thirty-five, was sleeping in the back room; she knew the owner, who "had been her boss when she was a domestic employee in the defendant's butcher shop." Lucía's statement put her in a position of subordination in relation to the owner but also clarified that, after many years of not working with her, in a desperate economic situation, the woman hired her as a waitress (DHJC, folder 569, file 1264, 1972). Lucía defended that she was hired to clean and not to sell sex; that is, she tried to separate two economic activities before the justice system to keep the owner from being defined as a pimp.

The ties between prostitutes and tenants could vary. The social capital with which these women operated was mediated by social hierarchies and material differences. When the women went to seasonal bars, they had to give part of their earnings to guarantee a place to spend the night next to the highway, something that, beyond the risk it assumed, favored tenants.

The bars located along the highways were also places where supply and demand interacted. They became the closest extension of the old brothels, and at their core the supply of sex coexisted with drinking, dancing, and games. Bars were places for meeting and socialization between men where friendship allowed information to travel from one truck driver to another, letting others know how to recognize and access paid sex. The police descriptions do not offer precise information about which signs facilitated the recognition of these women, but we know that among the consumers, information spread about how and where to access sexual services. Nighttime meetings in which the clientele changed from one night to the next allowed the prostitutes to meet different men and therefore avoid client scarcity. In the bars, they played erotic games of flirting, which unlike the brothels, did not always have rooms, so residential inns were popular places to have sex.

The Caballo Negro, located on RN 5 in Mercedes, was a space where women rotated through, offering paid sex throughout the decades. Flirting games were played there in which the women and clients exchanged words, glances, and gestures through which the man felt like he was the one doing the conquering. On the two occasions the police inspected the establishment—in 1969 and 1971—they noted that "it is public knowledge in the institution that it violates the Social Prophylaxis Law." This suggests there was an arrangement with police as well as a recognition spread throughout the community of men that you could find women there (DHJC, folder 465, file 55.404 and 1198, 1971).

These spaces and clients' knowledge of them indicate that the consumers of sex were also very mobile. The traveling men went in search of encounters in their free time. Raúl, a forty-three-year-old bricklayer who traveled with his nephew from Mercedes to the town of Suipacha to hunt, stopped to eat. He told his nephew that "he had heard there were women there." He asked the waiter, "Nothing's going on here?" and the answer was that there was a woman in a room at the back of the lot. There the man found Lidia, a thirty-year-old woman who had sex with him in exchange for 2,000 pesos (DHJC, folder 489, file 55.404, 1971).

As I have already argued, the possibility of dialogue between men around the sex market was cemented in a masculine register that stimulated these practices. Raúl's conversation with the waiter was part of a masculine performance in front of his nephew. In that interaction, gender and age difference acted as contiguous threads with which masculine identity was woven on a daily basis. At the same time, the fact that the man would ask about sexual services while on a hunting trip shows the popularity of consuming paid sex.

The relationship between selling and buying sexual services was arranged through dialectic interaction. Although it is true that typically the price of the offer was adjusted based on the specifics of the demand, when it came to the price, the men sometimes were the ones who shopped around looking for an offer that suited them. In 1972, in San Andrés de Giles, in a bar located on the side of RN 8, Pablo, a nineteen-year-old shopworker, testified that he took a taxi from Pilar (63 km) because "there were really good women there." The boy spent 5,000 pesos on the taxi, almost double "the 3,000 pesos he paid for the fuck." Another man testified something similar; he was a twenty-three-year-old truck driver who always stopped at the same bar. As he stated, he liked to have sex with a thirty-year-old woman he found there (DHJC, folder 507, file 51.269, 1972).

As such, it is possible to say that the supply of and demand for sex were constructed in the interaction between the mobility of the men and women.

On the one hand, the women used their encounters with truck drivers and travelers to earn a means of subsistence that tended to have fewer intermediaries and let them keep more of their money. On the other, some women were able to combine the possibility of mobility with the demand. The men had selection criteria to seek out an offer that would satisfy their desires. As such, I believe the highway was a territory of various uses.

Agrarian Patriarchs: Buying and Selling Sex in the "Campo"

The small towns and cities in Buenos Aires Province made up a distinct landscape for the exchange of sex for money. Defining this phenomenon by its rural setting is inscribed in a debate about the definition of the urban, a scale that includes midsize cities in the province but prioritizes the small villages and open fields that marked the diversity of the setting of towns that between 1945 and 1975 underwent an intense process of demographic decline (Girbal-Blacha, 2010).

The trial testimonies give insight into the reticent connections to the cultural and social transformations that historians have signaled as a "sexual revolution." I consider how the situated configuration of hierarchical relationships of gender mediated how sex was bought and sold. The campo, or "countryside," also functions as a metaphor that includes a heterogeneous landscape of relationships of production, cultures, and social hierarchies that influenced sexual notions and practices outside of the city (Johnson, 2013). Unlike the cities, imagined by doctors, lawyers, and intellectuals as at the heart of modernity's disruptions, the agrarian world was praised for its closeness to nature and the traditional social order.

The second half of the twentieth century saw a transformation of rural economies. Peronism drove the subsidization of agriculture through the Argentine Institute of Exchange Promotion, an organization that worked to centralize foreign business through modernization and urged greater production and savings through less consumption. In the 1950s, the "second agricultural revolution" took shape and rural production was placed on the state agenda as a solution to the imbalance of economic planning, but the two consecutive droughts forced the government to put into place the Emergency Economic Plan in 1952 (Barsky and Gelman, 2009). The fall of Peronism in 1955 strengthened the focus on the rural sector of the economy and consolidated subvention measures that associated countryside efficiency with intensive cultivation and the improvement of the soils, modernization, and a profitable productive unit that was no longer directly related to large tracts of land (Girbal-Blacha, 2010).

By 1970, land and capital were no longer in the same hands. Property was subdivided and segmented between landowners and owners of production technology. New figures were introduced, such as *"el tantero,"* who leased land for farming. The increase in farming income and the price of land fed "intensive" exploitations and decreased the size of productive units to gain in efficiency and yields. From 1960 to 1973, the volume of grains and oilseed crops, the base of Argentine exports, grew an average of 2.7 percent (Girbal-Blacha, 2010).

The drastic reduction of labor caused by the modernization in the modes of production modified the lives of rural families, who faced new challenges for survival. The decline of the small farming world contracted the opportunities for families and encouraged women's mobility. Facing this situation, official speeches spoke to family life and traditional roles, encouraging life tied to rural production (Gutierrez, 2010).

Though the borders between the urban and rural became increasingly blurred, the "campo" as national metaphor supported practices rooted firmly in patriarchy. Though the poor fringes of the large urban centers and the countryside had shared customs, the social lives of the latter group developed in settings of close-knit experience in which the community played a primary role. I studied rural zones of towns, villages, and *partidos* such as 9 de Julio, Chivilcoy, Chacabuco, Mercedes, and Navarro, which had between 800 and 39,000 inhabitants during the period of analysis.

Unpaid domestic labor was central in maintaining the poor, working-class families. Many girls experienced *colocación,* or "placement," as a way to contribute to their families. Living in new homes in an auxiliary role, sometimes receiving wages or just food, was unsettling, and the young women often ran away to try to build their own lives. Fifteen-year-old Karina was detained by the police on a Mercedes farm when she was servicing a fifty-year-old pig farmer. The minor had been "placed" by her mother in a family home. She was from Villa Ocampo, Santa Fe, a rural town 821 kilometers from Mercedes. She had seven siblings, and her widowed mother could not support them. Later, due to the abuse she sustained in the house where she was living, she ran away with a girl her age and roamed the countryside in search of men who would pay them to have sex (DHJC, folder 539, file 53.154, 1974).

We can ask about the auxiliary roles of these girls in their families and how they were constructed. That is, we can examine how this experience is revealing of arguments articulated in stories of patriarchal and age inequality that defined the subaltern condition of minors in specific contexts. In 1959 Mirta "placed" Julieta, twelve, as a servant in Vicenta's house in Navarro because she was incapable of supporting her nine children. Two years later, she filed a complaint at the police station that the woman was prostituting her daughter, which is why she had run away. With this report, the mother attempted to use legal proceedings to define the conditions she considered fair for her daughter's placement and to reject the offer of sexual services (DHJC, folder 480, file 22, 1961). For some poor, working-class parents, their children had to contribute to the household, which when headed by a widow was in an even worse position to ensure they were fed. Vicenta, the head of house where Julieta was placed, known by men as "La Rubia" for her blond hair, had also been "placed" when she was twelve years old. From one generation to the next, families reproduced the auxiliary condition of girls and looked to insert them in the labor market.

On the one hand, it is possible that the notion of being a minor was also a discursive foundation with which those minors found in sexual commerce a possibility of earning an income and independence. As I said, the girls left their jobs where their families had "placed" them due to disturbing conditions and sometimes turned to selling sex as a way to build a new private space. Julieta, fifteen, got together with a bricklayer employed in the countryside, and together they paid a rent of 140 pesos a month. Lucas, a thirty-five-year-old client who lived in Sol de Mayo, paid twenty-five pesos and traveled thirty-eight kilometers to visit her, perhaps to avoid rumors among neighbors and his wife finding out (DHJC, folder 480, file 17, 1964).

Persisting practices in rural areas were interconnected in a use of the territory where traditional notions of sexuality were expressed. The *monte*, or scrubland, was a place to have sex, as León pointed out; he was a sixty-nine-year-old dairy farmer who was Julieta's client and paid with "sugar, *yerba mate*, and other things." The undergrowth and clusters of trees allowed for meeting spots that were impermeable to community oversight. The client said, "I knew the girl went to the *monte* with company" (DHC, folder 480, file 17, 1964).

Although the places with low demographic density combined the methods of community control of morality with privileges to exercise masculine sexuality protected by double standards or the use of spaces outside of town, the traditional notions impacted the women's sexual experiences. In their subaltern condition of age, class, and gender, their sexuality was inspected, thought about, and talked about by others. When the public defender had to intervene to defend the woman for promoting Julieta's sexuality, Vicenta argued that "the minor often escaped. . . . She tended to leave for hours or days saying she was going to see her family, and it's possible she let herself be corrupted by individuals" (DHJC, folder 480, file 17, 1964). There was an explicit sense of the expected uses of time and appropriate places for women; leaving the house or free time were masculine privileges that for a girl could be seen as threatening her femininity.

The circulation of an androcentric narrative about female sexuality shaped the life paths of the women defendants. Fourteen-year-old Celeste was sexually abused by her stepfather and forced to have sex in exchange for money, according to a neighbor's report. Her stepfather stated that "the exponent would wear a nightgown that showed her chest and panties" and stated that in front of him "she touched her breasts and provoked me by sitting on my lap" (DHJC, folder 522, file 23, 1970). As Rita Segato (2017) emphasizes, the rapist acts as a moralizer performing the virile mandate to control female sexuality and makes statements to his male peers. The stepfather's language was founded on a punitive virile moralizing core, on a system of state male socialization in the presence of the police who took his statement.

The police doctor affirmed the girl was an alleged "compulsive liar." As I previously argued, the physicians employed by the justice system used various practices with which they described the minor's body. As such, with invasive practices such as touching the hymen, they noted she had been violated by force. Groups of up to four men would have sex in the back of the house in the open air with the girl, encouraged by the girl's stepfather, often around her eight-year-old little sister, who stated that they said "bad words" (DHJC, folder 522, file 23, 1970).

These misogynistically described nuclear families were not entirely widespread. The older sister of ten siblings from Mercedes, who had already become independent, requested custody of two sisters to get them away from that torture (DHJC, folder 522, file 23, 1970). But these virulent excesses were woven within multiple agreements in which male violence reinforced structural differences.

The forms of masculine domestic hierarchy marked how sex was offered. In 1973, on a rural farm in Chivilcoy, Margarita, sixteen, stated at the police station that she was forced with physical torture to sell sex by her boyfriend Rodrigo, a rural day laborer. The girl had traveled to Chacabuco to see her aunt. According to her testimony to the justice system, she decided not to go home because her father would hit her for leaving without letting anyone know, which a neighbor confirmed. The girl's fear gives indications how domestic hierarchies were handled. It is possible that some parents would continue asserting their power in the home through the use of force. The fact that no member of the defense or the prosecution would pay attention to that point indicates that there was consensus around what a man could do with his family (DHJC, folder 568, file 1827, 1973).

With nowhere for Margarita to spend the night, her boyfriend put her in a house with other day laborers. Several of the clients witnessed the blows with which the boy forced the girl to agree to service the men, and before the justice system they supported the minor's testimony and accused the boyfriend of pimping. This did not stop them from having sex with her on the ranch floor and later paying Rodrigo (DHJC, folder 568, file 1827, 1973). In this sense, we can imagine that the day laborers understood the sexual encounters immersed in a gendered narrative that gave their sexuality boundless sexual attributes and relegated Margarita to a secondary position. Lucas, a twenty-two-year-old rural day laborer, referred to the act as fulfilling "my physiological needs" (DHJC, folder 568, file 1827, 1973).

Margarita's attitude for the seven days she was forced to offer sex for money was not entirely subordinate. When the pimp asked her to take some pills so she would not get "pregnant," the girl refused. She testified that she did not take them because "she was not a whore." Back then, though the technological power of the contraceptive pills transformed sexuality by separating the sphere of pleasure from that of reproduction (Felitti, 2012), in nonmetropolitan zones their consumption could be interpreted as inappropriate. Along these lines, there was the idea that contraceptives did not have ontological properties that would strengthen the body's autonomy but that were marked by the limits that defined sexual cultures in which their consumption was situated.

The circulation of a heterogenous language of class impregnated with an androcentric imagination that placed women and children in an auxiliary position in regard to the survival of the domestic unit constituted the foundation of possible models for women to earn money. The interpretation of the notion of the auxiliary condition of nonadult girls among sectors where extreme poverty threatened their existence allowed, not without running afoul of the law, some families to accept and collaborate with the girls' activities.

In 1972 in the city 9 de Julio, Homero and Lucrecia, parents to three children, were accused of facilitating sixteen-year-old Jazmin's prostitution. The girl's mother was a laundrywoman, and her father was a photographer who regularly traveled to Bahía Blanca, where he earned 500 pesos a month. The father got sick, so his trips became more irregular. Jazmin had been born in Pehuajó, then lived with her mother in Carlos Casares and later settled in 9 de Julio. Due to this migration, she had not finished her studies and was illiterate. The discontinuities of the family's income created a precarious existence. As such, it is possible that the family, trying to increase their earnings, tried to get their daughter to sell sex as a legitimate activity, which the mother explained as the girl's "loose living." With the first client, which was also Jazmin's first sexual experience, the girl earned fifty pesos, a tenth of the father's monthly earnings (DHJC, folder 540, file 50.345, 1972).

Our notion of territory tries to emphasize how the social dynamics for the masculine demand for sex intervened in how the territory was used to sell sex (as well as how women selling sex negotiated these conditions). Jazmin's services were established through various networks that the girl used to move to locations where there were isolated men. To get a client list and earn money, she depended on numerous mediators among whom were her clients, a shopkeeper—who because of his job possibly had more information and social capital than other neighbors—and a taxi driver. Ismael worked during the day as a laborer in the region's fields and in the evening as a driver transporting inhabitants to farms and *estancias*. The low demographic density and intermittent relationships between neighbors spread across a huge area strengthened the role of intermediaries in the offering to customers, though unlike those described in chapter 4, these people said they did not receive any commission, perhaps to avoid being classed as pimps. Surely, they were guided by fraternity with groups of isolated men looking for some kind of entertainment.

Jazmin's clients included dairy farmers and construction workers. The girl first approached a group of bricklayers who were building silos to store grains. Her primary contact was a twenty-three-year-old Chilean worker nicknamed Francisco. By spending a day with the three men, she earned seventy pesos. Then Francisco visited her, and for one sexual encounter, for which they used the room where Jazmin's entire family lived, he gave her forty pesos, so she earned a total of 110 pesos (DHJC, folder 540, file 50.345, 1972).

The high number of salaried men in small zones marked a specific demand in which men invested in transportation and lodging to access sexual services. This allowed a girl like Jazmin to not be exposed to the urban practices of the circuit. It also guaranteed them a clientele that was not disposed to argue, was more consistent, and was prepared to pay more. Ricardo, a twenty-nine-year-old dairy farmer from 12 de Octubre, contacted Jazmin through a taxi driver. The solitary experience of a man located in a town with no more than 300 inhabitants marked the tone of his conversation with which, as he testified, he told the driver, "I need a woman" and explained that in his hometown this was "impossible." In a first encounter, Ricardo paid for the taxi, a hotel room located in her town, and fifteen pesos to Jazmin. Later, so the girl would spend three days with him on the farm where he worked, he spent 130 pesos. The money Jazmin earned was higher than other girls who sold sex in other areas, but less than the salary earned by the workers she serviced. Finally, an adult sister still living in Pehuajó went to the justice system and requested custody of all her siblings. She won, stripping her parents of a large part of their domestic unit (DHJC, folder 540, file 50.345, 1972).

The fluctuating relationships between selling and buying sex changed due as much to economic trends as to social hierarchies. In 1960 in Mercedes, Leandro, a twenty-year-old university student who was returning to town to visit his parents, met up with two friends in a bar. There they decided "to find a place to have a good time." With this goal and the help of a taxi driver, they headed to the outskirts of the city toward a farm where Andrea, a forty-nine-year-old woman, managed a house. The taxi driver warned the three boys that "clients were strictly selected based on whether they appeared to have a lot of money" (DHJC, folder 381, file 43.078, 1972).

It is possible that, when low populations meant inhabitants did not have anonymity, the social hierarchies were complex. The taxi driver's knowledge of a place of consumption for those who looked like they had money was proof not only of income but also of status where perhaps information like rustic dress and skin leathered by the sun defined an inability to transgress a border. Juan had to pay seventy pesos to have sex with Balbina, a rate twice what is found in other narratives from the period.

It was not only that the establishment's owner—that is, beginning with the offer—would select the clients; it was also the desire to differentiate the customers so as to not allow men who could be her employees to have sex with the women. The established relations in the bedrooms of that brothel put into play an ephemeral good that exposed the consumer's intimacy. That separation validated a specific way of embodying masculinity.

In sum, in the towns with low density that were based on agriculture, the auxiliary role of girls with respect to their families was the foundation of a range of practices for domestic survival that spanned from placement to the exchange of sex for money. In this framework, the landscape of groups of dispersed consumers, making intermittent connections, allowed women to travel to sell sex. And, out of necessity for continued social differentiation, there were spaces for elite sexual consumption.

· · · · · ·

In this chapter I addressed the complex systems in which the action, meanings, and practices of various actors were constitutive elements of the sexualized use of the territory. The selling and buying of sex during the 1960s and 1970s showed a varied capacity of offer and demand associated with characteristics of the social, cultural, and regional economic dynamic.

State agents made the criminalization of a long-standing moralizing policy a reality. In their actions, the police gave life to the notion of morality in which the construction of order associated sexuality and policy. The informal daily practices with which they agreed upon and renewed the negotiation of the sex-trade monopoly were the attempt to recuperate direct control lost with the abolition of regulation.

The range of pressures was met with varied acts of resistance with which some women who sold sex attempted to avoid the trappings of the law. Because of this, we can think that despite being exposed, they did not express in their daily lives the direct consequence of the practices criminalized by public agencies, but instead they had the capacity of daily inventiveness with which they created alternative forms of existence. It is also worth mentioning that the stigma that legitimized the practices of moral persecution were based in some notions of civil society, which expressed the borders between the public and private meanings.

I then reflected on the materiality of the relations that made up the territory. On the one hand, the highways are the pretext for thinking about how the appearance of new forms of sexual consumption and circulation of money collaborated with the emergence of ruteras as a specific form of selling sex. The potential of a mobile form of sale and the expansion of a space of circulation of women and men (parrillas, bars, and restaurants) allowed for a sizable group of ruteras to circulate to earn a living.

Finally, the practices of selling and buying sex in the rural settings were impacted by the intersection of gender, class, and age. There, the auxiliary status of underage girls to guarantee the subsistence of their families and future generations as a way to consolidate their subaltern position constituted the basis that legitimized their practices of exchanging sex for money to survive. At the same time, the complex traditional notions of sexuality filtered a female experience in which the varied discursive systems combined their existence as assistants of the physiological needs of men with public condemnation. Finally, it is possible that the existence of a particular demand, the concentration of men in the constructions or the presence of unaccompanied men who were employed in dairy farming, marked a kind of female mobility. Thus, the entertainment that they could bring men in areas where the number of inhabitants was low was an opportunity for these women to earn more money than expected.

The record of these complex, heterogeneous forms of relations allows us to sketch out a map in which the so-called radical transformation of sexual notions and practices draws the lines and establishes a scene profoundly impacted by conflict. The reference to the diversity of relations and the historicity of the connection of the exchange of sex for money is a way to understand the problematization of the homogenous notions of the territory to open the scene to the coexistence of interpretations, uses, and actors that through conflict would arrange its own support system.

Conclusion

· ·

In *Money Isn't Everything*, I have studied the diverse forms of buying and selling sex in Argentina in the (short) twentieth century. I have considered narratives of practices, social meanings, and life paths inscribed in the commercialization of sex as a space to understand the social, economic, and cultural processes that made (and make) up our social lives.

The first conclusion is that various forms of exchanging sex for money existed. This multiplicity challenges binary readings that tend to reduce selling sex either to enslavement or autonomous sex work, and suggests a flexible interpretive framework situated in space and time. Furthermore, working against those who see a binary of a subject's autonomous choices and systems of power, I describe the activities as structured means with greater or lesser durability and contemplate the risks and uncertainties in connection with conditions rooted in dissimilar spaces and times. By this, I am not denying the experiences of sex workers but trying to understand specific documents in their context. This is an important contribution for future research in the field as this project expands on who is studied and what their activities were; it scales the practices to interconnect social spheres without falling into the trap of hermetic or ontological approaches in the commercial sex circuit.

For example, in chapter 1, I study the discourses, practices, and notions of pimps, prostitutes, and civil servants in the transnational construction of "white slavery." That is, I emphasize the existence of a specific configuration of the sale of sex marked by the mobility of the sexual supply, the circulation of information and a male social capital, the network of mediators, and the use of various degrees of coercion to appropriate earned money. I point out that these mechanisms were in dialogue with a specific regulatory framework (licensed brothels), influenced by medium-term conditions of each city (such as the difficulty of accessing space to sell sex independently in Buenos Aires), and influenced by constantly changing patterns of intercontinental migration in which prostitutes and pimps were inscribed.

In chapter 2, I explain how the androcentric interpretations of sexuality as a national good on the part of the military influenced the transformation of abolitionist regulations and redefined the scope of that policy.

I explore how lobbying on the state can subvert the mechanisms of regulation that enabled specific forms of sex work, those protected by the state in the barracks, and forms of consumption that outlasted regulations, such as military encouragement for conscripts to pay for sex.

In chapters 5 and 6, I stress that consumption played a role in defining the sexual supply. Thus, for example, the existence of a mobile workforce in the south of Buenos Aires Province or the circulation of truck drivers on highways defined some of the possible forms of selling sex. As I demonstrate in chapters 3, 4, and 6, other types of structural factors played a role. First, the enduring restrictive state policy to control the territory, used by police officers, forced many women to avoid or negotiate with local powers. Second, domestic structures placed young women in service positions that were integral to their subaltern sexual relations and their auxiliary position in relation to men (fathers and then husbands or boyfriends).

A second conclusion is that diversity confirms that small aspects of social life, such as buying and selling a sexual service, are symptoms that articulate complex systems and actors. I thus bring to the fore life outside of the brothels to examine, always unequally, the conceptions and actions of social actors that transcended the model of the prostitute to reposition the action of consumers, pimps, civil servants, taxi boys, *travestis*, commission agents, investigators, police, judges, military officers, politicians, among others, as those who constructed and reproduced circuits for selling and buying sex. By broadening this universe, I examine a narrative history of women to connect quotidian experiences of commercial sex. For example, historicizing the purchase of sex by men undermines the idea of an uncontrollable male sexuality that was frequently blamed on women—and still is—when examining how this argument endured and was established. I also highlight how the practice of offering sexual services operated in precarious, mobile lives that became porous and involved multiple activities to survive.

A third conclusion is that the complex mechanisms by which the state intervened in the selling and buying of sex, which included the abolition of legal sex work and expanding punitive capacities, was part of a general reaction to the social and cultural transformations of sexualities in the country. In this sense, this book shows that the abolitionism employed in Argentina had an aggressive punitive nature that deprived people selling sex of their most basic rights. As I point out in chapter 3, there were at least two periods in the punitive interpretation of abolitionism. First, the introduction of loopholes to abolitionist policies and regional neo-regulationism

(1937–55) caused a spike in arrests, aimed at disciplining prostitutes "freed" by the previous administrative system. Second, the punitive consolidation of abolitionism between 1955 and 1966 involved a set of measures that increased police power and had at its core a punitive interpretation of state policy related to selling and buying sex. In 1984 this legal system began to end, but its echoes can still be felt today.

These centrifugal and centripetal tendencies of the legal system did not take place without conflict. First, the justice system generally rejected requests for prison time made by the police, which thus constructed a disciplinary system of the territory marked by short stays in prisons or jails. Second, this situation did not subsume women in prison discipline but, on the contrary, created spaces of socialization that, both inside and outside of institutions, allowed the circulation of knowledge and affective networks.

This process of institutionalizing morality as a form of violence is a phenomenon of medium duration. Since the 1930s, the cultural elites' perception of an apparent threat to the material foundations of the national identity led to the misdemeanor codes that regulated the social and sexual limits of the uses of public space. In this book, I argue that there was a set of policies that restricted the uses of the public space that transcended the swings between civil and military governments. These regulations consolidated an idea of morality in which sexuality and policy acted as complementary metaphors of order and criminalizing poor urbanites, young people, homosexuals, travestis, and prostitutes.

It was the collective and organized action of LGBTQIA+ organizations—especially of travesti and trans movements in the 1990s—in coordination with sex workers that opened the door to contest the repressive moralism of the Argentine state. In 1996, following a constitutional reform in 1994 that transformed the capital city into an autonomous territory, the Buenos Aires assembly called upon citizens to discuss a new local Magna Carta. In addition to other reforms, the assembly planned to reconsider the local codes that policed public spaces. A coalition of sex workers, travestis, gays, lesbians, human rights associations, and progressive feminists demanded the end of police repression. This coalition was a reaction against the politics of neighborhood groups and police officers who campaigned for the eviction of travestis from the city's wealthier districts. Finally, in 1998 this coalition forced the local government to abolish the moral codes under which police prosecuted citizens, expanding some of the rights of sex workers. While the legal transformation spread throughout the country, police officers kept deploying legal mechanisms to persecute those offering sexual services.

A fourth conclusion is that, beyond the constant regulatory changes, those who sold and bought sex deployed shared practices, knowledge, and meanings to negotiate their sexual and economic experiences. These systems were modified in dialogue with structural conditions and actions with which prostitutes and clients upheld their commercial sex relations. As I point out in chapters 3 and 4, there were patterns that defined the kind of paid sex offered; for example, the periods in which the labor force circulated between the harvest, exportation, and dock labor in the south of Buenos Aires Province stimulated the circulation of those who sold sex. At the same time, the circulation varied in response to prior traditions, as with the networks inherited from the regulation culture born in the licensed brothels outlawed in 1936. The examples I have presented are varied and emphasize the complexity of these practices. Thus, I can point out that the pimps who traveled at the beginning of the twentieth century from Europe to Buenos Aires found in the regulations mechanisms to set up their business model. They also benefited from the consolidation of an image of masculine sexuality.

The focus on forms of selling sex allowed me to recognize patterns in the lives of women in society. I thus emphasize how the disposition that marked their class identity and participation in households permeated bodily and sexual experiences that solidified inequalities of gender, class, and age, experiences integral to their life paths and without which it is possible that the sale of sex would not have emerged as an available option for survival.

Following this line of argument, a fundamental conclusion relates to the complexity of selecting categories that define the payment of a sexual service with contemporary concepts. As such, I focus my critical gaze on the meanings with which women and men made sense of their own experiences. There are many examples of this. In chapters 3, 4, and 6, I problematize the ways women negotiated with various state offices around the terms used to give meaning to their daily practice. In general terms, these women emphasized categories associated with domestic labor. Some did this because they exemplified the secondary jobs they held to survive; others did so because they wanted to avoid the risk of arrest or prosecution, but they also did so because they were guided by moral values that marked how they chose to define themselves. That is, why are we capable of recognizing their abilities to intervene in their destiny only when they test the moral character with which we view a class's history and not when they seem to reproduce some of the prejudices that, perhaps, subjugated them?

This question is part of a profound act of epistemological reflection. As I emphasize in chapter 5, something similar happens when the role of paying for sex in the construction of working cultures is ignored and instead the opposite is prioritized, such as other pleasure activities like sports or meeting at bars. As such, this book also calls attention to the moral prescriptions with which we historically imagine the lives of the working class, popular sectors, their families, and their leisure time. Sexual commerce was a porous vector of working-class lives. Here I am not denying that sex work was work or trying to erase women's agency. On the contrary, I am mapping the contradictory meanings with which they made sense of it or the language they used to negotiate with the state. Here I confirm the premise that there are no ties of preestablished solidarity with those whom we should organize, but on the contrary, it is in their own meanings and ways of existing in the world that we should try to understand them.

In this book I also pay attention to the circulation of categories produced in public organizations or the press, as well as their resignifications or the emergence of local terms in communities tied to commercial sex. The polysemic uses of different concepts allow us to reconnect with the disputes through the interpretation of these practices. Thus, for example, every ruling in which a judge named a woman who sold sex a prostitute was an act of symbolic ordering. In chapter 1, I observe the permeability between journalistic discourses related to "white slavery" and the translations with which pimps and prostitutes interpreted their actions at the beginning of the century. Thus, I signal how the narratives of the pimp as a symbol played an important role in the redefinition of the dominant value of "whiteness" in the national imagination. In chapters 2 and 5, I emphasize how language used by men, always variable in their social positions, legitimized that the military leadership would call for the installation of brothels or influence the rituals of nonsimultaneous sexual consumption. All these examples substantiate that the different terms used, also by us, define their polysemy in conditions of locution mediated by physical experiences of class and gender. They are always inscribed in contentious spaces where definitions are negotiated, and they are experienced as part of the embodiment of intimacies, sexualities, and affects.

A final conclusion responds to the centrality of sexuality for interpreting social, political, economic, and cultural phenomena. The embodiment of masculinity, the complementary uses of the sale of sex, the sexual satisfaction of the workforce, state repression, and representations in the redefinition of a "white" Argentina, among other issues, also connect to acts that are considered natural and that (sometimes) take place in bedrooms.

Though the connections that I highlight may be arbitrary, the progressive spatial displacement of the cities to the highways, the harvests and the cities and the rural towns of the interior of Buenos Aires Province, are a reminder that the changes were not always symmetrical, much less homogenous. The periods that seem well defined when we look at the city of Buenos Aires blur when we look at diverse social settings in midsize cities of the province. Thus as the material transformations of Peronism and the emergence of expectations among the popular classes or, much more, the weakening of parental restrictions over the lives of the youth contract from the margins, they also narrow in relation to reticent connections that are a reminder that social class and the patriarchy are upheld as verdicts over social life; they cling to and attempt to not be dragged under by the magnetic force of the center.

I do not want to emphasize an Argentina of eternal permanence, but on the contrary, I want to mark the tensions and quotidian actions that are necessary to, beyond the transformative fluctuations, maintain the profound structures that articulate the inequities of lives. That is, I want to emphasize the heterogeneity of processes that define what certain bodies can do, the vertical and horizontal restrictions, but also the singular displays of challenging the norms.

This book is a contribution to a promising research agenda about the scope of the study of sexuality(ies), its history as a way to understand the subjective systems that articulated and articulate us as individuals, with our fragile subjectivities, with our ability for action and our limits. It reminds us of the potential to study pleasure, suffering, and the body as symptoms of the social world that permeates us and is permeable by our everyday life, transforming it into an undeniably political setting.

Notes

Chapter 1

1. Pablo Urbanyi was born in Hungary in 1939, migrated to Argentina at the age of seven, and became naturalized. A journalist for *La Opinión*, he presented his book *El mercado erótico* as a compilation of journalistic and police sources on pimps in 1930.

Chapter 2

1. The letters cited in this chapter are contained in files of the Archivo de Asuntos Secretos del Ministerio del Interior: box 17, file no. 234; box 17, file no. 234; and box 3, file no. 31.

Chapter 4

1. A town in south-central Buenos Aires Province located in the Necochea *partido*. Its rural economy is based on the production of sunflowers and vegetables. According to the 1947 census, the town had 1,064 inhabitants (urban and rural zones).

2. A city partially located in the Salado River watershed, Buenos Aires Province. According to the 1960 census, it had 24,660 inhabitants.

3. The department included Tres Arroyos, Dolores, Juárez, Necochea, Lobería, Balcarce, Mar Chiquita, Ayacucho, Arenales, Rauch, Pilar, Vecino, Maipú, Molsalvo, Tuyú, Ajó, Tordillo y Catelli, and General Alvarado (until its later separation) (Calandria, 2016).

4. A city in the south of Buenos Aires Province and seat of the homonymous *partido*. Between 1914 and 1947, its population grew from 19,464 to 30,621. Its economy is based on livestock, grains, and produce.

5. Nerio Rojas (1890–1970) was an Argentine legal physician and psychiatrist with a strong influence in his field and with the state. He was an associate professor of forensic medicine (1924–46) at the University of Buenos Aires, and in 1955 he served as head of the institution. He was elected national deputy by the Radical Civic Union (UCR) for three nonconsecutive terms (1942–43, 1946–50, 1960–62). He held editorial positions in important specialized publications and was a UNESCO ambassador (1964–66).

6. City located in the south of Buenos Aires Province with a rural economy. It was the capital of wheat production in the province. In 1947 there were 48,757 inhabitants living there.

7. Both are neighboring port cities, centers of export for beef and grains. They are separated by the river Quequén Grande by four kilometers. Necochea is the headquarters of the homonymous *partido* and at the time had a population of 17,708.

8. Miramar is the coastal city that is the headquarters of the General Alvarado *partido*. At the time it had 3,537 inhabitants.

9. A city that was the headquarters of the justice system of the south of Buenos Aires Province dedicated to rural production. In 1947 there were 19,068 inhabitants.

10. Guatraché is a department in La Pampa Province. In the 1947 census, there were 9,147 inhabitants in the whole territory (there is no previous census data).

11. Balcarce is a mountain town in the south of Buenos Aires Province with a livestock, forestry, and agricultural economy. In 1947 there were 30,197 inhabitants.

12. A small rural city in the south of the province. In 1947 there were 13,429 inhabitants.

13. Lobería is a *partido* in the south of Buenos Aires Province whose economy is centered on rural production. The 1947 census reported 7,916 inhabitants.

Chapter 5

1. Lobería is a *partido* in the south of Buenos Aires Province whose economy is based on rural production. The 1947 census reported 7,916 inhabitants.

2. Mercedes is a town located in the north of Buenos Aires Province and is the seat of the homonymous *partido*. Its economy was traditionally centered on cattle and grain production. Between 1930 and 1950 its population was between 30,000 and 40,000. In 1970 there were 39,868 inhabitants.

3. City in central-west Buenos Aires Province dedicated to cattle. In 1947 the census recorded 19,621 inhabitants.

Chapter 6

1. *Partido* in the north of Buenos Aires Province. According to the 1960 census, it had 51,197 inhabitants. In the area, there is agrarian production as well as food and manufacturing industries.

2. A central-eastern *partido* located in Gran Buenos Aires.

3. A town in the western zone of Gran Buenos Aires. It is part of the *partido* La Matanza, the most populated in the province.

4. A town in the western zone of Gran Buenos Aires and seat of the homonymous *partido*.

5. A town in the northeast of Buenos Aires Province, capital of the homonymous *partido*, and on the peripheries of Mercedes dedicated to ranching and the food industry. In 1970 there were 11,456 registered inhabitants.

6. Calculated from the database of parity skill signed by the Union for Chauffeurs, Trucks, and Others in Buenos Aires Province, active between 1969 and 1978.

7. San Justo is the capital of the *partido* La Matanza, Buenos Aires Province.

Bibliography

Archives

Archivo digital del Instituto Iberoamericano de Berlín
Archivo digital Ruinas Digitales
Archivo General de la Nación
Archivo Nacional de la Defensa
Archiwum Urzad Wojewodzki Katowice
Biblioteca de la Facultad de Ciencias Jurídicas y Sociales de la UNLP
Biblioteca de la Facultad de Derecho y Ciencias Sociales de la UBA
Biblioteca de la Facultad de Medicina de la UBA
Biblioteca de la Legislatura de la Ciudad Autónoma de Buenos Aires
Biblioteca de la Salud Pública de la UBA
Biblioteca del Congreso de la Nación Argentina
Biblioteca digital de la Suprema Corte de la Provincia de Buenos Aires
Biblioteca Nacional Mariano Moreno
Biblioteka Narodowa
CEMLA
DHJC
DHJS
DIPBA
Hemeroteca Digital de España
Infoleg
Repositorio Digital de la ONU
Reservorio de Expedientes de la Cámara de Diputados de la Nación Argentina
Rockefeller Archive Center
SPB

Official Publications

Boletín del Patronato Real para la Represión de la Trata de Blancas
Boletín Mensual de la Sociedad de las Naciones
Censo de las cárceles nacionales, 1931
Censo Nacional de Población de la República Argentina (1947, 1960, 1970, 1980)
Diarios de sesiones de las Cámaras de Diputados y Senadores (1914–60)
International Bureau for the Suppression of Traffic of Women and Children
    (various publications)

Memorandum to the council on the comments submitted by the government
  regarding part II of the report of special body of experts, 30 November 1927.
Memorias del Ministerio de Guerra, Buenos Aires, t. i–ix, 1937–48.
Report of the Special Body of Experts on Traffic in Women and Children. Part i and ii.
  The Paul Kinsie reports for the League of Nations, Ginebra, 1927.

Periodical Publications

Anales de la Legislación Argentina
¡Así!
Caras y Caretas
Clarín
Crítica
Crónica
El Extranjero (Spain)
El Gladiador

Esto
La Pluma (Uruguay)
La Razón
Reflejos
Somos
Tacuara
Todo es Historia

Journals

Acta Médica de Córdoba
Archivos de la Secretaría de Salud
  Pública
Boletín de la Liga Argentina de
  Profilaxis Social
Boletín Departamento Nacional
  de Higiene
Iatría
La Semana Médica
Medicina Legal
Medicina Social

Publicaciones Médicas
Revista Argentina de Dermatosifilología
Revista de la Sociedad Argentina de
  Venerología y Profilaxis Social
Revista de Medicina Legal y
  Jurisprudencia
Revista de Policía y Criminalística
Revista Médica de Córdoba
Sindicato Unidos Portuarios Argentinos
Somos
Unión Confiteros

Primary Sources

Aftalion, E. 1944. "Bases para la reforma de la regulación jurídica de la prostitución en la República Argentina." *Revista Argentina de Dermatosifilología* xxviii (2): 180–85.

———. 1946. "Prostitución, proxenetismo y delito." *Revista de Policía y Criminalística* iv (19).

Alsogaray, J. 1933. *Trilogía de la trata de blancas (Rufianes, policía, municipalidad).* Buenos Aires: Rosso.

Anónimo. 1946. "Reglamentó el P. E. la ley de Profilaxis Social." *Revista de la Sociedad Argentina de Venerología y Profilaxis Social* x (18): 47–56.

Arlt, R. 2009 (1929). *Los siete locos.* Buenos Aires: Losada.

———. 2015. *The Seven Madmen.* Translated by Nick Caistor. New York: NYRB Classics.

Ayarragaray, L. 1937. *Cuestiones y problemas argentinos contemporáneos*. Buenos Aires: L. J. Rosso.

Baliña, L. 1954. "Sobre el consorcio abolicionista." *Iatría* xxv (123): 24–30.

Baliña, P. 1937. "Libreta de salud, obligatoria, y lucha antivenérea." *Revista Argentina de Dermatosifilología* xxi: 611–22.

——. 1942. "El problema venéreo al cumplir cinco años de vigencia la ley nacional de profilaxis Nº 12.331." *Revista Argentina de Dermatosifilología* xxvi: 759–64.

——. 1962. "Soluciones para reducir la oferta y la demanda de prostitución." *La Semana Médica* 569: 32–35.

Barrés, M. 1934. *El hampa y sus secretos*. Buenos Aires: Imprenta López.

Belvey, J. 1939. "Travestiment." *Revista de Medicina Legal y Jurisprudencia* 104: 57–78.

Bembo, M. 1912. *La mala vida en Barcelona*. Cataluña: Manucci.

Bossio, B. 1935. "¿La prostitución es una cualidad inherente a determinada nacionalidad, raza o credo religioso?" *Medicina Social* 24: 22–29.

Carrillo, R. 1948. "El abolicionismo no excluye la policía sanitaria." *Archivos de la Secretaría de Salud Pública* iv (5): 387–92.

Castaldo, E. 1938. "El problema médico-social de la prostitución." PhD Thesis, University of Buenos Aires.

Domínguez, S. 1947. *La policía sanitaria*. Policía de Buenos Aires.

Eiris, E. 1935. "Consideraciones médico-legales sobre la ley 12.331." *Revista de Medicina Legal y Juridisprudencia* 50: 109–13.

Eiris, E., and R. Cerini. 1939a. *La medicina y la sociología frente a la prostitución*. Rosario, Argentina: Comunicación del Círculo Médico.

——. 1939b. "La prostitución ante la medicina y la sociología." *Publicaciones Médicas* 5: 12–19.

Escudero, P. 1939a. *La alimentación de la familia en Buenos Aires*. Buenos Aires: Instituto Nacional de Nutrición.

——. 1939b. *La política nacional de alimentación en la República Argentina*. Buenos Aires: Ministerio de Relaciones Exteriores y Culto-Instituto Nacional de Nutrición.

Gálvez, M. 1905. *La trata de blancas*. Buenos Aires: Tragant.

García, G. L. 1968. *Nanina*. Buenos Aires: Editorial Jorge Álvarez.

Garzón, R. 1961. "Experiencia sobre la vigencia de la ley 12.331." *Acta Médica de Córdoba* vi (4–6): 4–10.

Giménez, A. M. 1919. *Contra la reglamentación de la prostitución: Abolición de las ordenanzas municipales y profilaxis de las enfermedades venéreas: Proyectos y discursos pronunciados por el Consejo Deliberante de Buenos Aires, en las sesiones*. Buenos Aires: Talleres Gráficos Optimus de A. Cantiello.

——. 1930. *La reglamentación de la prostitución y la represión de la trata de blancas ante la justicia penal*. Buenos Aires: Imprenta La Vanguardia.

Hackett, L. 1944. *Diary*. Rockefeller Archive.

Jiménez de Asúa, L. 1953. *Cuestiones de derecho penal*. Quito, Ecuador: Talleres Gráficos Nacionales.

Jozami, M. 1930. *¡Vendida! Memorias íntimas de Cosia Zeilon: La Zwi Migdal vista por dentro*. Buenos Aires: Tor.

Landaburu, L., and E. Aftalion. 1942. "Aspectos civiles, penales y administrativos de la ley 12.331 de profilaxis antivenérea." *Revista Argentina de Dermatosifilología* xxvi: 763–74.

Londres, A. 2007 (1927). *El camino a Buenos Aires: La trata de blancas*. Buenos Aires: Del Zorzal.

Lugones, L. 1930a. *La grande Argentina*. Buenos Aires: Huemul.

———. 1930b. *La patria fuerte*. Buenos Aires: Taller Gráfico de L. Bernard.

Luisi, P. 1926. *El problema de la prostitución: ¿Abolicionismo o reglamentarismo?* Montevideo, Uruguay: La Industrial.

Mendoza, A. 1933. *La cárcel de mujeres*. Buenos Aires: Claridad.

Moreno, R. 1917. *Proyecto de código penal para la Nación Argentina*. Buenos Aires.

O'Connor, J. 1931. *Estado del sistema penitenciario*. Marcos Paz: Talleres Gráficos de la Colonia Hogar.

Opizzo, J. 1963. *Alteraciones sexuales: Diagnóstico y orientación del enfermo sexual*. Buenos Aires: Edición del autor.

Pareja, E. 1937. *La prostitución en Buenos Aires*. Buenos Aires: Tor.

———. 1940. "Los artículos 15 y 17 de la ley no han resuelto un serio problema social." *Revista de Policía y Criminalística* iv (18–19): 29–31.

Pellegrini, R. 1950. *Sexuollogia*. Madrid: Morata.

Pinazo, M. 1918. *Delitos y delincuentes: El trasplante siniestro*. Buenos Aires: Imprenta Cúneo.

Puente, J. 1940. "Estado actual de la profilaxis de las enfermedades venéreas en la República Argentina." *Boletín Departamento Nacional de Higiene* iv: 426–27.

Queirel, L. 1978. "Sin precio no hay prostitución." *Iatría*, 98: 10–14.

Quevedo, J. 1951. *El sindicalismo y el problema de la prostitución*. Buenos Aires: Publicaciones del Laboratorio Social Argentino de la Peña Sindicalista.

Riesco, L. 1963. "Una encuesta sociosanitaria en un barrio de la ciudad de Córdoba: La prostitución como enfermedad social." *Revista Médica de Córdoba* 8: 13–16.

Rojas, N. 1943. "Jurisprudencia comentada: Impotencia, desfloración y anulación del matrimonio." *Medicina Legal* 5 (4): 25–36.

Rosenblatt, M., and C. Benertervide. 1935. *Endocrinología y el problema de la prostitución*. Buenos Aires: El Ateneo.

Russo, F. 1937. "Profilaxis en los cafetines." *Revista de la Sociedad Argentina de Venerología y Profilaxis Social* i (1): 95–97.

———. 1944a. "Un agregado indispensable al decreto reglamentario de la ley 12.331." *Revista de Venerología y Profilaxis Social* vii (13): 17–23.

———. 1944b. "Los artículos 15 y 17, modificados por la ley 12.331." *Revista de Venereología y Profilaxis Social* vii (14): 21–25.

Sirlin, L. 1922. *Hacia una cultura sexual*. Buenos Aires: Claridad.

Urbanyi, P. 1976. *El mercado erótico*. Buenos Aires: Analítica.

Vargas Llosa, M. 1990. *Captain Pantoja and the Special Service*. Translated by Gregory Kolovakos and Ronald Christ. New York: Farrar, Straus and Giroux.

Secondary Sources

Ablard, J. D. 2017. "'The Barracks Receives Spoiled Children and Returns Men': Debating Military Service, Masculinity and Nation-Building in Argentina, 1901–1930." *Americas* 74 (3): 299–329.

Acha, O. 2007. "Cartas de amor en la Argentina peronista: Construcciones epistolares del sí mismo, del sentimiento y del lazo político populista." *Nuevo Mundo*. Available at http://nuevomundo.revues.org/document12272.html.

———. 2014. *Crónica sentimental de la Argentina peronista: Sexo, inconsciente e ideología, 1945–1955*. Buenos Aires: Prometeo.

Adamovsky, E. 2012. *Historia de las clases populares en la Argentina: Desde 1880 hasta 2003*. Buenos Aires: Sudamericana.

———. 2014. "La cuarta función del criollismo y las luchas por la definición del origen y el color del ethnos argentino (desde las primeras novelas gauchescas hasta c. 1940)." *Boletín del Instituto de Historia Argentina y Americana Dr. Emilio Ravignani* 41: 50–92.

Aguiló, I. 2018. "The Darkening Nation: Race, Neoliberalism and Crisis in Argentina." Available at http://search.ebscohost.com/login.aspx?direct=true&scope=site&db=nlebk&db=nlabk&an=1839739.

Alberto, P., and E. Elena. 2016. *Rethinking Race in Modern Argentina*. Cambridge: Cambridge University Press.

Albornoz, M., and D. A. Galeano. 2016. "El momento Beastly: La policía de Buenos Aires y la expulsión de extranjeros (1896–1904)." *Astrolabio* 17: 6–41.

Allemandi, C. L. 2017. *Sirvientes, criados y nodrizas: Una historia del servicio doméstico en la ciudad de Buenos Aires (fines del siglo xix y principios del xx)*. Buenos Aires: Teseo.

Allen, J. A. 2002. "Men Interminably in Crisis? Historians on Masculinity, Sexual Boundaries, and Manhood." *Radical History Review* 82 (1): 191–207.

Ansaldi, W., and V. Giordano. 2014. *América Latina: Tiempos de violencias*. Buenos Aires: Planeta.

Armus, D. 2007. *La ciudad impura: Salud, tuberculosis y cultura en Buenos Aires, 1870–1950*. Buenos Aires: Edhasa.

Arnold, J. H., and D. S. Brady. 2011. *What Is Masculinity?* New York: Springer.

Ballent, A. 2005. *Las huellas de la política: Vivienda, ciudad, peronismo en Buenos Aires, 1943–1955*. Bernal, Argentina: Universidad Nacional de Quilmes.

Balsa, J. 2006. *El desvanecimiento del mundo chacarero: Transformaciones sociales en la agricultura bonaerense 1937–1988*. Bernal, Argentina: Universidad Nacional de Quilmes.

Barclay, K. 2014. "Singing, Performance, and Lower-Class Masculinity in the Dublin Magistrates' Court, 1820–1850." *Journal of Social History* 47 (3): 746–68.

Barrancos, D. 2006. "Problematic Modernity: Gender, Sexuality, and Reproduction in Twentieth Century Argentina." *Journal of Women's History* 18 (2): 123–50.

———. 2008. "Feminismo, trata y nuevos tratos." *Mora* 14 (2): 161–64.

———. 2012. *Mujeres en la sociedad argentina: Una historia de cinco siglos*. Buenos Aires: Sudamericana.

———. 2014. "Sentidos, sentimientos y sensibilidades (1880–1930)." *Revista Latinoamericana de Estudios sobre Cuerpos, Emociones y Sociedad* 15 (11): 27–39.

Barreneche, O. 2009. "Por mano propia: La justicia policial de la provincia de Buenos Aires en el primer peronismo." *Sociohistórica* 25: 123–52.

———. 2010. "De brava a dura: La policía de la provincia de Buenos Aires durante la primera mitad del siglo XX." *Cuadernos de Antropología Social* 32: 31–56.

Barrés, M. 1934. *El hampa y sus secretos*. Buenos Aires: Imprenta Lopéz.

Barsky, O., and J. D. Gelman. 2009. *Historia del agro argentino: Desde la conquista hasta comienzos del siglo xxi*. Buenos Aires: Sudamericana.

Bazán, O. 2006. *Historia de la homosexualidad en la Argentina: De la conquista de América al siglo xxi*, vol. 1. Buenos Aires: Marea.

Bembo, M. 1912. *La mala vida en Barcelona*. Barcelona: Manucci.

Ben, P. 2009. *Male Sexuality, the Popular Classes and the State: Buenos Aires, 1880–1955*. Chicago: University of Chicago Press.

———. 2014. "Historia global y prostitución porteña: El fenómeno de la prostitución moderna en Buenos Aires, 1880–1930." *Revista de Estudios Marítimos y Sociales* 5–6: 13–26.

Berger, A. 2016. *El gran teatro del género: Identidades, sexualidades y feminismos*. Buenos Aires: Mardulce.

Berlant, L. 2007. "Slow Death (Sovereignty, Obesity, Lateral Agency)." *Critical Inquiry* 33 (4): 754–80.

Berrotarán, P. M. 2008. "Educar al funcionario: "De la frialdad de las leyes a las innovaciones doctrinarias" (Argentina 1946–1952)." *Nuevo Mundo*. Available at https://journals.openedition.org/nuevomundo/3660.

Biernat, C. 2007. "Médicos, especialistas, políticos y funcionarios en la organización centralizada de la profilaxis de las enfermedades venéreas en la Argentina (1930–1954)." *Anuario de Estudios Americanos* 64 (1): 257–88.

———. 2013. "Entre el abolicionismo y la reglamentación: Prostitución y salud pública en Argentina (1930–1955)." *Cuadernos del Sur* 40 (3): 29–48.

———. 2018. "Cuando los enfermos van a la justicia: Denuncias de varones por contagio venéreo y prácticas punitivas en la provincia de Buenos Aires (1936–1954)." *Historia y Justicia* 10: 104–29.

Biernat, C., and K. I. Ramacciotti. 2013. *Crecer y multiplicarse: La política sanitaria materno–infantil, Argentina 1900–1960*. Buenos Aires: Biblos.

Biernat, C., and P. Simonetto. 2017. "Imaginar a los enfermos: Campañas privadas y públicas de profilaxis venérea en la Argentina de la primera mitad del siglo xx." *Meridional. Revista chilena de estudios latinoamericanos* 9: 113–43.

Bjerg, M. 2013. *Historias de la inmigración en Argentina*. Buenos Aires: Edhasa.

Bloch, M. 2000. *Introducción a la historia*. México City: FCE.

Blum, A. S. 2009. *Domestic Economies: Family, Work, and Welfare in Mexico City, 1884–1943*. Lincoln: University of Nebraska Press.

Bohoslavsky, E. 2006. "Los mitos conspirativos y la Patagonia en Argentina y Chile durante la primera mitad del siglo xx: Orígenes, difusión y supervivencias." PhD diss. Universidad Complutense de Madrid, Geography and History.

Bourdieu, P. 1997. "Espíritu de familia." *Razones prácticas: Sobre la teoría de la acción*. Barcelona: Anagrama, 126–38.

———. 2015. *La dominación masculina*. Barcelona: Anagrama.

Brah, A., and A. Phoenix. 2004. "Ain't I a Woman? Revisiting Intersectionality." *Journal of International Women's Studies* 5 (3): 75–86.

Breckenridge, K. 2000. "Love Letters and Amanuenses: Beginning the Cultural History of the Working Class Private Sphere in Southern Africa, 1900–1933." *Journal of Southern African Studies* 26 (2): 337–48.

Butierrez, M., and P. Simonetto. 2020. "Las embajadoras de Travestilandia." *Moleculas Malucas*. Available at www.moleculasmalucas.com/post/las-embajadoras-de-travestilandia.

Butler, J. 2015. *Cuerpos que importan: Sobre los límites materiales y discursivos del "sexo."* Buenos Aires: Paidós.

Cahn, S. K. 2007. *Sexual Reckonings: Southern Girls in a Troubling Age*. Cambridge, MA: Harvard University Press.

Caimari, L. 1995. *Perón y la Iglesia Católica: Religión, Estado y sociedad en la Argentina (1943–1955)*. Buenos Aires: Ariel.

———. 2004. *Apenas un delincuente: Crimen, castigo y cultura en Buenos Aires, 1880–1940*. Buenos Aires: Siglo XXI.

———. 2012. *Mientras la ciudad duerme: Pistoleros, policías y periodistas en Buenos Aires, 1920–1945*. Buenos Aires: Siglo XXI.

Calandria, S. 2015. "Maternidades en cuestión: Modelos idílicos y prácticas de las madres en Argentina 1892–1936." *Trabajos y Comunicaciones* 41: 1–14.

———. 2016. "En busca de un nuevo orden provincial: El Poder Judicial y el fuero penal en la Provincia de Buenos Aires (1881–1915)." *Revista de Historia del Derecho* 51: 17–48.

Cammarota, A. 2014. *Somos bachiyeres: Juventud, cultura escolar y peronismo en el Colegio Nacional Mixto de Morón (1949–1969)*. Buenos Aires: Biblos.

Chaumont, J. M., M. Rodríguez García, and P. Servais, eds. 2017. *Trafficking in Women 1924–1926: The Paul Kinsie Reports for the League of Nations*, vol. 1. Geneva: UN.

Chaumont, J. M., and A. L. Wibrin. 2007. "Traite des Noirs, traite des Blanches: Même combat?." *Cahiers de recherche sociologique* 43: 121–32.

Conlon, D. 2004. "Productive Bodies, Performative Spaces: Everyday Life in Christopher Park." *Sexualities* 7 (4): 462–79.

Cooper, F., T. C. Holt, and R. J. Scott. 2014. *Beyond Slavery: Explorations of Race, Labor, and Citizenship in Postemancipation Societies*. Chapel Hill: University of North Carolina Press.

Corbin, A. 1988. "La prostituta en la Francia del siglo xix." *Debats* 24: 4–9.

Corrales, J., and M. Pecheny. 2010. *The Politics of Sexuality in Latin America*. Pittsburgh, PA: University of Pittsburgh Press.

Cosse, I. 2006. *Estigmas de nacimiento: Peronismo y orden familiar, 1946–1955*. Buenos Aires: Universidad San Andrés.

———. 2010. *Pareja, sexualidad y familia en los años 60: Una revolución discreta en Buenos Aires*. Buenos Aires: Siglo XXI.

Cowan, B. A. 2016. *Securing Sex: Morality and Repression in the Making of Cold War Brazil.* Chapel Hill: University of North Carolina Press.

Cutuli, M. S. S. 2013. "Maricas y travestis: Repensando experiencias compartidas." *Sociedad y Economía* 24: 183–204.

Daich, D. 2012. "Prostitución, trata y abolicionismo: Conversaciones con Dolores Juliano y Adriana Piscitelli." *Avá* 20: 1–10.

Daich, D., and M. Sirimarco. 2015. "Policías y prostitutas: El control territorial en clave de género." *Publicar en Antropología y Ciencias Sociales* 17. Available at http://ppct.caicyt.gov.ar/index.php/publicar/article/view/4702.

Daich, D., and C. Varela. 2014. "Entre el combate a la trata y la criminalización del trabajo sexual: Las formas de gobierno de la prostitución." *Delito y Sociedad* 23 (38): 63–86.

Dalle, P. 2016. *Movilidad social desde las clases populares: Un estudio sociológico en el Área Metropolitana de Buenos Aires (1960–2013).* Buenos Aires: Ciccus.

D'antonio, D. C. 2016. *La prisión en los años 70: Historia, género y política.* Buenos Aires: Biblos.

De Fanelli, A. M. G. 1991. "Empleo femenino en la Argentina: De la modernización de los 60 a la crisis de los 80." *Desarrollo Económico* XXXI (123): 95–414.

De Luca, J., and V. Lancman. 2010. *Promoción y facilitación de la prostitución.* Available at www.pensamientopenal.com.ar/system/files/cpcomentado/cpc37752.pdf.

Devoto, F. J. 2001. "El revés de la trama: Políticas migratorias y prácticas administrativas en la Argentina (1919–1949)." *Desarrollo Económico* 41 (162): 81–304.

———. 2003. *Historia de la inmigración en la Argentina.* Buenos Aires: Sudamericana.

Doezema, J. 1999. "Loose Women or Lost Women? The Re-Emergence of the Myth of White Slavery in Contemporary Discourses of Trafficking in Women." *Gender Issues* 18 (1): 23–50.

Drinot, P. 2006. *Moralidad, moda y sexualidad: El contexto moral de la creación del Barrio Rojo de Lima.* Lima: Instituto Riva Agüero.

Eidelman, A. E. 2015. "El desarrollo de los aparatos represivos del Estado argentino durante la 'revolución Argentina,' 1966–1973." PhD diss., University of Buenos Aires.

Elena, E. 2005. "What the People Want: State Planning and Political Participation in Peronist Argentina, 1946–1955." *Journal of Latin American Studies* 37 (1): 81–108.

Farge, A. 2008. *Efusión y tormento, el relato de los cuerpos: Historia del pueblo en el siglo xviii.* Buenos Aires: Katz.

———. 2013. *The Allure of the Archives.* New Haven, CT: Yale University Press.

Federici, S. 2017. *Revolución en punto cero: Trabajo doméstico, reproducción y luchas feministas.* Madrid: Traficantes de Sueños.

Felitti, K. 2012. *La revolución de la píldora: Política y sexualidad en la Argentina de los 60.* Buenos Aires: Edhasa.

Foucault, M. 2012. *Historia de la sexualidad*, vol. 1: *La voluntad del saber.* Madrid: Biblioteca Nueva.

Freidenraij, C. 2016. "Intervenciones policiales sobre la infancia urbana. Ciudad de Buenos Aires, 1885–1920." *Historia y Justicia* 6: 164–97.

Galeano, D. 2016. *Criminosos viajantes: Circulações transnacionais entre Rio de Janeiro e Buenos Aires, 1890–1930.* Río de Janeiro: Ministério da Justiça, Arquivo Nacional.

Gallagher, C., and T. W. Laqueur. 1987. *The Making of the Modern Body: Sexuality and Society in the Nineteenth Century.* Oakland: University of California Press.

Garazi, D. 2016. "Del 'trabajo de servidor' al 'trabajo asalariado': Debates en torno a la remuneración de los trabajadores del sector hotelero–gastronómico en Argentina en las décadas centrales del siglo xx." *Pasado Abierto* 2 (3): 106–27.

García, M. R. 2012. "The League of Nations and the Moral Recruitment of Women." *International Review of Social History* 57 (S20): 97–128.

Gayol, S. 2000. *Sociabilidad en Buenos Aires: Hombres, honor y cafés, 1862–1910.* Buenos Aires: Del Signo.

Giddens, A. 2000. *The Transformation of Intimacy: Sexuality, Love and Eroticism in Modern Societies.* Stanford, CA: Stanford University Press.

Gilfoyle, T. J. 1999. "Prostitutes in History: From Parables of Pornography to Metaphors of Modernity." *American Historical Review* 104 (1): 117–41.

Ginzburg, C. 1991. "O inquisidor como antropólogo." *Revista Brasileira de História* 21: 9–20.

Giordano, V. 2012. *Ciudadanas incapaces: La construcción de los derechos civiles de las mujeres en Argentina, Brasil, Chile y Uruguay en el siglo xx.* Buenos Aires: Teseo.

Giordano, V., K. I. Ramacciotti, and A. M. Valobra, eds. 2015. *Contigo ni pan ni cebolla: Debates y prácticas sobre el divorcio vincular en Argentina, 1932–1968.* Buenos Aires: Biblos.

Girbal-Blacha, N. 2010. "La memoria rural de la Argentina del Bicentenario." *Revista Pilquen* 12. Available at http://170.210.83.53/htdoc/ revele/index.php /Sociales/article/view/1921.

Godelier, M. 2000. *Cuerpo, parentesco y poder: Perspectivas antropológicas y críticas.* Quito: Pontificia Universidad Católica del Ecuador-Abya-Yala.

González Leandri, R., P. González Bernaldo de Quirós, and J. Suriano. 2010. *La temprana cuestión social. La ciudad de Buenos Aires durante la segunda mitad del siglo xix.* Madrid: CSIC.

Grammático, K. 2002. *Obreras, prostitutas y mal venéreo: Un Estado en busca de la profilaxis.* Buenos Aires: Taurus.

Gutiérrez, T. V. 2007. *Educación, agro y sociedad: Políticas educativas agrarias en la región pampeana, 1897–1955.* Bernal, Argentina: Universidad Nacional de Quilmes.

Guy, D. 1991. *Sex and Danger in Buenos Aires: Prostitution, Family, and Nation in Buenos Aires.* Lincoln: University of Nebraska Press.

———. 2000. *White Slavery and Mothers Alive and Dead: The Troubled Meeting of Sex, Gender, Public Health, and Progress in Latin America*. Lincoln: University of Nebraska Press.

———. 2003. *Rape and the Politics of Masculine Silence in Argentina*. Durham, NC: Duke University Press.

———. 2008. *Women Build the Welfare State: Performing Charity and Creating Rights in Argentina, 1880–1955*. Durham, NC: Duke University Press.

———. 2017. *La construcción del carisma peronista: Cartas a Juan y Eva Perón*. Buenos Aires: Biblos.

Hershatter, G. 1997. *Dangerous Pleasures: Prostitution and Modernity in Twentieth Century Shanghai*. Oakland, CA: University of California Press.

Herzog, D. 2008. *Brutality and Desire: War and Sexuality in Europe's Twentieth Century*. New York: Springer.

———. 2011. *Sexuality in Europe: A Twentieth Century History*. Cambridge: Cambridge University Press.

Hofman, E. 2017. "Managing Stigma: Prostitutes and Their Communities in the Southern Netherlands, 1750–1800." *Histoire Sociale/Social History* 50 (101): 3–18.

Howell, P. 2004. "Race, Space and the Regulation of Prostitution in Colonial Hong Kong." *Urban History* 31 (2): 229–48.

Insausti, S. J. 2011. "Selva, plumas y desconche: Un análisis de las performances masculinas de la feminidad entre las locas del Tigre durante la década del 80." Available at https://dialnet.unirioja.es/servlet/ articulo?codigo= 3804693.

Jeffreys, S. 2011. *La industria de la vagina*. Buenos Aires: Paidós.

Johnson, C. R. 2013. *Just Queer Folks: Gender and Sexuality in Rural America*. Philadelphia: Temple University Press.

Jones, G. S. 1983. *Languages of Class: Studies in English Working Class History 1832–1982*. Cambridge: Cambridge University Press.

Jordan, J. 2007. *Josephine Butler*. New York: Hambledon Continuum.

Kalifa, D. 2013. *Les bas-fonds. Histoire d'un imaginaire*. Paris: Seuil.

Klubock, T. M. 1998. *Contested Communities: Class, Gender, and Politics in Chile's El Teniente Copper Mine, 1904–1951*. Durham, NC: Duke University Press.

Knepper, P. 2011. *International Crime in the 20th Century: The League of Nations Era, 1919–1939*. New York: Springer.

Kozma, L. 2016. "Women's Migration for Prostitution in the Interwar Middle East and North Africa." *Journal of Women's History* 28 (3): 93–113.

Laite, J. 2011. "Common Prostitutes and Ordinary Citizens: Commercial Sex in London, 1885–1960." New York: Springer.

———. 2017. "Between Scylla and Charybdis: Women's Labour Migration and Sex Trafficking in the Early Twentieth Century." *International Review of Social History* 62 (1): 37–65.

Lamas, M. 2017. *Fulgor de la noche: El comercio sexual en las calles de la Ciudad de México*. Océano: Ciudad de México.

Ledesma Prietto, N. F., and K. Ramacciotti. 2014. "Saberes médicos y legales en la legitimación de la separación y el divorcio en la Argentina (1930–1955)." Available at https://revistas.unc.edu.ar/index.php/anuariohistoria/article /view/9367.

Leite Lopes, J. S. 2011. *El vapor del diablo: El trabajo de los obreros del azúcar.* Buenos Aires: Antropofagia.

Levi, G. 1990. *La herencia inmaterial: La historia de un exorcista piamontés del siglo xvii.* Madrid: Nerea.

Limoncelli, S. A. 2006. "International Voluntary Associations, Local Social Movements and State Paths to the Abolition of Regulated Prostitution in Europe, 1875–1950." *International Sociology* 21 (1): 31–59.

Linares, L. 2016. "La ley en los cuerpos ajenos: Prostitución rural y tensiones entre práctica y discurso médico en relación con las enfermedades venéreas: El caso del sudeste bonaerense en las primeras décadas del siglo xx." PhD diss., Universidad Nacional de Mar del Plata.

Lobato, M. Z. 2008. "Trabajo, cultura y poder: Dilemas historiográficos y estudios de género en Argentina." *Estudios de Filosofía Práctica e Historia de las Ideas* 10 (2): 29–45.

Losada, L. 2009. *Historia de las elites en la Argentina: Desde la conquista hasta el surgimiento del peronismo.* Buenos Aires: Sudamericana.

Loyola, M., and H. Camarero. 2016. *Política y cultura en los sectores populares y de las izquierdas latinoamericanas en el siglo XX.* Santiago de Chile: Ariadna.

Maynes, M. J., J. L. Pierce, and B. Laslett. 2012. *Telling Stories: The Use of Personal Narratives in the Social Sciences and History.* Ithaca, NY: Cornell University Press.

McGee Deutsch, S. 2005. "Contra 'el gran desorden sexual': Los nacionalistas y la sexualidad, 1919–1940." *Sociohistórica* 17–18: 127–50.

Ménétra, J. L., R. Darnton, and A. Goldhammer. 1986. *Journal of My Life.* New York: Columbia University Press.

Milanesio, N. 2005. "Redefining Men's Sexuality, Resignifying Male Bodies: The Argentine Law of Anti-Venereal Prophylaxis, 1936." *Gender & History* 17 (2): 463–91.

———. 2014. "A Man Like You: Juan Domingo Perón and the Politics of Attraction in Mid-Twentieth Century Argentina." *Gender & History* 26 (1): 84–104.

Milanich, N. B. 2010. *Children of Fate: Childhood, Class, and the State in Chile, 1850–1930.* Durham, NC: Duke University Press.

Miranda, M. 2011. *Controlar lo incontrolable: Una historia de la sexualidad en la Argentina.* Buenos Aires: Biblos.

———. 2012. "Buenos Aires, entre Eros y Tánatos: La prostitución como amenaza disgénica (1930–1955)." *Dynamis* 32 (1): 93–113.

Mirelman, V. A. 1984. "The Jewish Community Versus Crime: The Case of White Slavery in Buenos Aires." *Jewish Social Studies* 46 (2): 145–68.

Morcillo, S. 2010. "De cómo vender sexo y no morir en el intento: Fronteras encarnadas y tácticas de quienes trabajan en el mercado sexual." *Revista Latinoamericana de Estudios sobre Cuerpos, Emociones y Sociedad* 2 (7): 17–28.

———. 2014. "'Como un trabajo.' Tensiones entre sentidos de lo laboral y la sexualidad en mujeres que hacen sexo comercial en Argentina." *Sexualidad, Salud y Sociedad. Revista Latinoamericana* 18: 12–40.

Múgica, M. L. 2001. *Sexo bajo control: La prostitución reglamentada, un escabroso asunto de política municipal (Rosario entre 1900 y 1912)*. Rosario, Argentina: Universidad Nacional de Rosario.

———. 2014. *La ciudad de las Venus impúdicas: Rosario, historia y prostitución, 1874–1932*. Rosario, Argentina: Laborde.

Nari, M. M. A. 2004. *Políticas de maternidad y maternalismo político: Buenos Aires, 1890–1940*. Buenos Aires: Biblos.

Navarro Floria, P., and P. G. Núñez. 2012. "Un territorio posible en la República imposible: El coronel Sarobe y los problemas de la Patagonia argentina." *Andes* 23 (2): 1–18.

Nouwen, M. L. 2013. *Oy, My Buenos Aires: Jewish Immigrants and the Creation of Argentine National Identity*. Albuquerque: University of New Mexico Press.

Otero, H. 2006. *Estadística y nación: Una historia conceptual del pensamiento censal de la Argentina moderna, 1869–1914*. Buenos Aires: Prometeo.

Pagani, E., and M. V. Alcaraz. 1991. *Mercado laboral del menor (1900–1940)*. Buenos Aires: Ceal.

Palacio, J. M. 2004. *La paz del trigo: Cultura legal y sociedad local en el desarrollo agropecuario pampeano, 1890–1945*. Buenos Aires: Edhasa.

Panter-Brick, C., and M. T. Smith, eds. 2000. *Abandoned Children*. Cambridge: Cambridge University Press.

Pastoriza, E. 2008. "El turismo social en la Argentina durante el primer peronismo. Mar del Plata, la conquista de las vacaciones y los nuevos rituales obreros, 1943–1955." *Nuevo Mundo*. Available at https://journals. openedition .org/nuevomundo/36472.

Pateman, C. 2018. *The Sexual Contract*. Stanford, CA: Stanford University Press.

Peralta, P. J. F. 2015. *The Oldest Professions in Revolutionary Times: Madames, Pimps, and Prostitution in Mexico City, 1920–1952*. Toronto: York University.

Pereira, C. S. 2005. "Lavar, passar e receber visitas: Debates sobre a regulamentação da prostituição e experiências de trabalho sexual em Buenos Aires e no Rio de Janeiro, fim do século xix." *Cadernos Pagu* 25: 25–54.

Pérez, I. 2016. "Hurto, consumo y género en el servicio doméstico: Mar del Plata, 1950–1980." *Anuario del iehs* 31 (2): 57–78.

———. 2017. "Consumo y género: Una revisión de la producción historiográfica reciente sobre América Latina en el siglo xx." *Historia Crítica* 65: 29–48.

Pérez, I., and S. Canevaro. 2016. "Entre lo público y lo privado: Empleadores y trabajadoras domésticas frente al Tribunal del Trabajo Doméstico de la ciudad de Buenos Aires." *Política y Sociedad* 53 (1): 169–86.

Pérez, I., R. Cutuli, and D. Garazi. 2018. *Senderos que se bifurcan: Servicio doméstico y derechos laborales en la Argentina del siglo XX*. Mar del Plata, Argentina: Eudem.

Pérez, I., and D. Garazi. 2014. "Mucamas y domésticas: Trabajo femenino, justicia y desigualdad (Mar del Plata, Argentina, 1956–1974)." *Cadernos Pagu* 42: 313–40.

Perlongher, N. O. 1999. *El negocio del deseo: La prostitución masculina en San Pablo*, vol. 3. Buenos Aires: Paidós.

Piglia, M. 2014. *Autos, rutas y turismo: El Automóvil Club Argentino y el Estado*. Buenos Aires: Siglo XXI.

Pinazo, M. 1918. *Delitos y delincuentes (el transplantetrasplante siniestro)*. Buenos Aires: Cúneo.

Piscitelli, A., and L. Lowenkron. 2015. "Categorias em movimento: A gestão de vítimas do tráfico de pessoas na Espanha e no Brasil." *Ciência e Cultura* 67 (2): 35–39.

Pite, R. E. 2016. *La mesa está servida: Doña Petrona C. de Gandulfo y la domesticidad en la Argentina del siglo XX*. Buenos Aires: Edhasa.

Plumauzille, C., and M. Rossigneux-Méheust. 2014. "Le stigmate ou 'la différence comme catégorie utile d'analyse historique.'" *Hypothèses* 17 (1): 215–28.

Potash, R. A. 1994. *El Ejército y la política en la Argentina, 1945–1962: De Perón a Frondizi*. Buenos Aires: Sudamericana.

Premo, B. 2017. *The Enlightenment on Trial: Ordinary Litigants and Colonialism in the Spanish Empire*. Oxford: Oxford University Press.

Putnam, L. 2013. *Género, poder y migración en el Caribe costarricense, 1870–1960*. San José, Costa Rica: Instituto Nacional de la Mujer.

Queirolo, G. 2014. "Género y sexualidad en tiempos de males venéneros (Buenos Aires, 1920–1940)." *Nomadías* 17: 67–87.

———. 2018. *Mujeres en las oficinas: Trabajo, género y clase en el sector administrativo: Buenos Aires, 1910–1950*. Buenos Aires: Biblos.

Ramacciotti, K. I., and A. M. Valobra. 2008. "El campo médico argentino y su mirada al tribadismo, 1936–1955." *Estudos Feministas* 16 (2): 493–516.

Rein, R. 1999. "Preparando el camino para el peronismo: Juan A. Bramuglia como interventor federal en la provincia de Buenos Aires." *Revista Europea de Estudios Latinoamericanos y del Caribe* 67: 35–55.

Revenin, R. 2005. *Homosexualité et prostitution masculines à Paris, 1870–1918*. París: L'Harmattan.

Rey, F. 2009. *Cárcel y mujeres: ¿Delito o pecado?* La Plata: SPB.

Ribeiro, V. V. 2008. *Cuestiones agrarias en el varguismo y el peronismo: Una mirada histórica*. Bernal, Argentina: Universidad Nacional de Quilmes.

Riobó, C. 2019. *Caught Between the Lines: Captives, Frontiers, and National Identity in Argentine Literature and Art*. Lincoln: University of Nebraska Press.

Riva, B. C. 2011. *El perito médico en los delitos sexuales*. PhD diss., Facultad de Humanidades y Ciencias de la Educación.

Roberts, M. L. 2010. "The Price of Discretion: Prostitution, Venereal Disease, and the American Military in France, 1944–1946." *American Historical Review* 115 (4): 1002–30.

Rodríguez García, M., E. van Nederveen Meerkerk, and A. F. Heerma van Voss. 2016. *Selling Sex in the City: Prostitution in World Cities, 1600 to the Present*. Leiden, Germany: Brill.

Roediger, D. R. 1999. *The Wages of Whiteness: Race and the Making of the American Working Class*. London: Verso.

Rossiaud, J. 1976. "Prostitution, jeunesse et société dans les villes du Sud-Est au XVe siècle." *Annales. Histoire, Sciences Sociales* 31 (2): 289–325.

Ruocco, L. 2008. "De las obreras de la conserva a las fileteras: Cambios y continuidades del trabajo femenino en la industria del pescado, Mar del Plata 1942–1975." *Revista de Estudios Marítimos y Sociales* 1: 127–30.

Sabsay, L. 2011. *Fronteras sexuales: Espacio urbano, cuerpos y ciudadanía.* Buenos Aires: Paidós.

Salessi, J. 2000. *Médicos, maleantes y maricas: Higiene, criminología y homosexualidad en la construcción de la Nación Argentina (Buenos Aires 1871–1914).* Rosario, Argentina: Beatriz Viterbo.

Salvatore, R. D. 2013. *Subalternos, derechos y justicia penal: Ensayos de historia social y cultural argentina 1829–1940.* Buenos Aires: Gedisa.

Sanders, T. 2017. "The Risks of Street Prostitution: Punters, Police and Protesters." *Feminist Theories of Crime.* Edited by Mary Morash. London: Routledge.

Scheinkman, L. 2017. "Trabajo femenino, masculino e infantil en la industria del dulce porteña en la primera mitad del siglo xx: Experiencias laborales, protesta y vida cotidiana." PhD diss., Universidad de Buenos Aires.

Schettini, C. 2014. "Conexiones transnacionales: Agentes encubiertos y tráfico de mujeres en los años 1920." *Nuevo Mundo.* Available at https://journals .openedition.org/nuevomundo/67440.

———. 2016. "Ordenanzas municipales, autoridad policial y trabajo femenino: La prostitución clandestina en Buenos Aires, 1870–1880." *Historia y Justicia* 6: 72–102.

Scott, J. W. 2001. "Experiencia." *La Ventana* 2 (13): 42–74.

———. 2016. "Género: ¿Todavía una categoría útil para el análisis?" *La Manzana de la Discordia* 6 (1): 95–101.

Scoular, J. 2004. "The 'Subject' of Prostitution: Interpreting the Discursive, Symbolic and Material Position of Sex/Work in Feminist Theory." *Feminist Theory* 5 (3): 343–55.

Sedgwick, E. K. 1998. *Epistemología del armario.* Barcelona: De la Tempestad.

Segato, R. 2017. "La estructura de género y el mandato de violación." In *Mujeres intelectuales: feminismo y liberación en América Latina y el Caribe,* edited by A. de Santiago Guzmán, E. Caballero Borja, and G. González Ortuño. Buenos Aires: Clacso.

Sewell, W. H., Jr. 2005. *Logics of History: Social Theory and Social Transformation.* Chicago: University of Chicago Press.

Simonetto, P. 2016. "La moral institucionalizada: Reflexiones sobre el Estado, las sexualidades y la violencia en la Argentina del siglo xx." *e–l@tina. Revista electrónica de estudios latinoamericanos* 14 (55): 1–22.

———. 2017. "Fronteras del deseo: Homosexualidad." *Cadernos Pagu* 49: e174914.

———. 2018. "Intimidades disidentes: Intersecciones en las experiencias de homosexuales y lesbianas en Buenos Aires durante los 60 y 70." *Trashumante. Revista americana de historia social* 11: 28–50.

———. 2019. "Perón and the Female Visitors: Masculinity, Sex Consumption and Military Opposition to the Abolition of Regulated Prostitution, Argentina,

1936–1955." Translated by Catherine Jagoe. *História, Ciências, Saúde-Manguinhos* 26 (2): 427–43.

Soprano, G. 2016. "Culturas militares na Argentina do século xix ao inicio do xxi." *Militares e democracia: Estudos sobre a identidade militar.* Edited by D. Zirker and K. Suzeley. São Paulo: Cultura Acadêmica.

Stagno, L., and N. Giovagnetti. 2010. *Una infancia aparte: La minoridad en la provincia de Buenos Aires (1930–1943).* Buenos Aires: Flacso. Available at http://site.ebrary.com/id/10664969.

Stearns, P. N. 2017. *Sexuality in World History.* London: Routledge.

Suriano, J. 1988. *Trabajadores, anarquismo y Estado represor: De la Ley de Residencia a la Ley de Defensa Social (1902–1910).* Buenos Aires: Ceal.

———. 2009. "¿Cuál es hoy la historia de los trabajadores en la Argentina?" *Mundos do Trabalho* 1 (1): 27–50.

Swedberg, G. 2017. "Moralizing Public Space: Prostitution, Disease, and Social Disorder in Orizaba, Mexico, 1910–1945." *Journal of Social History* 52 (1): 54–73.

Tanaka, Y. 2003. *Japan's Comfort Women.* London: Routledge.

Tenti, M. M. 2012. "Los estudios culturales, la historiografía y los sectores subalternos." *Trabajo y Sociedad* 18: 317–29.

Thomas, L. M. 2016. "Historicising Agency." *Gender & History* 28 (2): 324–39.

Thompson, E. P. 1989. "Folklore, antropología e historia social." *Historia Social* 3: 81–102.

Tinsman, H. 1995. "Patrones del hogar: Esposas golpeadas y control sexual en el Chile rural, 1958–1988." *Disciplina y desacato: Construcción de identidad en Chile, siglos xix y xx.* Edited by L. Godoy, E. Hutchison, K. Rosemblatt, and M. S. Zárate. Santiago de Chile: Sur-Cedem, 111–46.

Torrado, S. 2003. *Historia de la familia en la Argentina moderna (1870–2000).* Buenos Aires: De la Flor.

Tosh, J. 2007. *A Man's Place: Masculinity and the Middle-Class Home in Victorian England.* New Haven, CT: Yale University Press.

Toulalan, S., and K. Fisher. 2013. *The Routledge History of Sex and the Body: 1500 to the Present.* London: Routledge.

Valobra, A. M. 2008. "Feminismo, sufragismo y mujeres en los partidos políticos en la Argentina de la primera mitad del siglo XX." *Amnis. Revue de civilisation contemporaine Europes/Amériques* 8. Available at www.memoria.fahce.unlp .edu.ar/art_revistas/pr.7382/pr.7382.pdf.

———. 2015. "El Estado y las mujeres, concepciones en clave feminista." *Estudios Sociales del Estado* 1 (2): 33–57.

Van der Linden, M. 2008. *Workers of the World: Essays Toward a Global Labor History*, vol. 1. Leiden, Germany: Brill.

Villalta, C. 2012. *Entregas y secuestros: El rol del Estado en la apropiación de niños.* Buenos Aires: Del Puerto.

Villulla, J. M. 2014. *Las cosechas son ajenas: Historia de los trabajadores rurales detrás del agronegocio.* Ituzaingó, Argentina: Cienflores.

Wacquant, L., and H. Moreno. 2007. "Carisma y masculinidad en el boxeo." *Debate Feminista* 36: 30–40.

Walkowitz, J. R. 1982. *Prostitution and Victorian Society: Women, Class, and the State*. Cambridge: Cambridge University Press.

Widdows, H. 2013. "Rejecting the Choice Paradigm: Rethinking the Ethical Framework in Prostitution and Egg Sale Debates." *Gender, Agency, and Coercion*. Edited by S. Madhok. New York: Springer, 157–80.

Yarfitz, M. 2012. "Polacos, White Slaves, and Stille Chuppahs: Organized Prostitution and the Jews of Buenos Aires, 1890–1939." PhD diss., University of California Los Angeles.

———. 2019. *Impure Migration: Jews and Sex Work in Golden Age Argentina*. Brunswick, NJ: Rutgers University Press.

Zapiola, M. 2008. "La Ley de Patronato de 1919: Una reestructuración parcial de los vínculos entre Estado y 'minoridad.'" *Jornadas de Historia de la Infancia en Argentina "1880–1960. Enfoques, problemas y perspectivas."* Los Polvorines, Argentina: Universidad Nacional de General Sarmiento.

Zelizer, V. A. R. 2005. *The Purchase of Intimacy*. Princeton, NJ: Princeton University Press.

Index

Italic page numbers refer to illustrations.

Benjamin, Walter, 1
Board of Catholic Action, 73
body, symbolism of: and Evita, 71;
   genitalia, 112–13, 157–58; male
   performance, 147, 149–50; penetration, 112–13
*Boletín Mensual de la sociedad de las
   Naciones,* 26
borders, national, and human trafficking, 18, 23, 48–49, 64
brothels: in Buenos Aires, 41; design
   and architecture of, 64; emergency,
   65; Kinsie's interviews, 39–40;
   replacement of, 180–81; as space for
   men, 148. *See also* abolitionism;
   military brothels
Buenos Aires: arrest and detention of
   women in, 88–89; court system of,
   84; economic frameworks, 107;
   housing access, 36; migration to, 99;
   in prostitution chains, 46–48
Buenos Aires Penitentiary Service
   (SPB), 59
Butierrez, Marce Joan, 170
Butler, Josephine, 23

Caistor, Nick, 148
Captain Pantoja and the Special Service
   (Vargas Llosa), 51, 63
Carrillo, Ramón, 55–56, 67, 74
Casa y Caretas (magazine), 137
Castaño, Enrique, 65
catcalls, 155, 158
Catholic Action, 71, 73
Catholic Church: culture in military, 56;
   and Eva/Evita Perón, 71; opposition
   to licensed brothels, 51–52; resistance
   to reforms of Prophylaxis Law, 72–73;
   women's organizations, 55–56; and
   women's roles, 73–74
CEMLA (Centro de Estudios Migratorios
   Latinoamericanos), 33
children. *See* minors
Chile, legislation in, 26
Circle of Catholic Women, 73

Circle of Housewives, 73
cities. *See* urban areas
class stratification, 113, 114–15; and
   consumption of sexual services, 138;
   and men's group rituals, 151; social
   control of working class, 15; and
   "whiteness," 27
Coll, Jorge Eduardo, 82
Committee for the Defense of the
   Woman's Dignity, 72
Committee for the Suppression of
   Traffic in Women and Children, 18,
   26, 43
Committee in Defense of Women's
   Dignity, 73
Comodoro Rivadavia (military zone), 55
condom use, 151, 155, 157–58, 168
Contagious Diseases Act (UK/1864), 54
Córdoba, Argentina, 49
Cosse, Isabella, 9
Costa Rica, 123–24
courtship, 41, 121–22, 128, 132
Crespo, Horacio, 63
Crónica (newspaper), 174
cross-dressing, 169–70
Cuba, legislation in, 26

Darnton, Robert, 147–48
Dávila, Pablo, 61–62
Delfino, Victor, 72
deportation, 13–14, 18–19; illicit
   payments to state officials, 47;
   Ministry of Interior documents, 21; of
   procurers and pimps, 40, 46–47
divorce: and Catholic Church, 52; and
   infidelity, 143; law, 71, 119. *See also*
   marriage
domestic labor: definitions of, 94; and
   women, 114; as workforce classification, 90, 107–8, 166
Dominican Republic, legislation in, 26

Echeverria, Esteban, 23–24
Egypt, legislation in, 25
Elena, E., 24

El Extranjero (newspaper), 48
El Gladiador, 28, 29
Emergency Economic Plan (1952), 182
erectile dysfunction, 150
¡Esto! (magazine), 169
eugenics, 24, 72
Eva Perón Foundation, 92
Eyle, Petrona, 28

familial relationships: hierarchical, 43;
and housing policy, 69; idealized, 71
Farrell, Edelmiro, 51–52
Federation of Argentine Marian
Congregations, 73
Federation of Mercy Alumni Centers, 73
feminism: approaches to prostitution,
28; perspectives, 6; pro-sex, xi; and
women's rights, 73
Fiscal Oilfields (YPF), 55, 62
France: legislation in, 25; procurement
networks, 37–38
Frente de Liberación Homosexual, 169

Galli, Eugenio, 55, 61, 64–65
Gálvez, Manuel, 28, 30, 119
García, Enrique, 66
García, Germán, 149
Garzón, Rafael, 167
Gayol, Sandra, 150
Gelblum, Cecilia, 43
gendered roles: androcentric ap-
proaches to female sexuality, 185;
feminization of imprisoned women,
88; history of, 10; in imprisoned
populations, 90–91, 94–95, 95,
96–100; male sexuality, 136–38;
masculine performance in courtship,
121–22; traditional, 30. See also male
sexuality; masculinity; women
genitalia, symbolism of, 112–13, 157–58
German League Against White
Slavery, 47
Gilbert, Luis Alberto, 55, 60–61
Giménez, Ángel, 31
Global South, stereotypes of, x, 25

Gobatto, Matías, 139
Goldberg, Motche, 20, 34–36, 38–42,
44–48
Goldestein, Isidoro, 42
Gómez, Eusebio, 82
gonorrhea, 58–59. See also venereal
disease
Gothier, Alce, 43
Guy, Donna, 10

Hackett, Lewis, 65–66
health. See public health
Heit, Sabina, 42
heteronormativity, 2–3, 22, 71, 105, 140
highway system, 161, 163, 167, 168, 170,
177–80, 192
historiography, 2, 5, 8, 15–16, 23
homosexuality, 113; attitudes toward,
41; fear of, 60, 61; jail detention of
gay men, 70; men as sex workers,
168–69; and prostitution, 86–87;
uranistas (gay men), 113
human trafficking: media coverage of,
31; UN treaty, 85

Illia, Arturuo Umberto, 164
illiteracy/literacy, 91, 98, 109, 166–67
immigration, 18–19; from Europe,
26–27; and labor force, 27–28; and
moral panic, 30; reform (1923), 43;
selection processes, 19; of single
women, 40. See also deportation
imprisonment: agency of prisoners,
91–92; education during, 93; gender
binaries and work roles, 90–91;
medical treatments, 92–93; Peronist
reforms, 93; prison knowledge
networks, 101; self-definitions of
women, 94–95, 95; women's lived
experiences, 96–100; of women with
children, 90
infidelity, marital, 143
Institute for Hygiene and Social
Medicine, 167
International Congress of Women, 28

minors: children's aid, 26; domestic arrangements for, 109–11; juvenile court system, 110–11; legal age limits, 113–14; "placement" of girls, 165, 184; and sale of sex, 82, 165

misdemeanor codes, 57, 70, 74–75, 81–82, 86, 162, 172, 176

moral issues: institutionalization of morality, 193–94; judgment of sex work, 124; judgment of women, 105–6; moral panic and violence, 9, 87; public debate regarding, 69, 78; public morality (concept), 105–6, 172; public morality and legal system, 86

Moreno, Rodolfo, 82

National Autonomist Party, 129

National Board for Health and Social Welfare, 65

National Conference on Venereal Diseases, 65

National Democratic Party, 129

National Department of Hygiene, 55

National Institute of Nutrition, 108

nationalism: border fears, 49; and male sexuality, 57–62; nation-building and borders, 23; and whiteness, 119

National Military College cadet incident, 61, 87

National Patronage of Juveniles, 110–11

National Professional School, 73

neighborhoods, 115–16; "neighbor," concept of, 106

Neiman, Nysel, 43

Nicaragua, legislation in, 26

Olite, Milena, 43

Olmos prison (La Plata), 14, 16, 79, 87–88

onanism, 142; law 12.331, 60

Onganía, Juan Carlos, 172, 174

Opizzo, José, 150

Order of the Good Shepherd, 87. *See also* Olmos, La Plata, prison

"Paisano Díaz" (pseudonym), 21–22

Palacios, Alfredo, 18, 31

Pareja, Ernesto, 32, 59, 119, 139

Patagonia: metaphor for empty country, 56; Patagonia Association, 55

patriarchy: androcentric approaches to female sexuality, 185; "droit du seigneur," 114–15

Patronage of Minors law, 110

Perlinger, Luis César, 55, 57, 63, 64–65

Perón, Eva/Evita, 71

Perón, Juan Domingo, 1, 14, 16, 51, 137; decree 22.532, 81; executive order 22.532, 51–52; law 12.331, 60; law 12.912, 67; law 12.912 (1947), 51; letters defending military brothels, 55; as public symbol, 57; and return to regulationist systems, 66

Peronism: decree 22.532, 74; misde- meanor codes, 74–75; Peronist cultural constructions, 52; potential vs. limitations, 52–53

Petijón, Santiago, 42–43

pimping, 32–35; commission agents, 40, 46; contextual aspects, 7, 19, 21; ethnic identities of, 38; familial and marriage relationships, 42–43; in First World War, 37–38; international networks, 37; narratives of, 21–32; nicknames of, 40–41; in popular culture, 22, 28; practices and social meanings, 38–45; role of, 18–20; rufianes vs. canflineros, 38–39, 162; and selection of women, 42; social networks, 35–38; state officials and bribery, 47–48; transnational movement, 11, 12, 45–49

Pittarino, Juan, 43

police: abolitionism models, 80; abuse by, 161; militarization of, 82; misdemeanor codes and public morality, 172–73; oversight of detained women, 85–86, 105, 106; portrayal as ineffective, 31–32; prohibitionism models, 80; punitive

police (cont.)
law, 78; and raids, 174–75; regulationism models, 80; territorial power,
171–77; training and working
conditions of, 34
Polish prostitution, 44
pornography, 68
poverty: in Buenos Aires, 107; and
domestic placement, 115; and
parental custody, 116; and placement
of minors, 110–12; in rural areas, 165;
women's self-sufficiency, 117; and
workforce, 107–8
private vs. public space. See spaces
procurement. See pimping
prohibitionism model, 80
Prophylaxis Law (law 12.331) (1936):
articles and provisions, 80–87;
defense of, 68; eugenic reforms to,
72; health care objectives, 100;
impact of, 19; influence of, 64–65;
interpretation of, 59; and jail
sentences, 81; loopholes, 103; and
masculine norms, 51, 58; medical
support for, 65; and police power,
81–82; and public health measures,
85; reforms to, 3, 64–65, 72–73,
82–85; regulationist vs. abolitionist
debates, 86–87; as restrictive, 60
prostitution: arrests and prison
sentences for, 77, 83, 83–93; criteria
for pimps' selection of, 42; definitions
and terms, 3, 7–8; demographics of
sex consumers, 141; diversity and
complexity of, 191–92; domestic
construction of, 109–16; group
payment for, 148; history of, 10; and
homosexuality, 86–87; identity and
meaning, 11, 93–96, 102, 123–24; men
as sex workers, 168–69; mobility and
migration, 109, 126–31, 178–82;
negotiated networks, 120–26, 194;
negotiation of price, 144–45; profiles
and pathways to, 104–9; regulatory
system, 51–52; scholarly approaches

to, 10–11; sex as entertainment,
140–47; and state intervention,
192–93; status by ethnicity, 44;
stigma, 89, 93–96, 124; tactics to
avoid police, 176–77; transnational
movement, 11, 12; *travestismo*
(cross-dressing), 169–70;
unionization, 69; and use of family
home for, 125
prostitution, legal frameworks for: 1917
bill, 82; 1921 code, 82; 1937 bill, 82;
1941 bill, 82; 1953 bill, 82–83; article
126 (1960), 83; court systems, 84; law
12.912 (1947), 51, 67; Law 16.666
(1965), 162, 173; law 19.903 (1919)
(Patronage of Minors), 110; law
21.338 (1976), 83; military decree, 85;
misdemeanors code (1956), 57, 70,
74–75, 81–82, 86, 162, 172, 176; penal
code bill (1906), 82; regulation and
licensure (1875), 10, 19, 77, 105. See
also Prophylaxis Law (law 12.331)
(1936)
public health: ambiguity of regulations,
85; androcentric concepts, 31, 59,
157; policies, 27. See also venereal
disease
public space. See spaces
Putnam, Lara, 123–24

Quevedo, José, 62, 67–69, 136–37

racial issues: Argentina as "white"
nation, 24, 27, 30–31, 32, 118–19, 195;
white masculinity, 19
railroad workers, raid in San
Martín, 70
Rama, Ramón, 43
Ramírez, Pedro Pablo, 1, 51, 55
rape, 61–62, 185
Reflejos (newspaper), 42
regulationism model, 80, 87
Reiss, León, 18, 35, 46–47
Rivadavia Nuns, 73
Roche, David, 147–48

Rockefeller Foundation, 25; on hygiene policy in Latin America, 65–66
Rojas, Nerio, 112–13, 197n5
Rosario, Argentina, 49, 84
Rosario Democratic Social Action Group, 74
rufiánes. *See* pimping
rural economies, 182
"Rutas Argentinas" (Almendra), 177
Ruzo, Guillermo, 54; on health effects of sexual abstinence, 60

safe sex, 157–58. *See also* condom use
Salteña Catholic Action, 73
San Juan, Argentina, 49
San Luis, Argentina, 49
Schettini, Cristiana, 11
Scolari, Pedro, 65
Scoular, Jane, 6
seasonal workers, 103, 107, 109
Segato, Rita, 185
Segundo Plan Quinquenal, 92
The Seven Madmen (Arlt), 148
sexology manuals, 60, 136, 138
sexual contract, 6
sexual education, 68; Catholic concepts of, 74
sexuality: androcentric narratives of, 185; in private vs. public life, 1–2; and social relations, 2
slavery: comparisons with commercialized sex, 5, 23, 28; "white slavery," 12, 19–20, 22–24, 26, 28, 30–32, 191
Sociedad de Beneficencia, 104
Society of Women Protecting Orphans, 73–74
Solari, Ángel, 55, 59, 61, 63–64
Somos (magazine), 169
Soriano de Rocha, Mariana, 71–72
Southern Cone: prostitution within, 45; and "white slavery," 30
spaces: domestic, 108, 111–12; family home and prostitution, 125–26; men's access to, 153–54; public vs. private,

81, 121, 152; rural, and selling of sex, 182–89
syphilis, 58–59. *See also* venereal disease

Tacuara (magazine), 178
Tarnosky, Elías, 43
"taxi boys," 168–69
taxi drivers, 70–71, 152, 154, 187–88
Thompson, Edward P., 141
Torres, Magdalena, 48
travestismo (cross-dressing), 169–70
Trilogía de la trata de blancas (Alsogaray), 31–32
tuberculosis, 142
Tucumán, Argentina, 49

Unión Cívica Radical (UCR), 112–13
Unionism and the Problem of Prostitution, 62
Unionist Club, 62
union members, 67–70
United Nations, treaty on trafficking of persons, 164
United Officers' Group (GOU), 53
Universidad Popular Sudamerican, 93
uranistas (gay men), 113
urban areas: vs. peripheries, 9–10; urbanization, 81; urban settings vs. rural settings, 128–29, 163, 183
Uruguay, legislation in, 26

vagrancy, 161
Vargas Llosa, Mario, 51, 63–64
Varsovia Society. *See* Zwi Migdal
venereal disease, 31, 44, 156–57; antibiotic treatment for, 168; criminalization of transmission of, 59, 67, 92–93; and military brothels, 58–59; women as foci of, 100
violence: between males, 125; against *travestis,* 170; against women, 117, 118, 185–86
virginity, 44, 111; "deflowering" exams, 112–13, 120; male loss of, 149
virility. *See* male sexuality

Printed in the USA
CPSIA information can be obtained
at www.ICGtesting.com
CBHW030228091124
17166CB00001B/3

9 781469 681221